SECOND CUSTOM EDITION FOR JROTC
A CHARACTER AND LEADERSHIP DEVELOPMENT PROGRAM

GEOGRAPHY, MAP SKILLS AND ENVIRONMENTAL AWARENESS

With material selected from:

World Geography: Building a Global Perspective, Second Edition
by Thomas J. Baerwald and Celeste Fraser

and

World Explorer: People, Places, and Cultures
by James B. Kracht

PEARSON
Custom
Publishing

PEARSON
Prentice
Hall

Printed in the United States of America

10 9 8 7 6 5 4 3 2

ISBN 0-536-81438-4

2005420129

EM/JS

Please visit our web site at *www.pearsoncustom.com*

PEARSON CUSTOM PUBLISHING
75 Arlington Street, Suite 300, Boston, MA 02116
A Pearson Education Company

Table of Contents

Geography, Map Skills, and Environmental Awareness

Map Skills

Chapter 1

LESSONS

1. The Globe: An Overview
2. Introduction to Maps
3. Introduction to Topographic Maps
4. Grid Reference System
5. Contours and Landforms
6. Determining Distance
7. Determining Direction
8. Converting the Grid-Magnetic Angle
9. Determining Location
10. Orienteering
11. Air Navigation

Lesson 1
The Globe: An Overview

Key Terms

continent
degrees
equator
globe
hemisphere
latitude
longitude
meridians
ocean
parallel
polar regions
poles
prime meridian

WHAT YOU WILL LEARN TO DO

- Explore the components of a globe

LINKED CORE ABILITIES

- Apply critical thinking techniques

SKILLS AND KNOWLEDGE YOU WILL GAIN ALONG THE WAY

- Identify the seven continents on a globe

- Identify the four oceans on a globe

- Distinguish between the two poles on a globe

- Distinguish between the longitude and latitude lines on a globe

- Differentiate between the equator and the prime meridian

- Define key words contained in this lesson

Introduction

For you to be a better citizen, it is important that you know about the world around you. How often while watching a news program, have you heard the name of a country and wondered where it was? Or while enjoying a movie filmed in a beautiful location have you thought that you would like to visit there someday? An understanding of the globe can help you readily identify a location and provide you with a visual or mental picture of it.

An overview of the globe will give you a basic understanding of the world in which you live. This overview will include the seven continents, four oceans, two poles, as well as longitude and latitude lines.

A Globe Defined

A **globe** is a sphere-shaped model of the earth. It is a representation of the Earth as it really is, round or like a ball. Looking at photos of the earth taken from space, you will only see half of the earth, or one **hemisphere**. A globe shows the whole earth. It shows the water and land formations on the earth's surface and helps you to understand natural events such as day and night and the seasons.

The Continents

Continents are the seven large landmasses on the planet. It is believed that there was only one continent over 225 million years ago. This continent slowly broke apart, shifted and drifted over millions of years until it assumed the shapes and positions of the seven continents that exist today. The seven continents (shown in Figure 1.1.1) from largest to smallest are Asia, Africa, North America, South America, Antarctica, Europe and Australia.

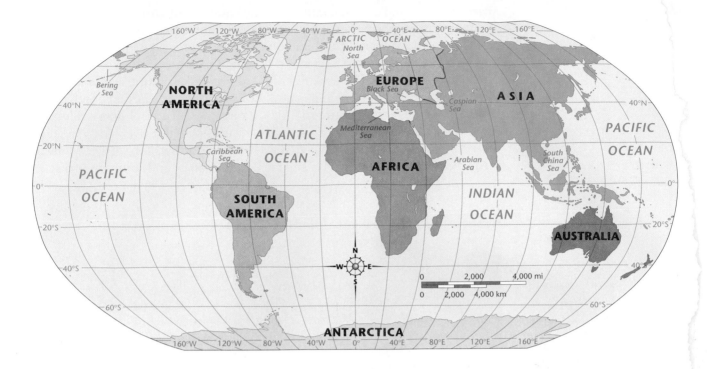

Asia is the largest continent in both size and population. It covers almost a third of the world's land area (16.9 million square miles) and has about three-fifths of its people (3.7 billion). It has 49 independent countries. Asia extends from Africa and Europe in the west to the Pacific Ocean in the east. The northernmost part of the continent lies within the frozen Arctic. In the south, Asia reaches into the steaming tropics near the equator.

Asia has some of the world's longest rivers, largest deserts, and thickest forests and jungles. The highest and lowest places on the earth are in Asia. Figure 1.1.2 depicts the highest, Mount Everest, which rises 29,028 feet above sea level and is along the Nepal-Tibet border. In contrast the Dead Sea shore, located between Israel and Jordan, is the world's lowest land, lying about 1,310 feet below sea level.

Figure 1.1.1: The World continents, oceans and seas.

Courtesy of MapQuest.com, Inc.

Figure 1.1.2: Mount Everest.

Courtesy of Getty Images.

Africa is the second largest continent in area and population. Africa covers about one fifth of the world's land area (11.6 million square miles) and is home to one-eighth of its people (824 million). The continent is an immense plateau, broken by a few mountain ranges and bordered in some areas by a narrow coastal plain. It is a land of striking contrasts and great natural wonders. Tropical rain forests inhabit western and central Africa. The world's largest desert, the Sahara, stretches across northern Africa. It occupies an area almost as large as the entire United States. Africa also has the world's longest river—the Nile (Figure 1.1.3). It flows more than 4,000 miles through northeastern Africa. Much of the rest of the continent is grassland located in eastern and southern Africa.

Figure 1.1.3:
The Nile River.

Courtesy of Stock Boston.

North America is the third largest continent in area (9.3 million square miles) making up about one-sixth of the world's land area. It extends from the Arctic Ocean in the north to South America in the south. It ranks fourth among the continents in population. (Asia, Africa, and Europe are larger in population.) The continent is roughly triangular in shape with the Arctic, Atlantic, and Pacific Oceans bordering its three sides. At its northern end, North America stretches more than 5400 miles from Alaska's Aleutian Islands to the Canadian province of Newfoundland. At the southern end of the continent, the narrowest parts of Panama are only about 30 miles wide (see Figure 1.1.4).

Figure 1.1.4:
The Panama Canal.

Courtesy of Photo
Researchers.

South America is the fourth largest continent in area (6.8 million square miles).
Only Asia, Africa, and North America are larger. It ranks fifth among the continents in population (346.9 million). Asia, Europe, Africa, and North America all
have more people. South America covers about 12 percent of the world's land
area and has about 6 percent of the total world population.

South America has nearly every type of landscape and climate, however, it is
only 600 miles from Antarctica. The world's largest tropical rain forest grows in
the Amazon River Basin (Figure 1.1.5). This basin occupies about two-fifths of
the continent. By contrast, the Atacama Desert in northern Chile is one of the
driest places in the world. Also to be found are snowy peaks and active volcanoes rising along the crest of the lofty Andes Mountains of western South America. Not to be forgotten are the rolling grasslands that stretch endlessly through
much of Argentina and Venezuela. South America's varied landscape also
includes spectacular waterfalls, huge lakes, and rocky, windswept islands.

Figure 1.1.5: The Amazon
River Basin.

Courtesy of Photo
Researchers.

South America is almost totally surrounded by water. The Caribbean Sea lies to the north and the Atlantic Ocean borders South America on the northeast and east. To the south, the Drake Passage separates South America from Antarctica. The Pacific Ocean is located on the west coast. South America borders land only at the Isthmus of Panama. This narrow strip of land links Central America with Colombia, in the northwestern part of South America.

Antarctica is an ice-covered continent located in the South Pole—the earth's most southerly region. As seen in Figure 1.1.6, its nearly barren land forms the coldest and iciest region in the world. It is slightly colder than the region around the North Pole because the North Pole is located in the Arctic Ocean. The South Pole lies near the center of the Antarctic continent, on a high windy plateau of ice and snow. Antarctica's deepest ice is more than 10 times the height of the Sears Tower, one of the world's tallest buildings.

Figure 1.1.6: The Ice Sheets of Antarctica.

Courtesy of National Geographic Society.

Antarctica covers about 5.4 million square miles, making it larger in area than either Europe or Australia. But, it would be the smallest continent if it did not have its icecap. This icy layer which averages 7,100 feet thick increases Antarctica's surface area and also makes Antarctica the highest continent in terms of average elevation.

Stormy waters of the Atlantic, Indian, and Pacific Oceans isolate Antarctica from the other continents. The world's lowest temperatures have been recorded in Antarctica. Ice and snow cover 98 percent of the continent. Underneath the ice, Antarctica has mountains, lowlands, and valleys—much like the landforms of other countries.

Europe is one of the smallest of the world's seven continents in area but one of the largest in population. It covers an area of about 4 million square miles and has a population of 707.8 million. Only Asia and Africa have more people. About one-eighth of the world's people live in Europe. Europe extends from the Arctic Ocean in the north to the Mediterranean Sea in the south and from the Atlantic Ocean in the west to the Ural Mountains in the east. Because Europe and Asia occupy the same landmass, they are sometimes collectively called Eurasia. Figure 1.1.7 shows Monaco, a popular European travel destination on the Mediterranean Sea.

Figure 1.1.7: Monaco: A Mediterranean location.

Courtesy of National Geographic Society.

Australia is the only country that is also a continent. As a country, Australia is the sixth largest in the world. As a continent, however, it ranks smallest in size. It is a stable landmass that lies between the Indian and Pacific Oceans. The northern third of Australia lies in the tropics and is warm the year round. The rest of the continent has warm summers and cool winters. About a third of the country is desert, as shown in Figure 1.1.8. Since it lies south of the equator, its seasons are the opposite of those in the Northern Hemisphere.

Figure 1.1.8: Ayers Rock in the Australian desert.

Courtesy of Comstock Stock Photography.

Key Note Term

ocean – one continuous body of salt water that is broken up by landmasses, given four different names based on where it is divided by continents: Pacific Ocean, Atlantic Ocean, Indian Ocean, and Arctic Ocean

Oceans

Did you know that the ocean is one continuous body of water interrupted by landmasses? It has been assigned four different names based on where it is divided by these landmasses: Pacific Ocean, Atlantic Ocean, Indian Ocean and Arctic Ocean.

The Pacific Ocean is the largest and deepest of the four oceans and covers a third of the globe, over 64 million square miles or 165.8 billion square kilometers. Its average depth is 12,900 feet. It is so large that all seven continents could fit in it and there would still be room for one more continent the size of Asia. It separates North and South America from Asia and Australia.

The Atlantic Ocean is the second largest body of water on the globe covering 33 million square miles or 867.7 billion square kilometers. It is continually widening and has an average depth of 11,700 feet. The Atlantic Ocean is bordered by Europe and Africa on the east and by North America and South America on the west.

The Indian Ocean is the third largest ocean and covers an area of about 28.3 million square miles or 73.3 billion square kilometers. At 12,600 feet deep, it is deeper than the Atlantic Ocean but smaller in size. It is the only ocean that is bordered by land on the north rather than water. On the eastern border is Indonesia and Australia. Africa is to the west and Antarctica to the south.

The Arctic Ocean is the smallest and shallowest of the four oceans. It is about 5 million square miles or 13 million square kilometers and averages about 4,000 feet deep. It is located at the top of the globe and is bordered primarily by northern Asia, Europe, and North America.

These four oceans are salt water and cover more than seventy percent of the earth's surface. They contain the highest mountain range, deepest valley, and some of the most unusual animals on earth.

Poles

Key Note Terms

poles – the points on a globe representing the northernmost and southernmost points of the earth, located at each end of the earth's imaginary axis

polar regions – the areas surrounding the North and South Poles

The points on the globe representing the northernmost and southernmost points of the earth are the North Pole and South Pole. These **poles** are located on each end of the earth's imaginary axis. The areas around them are sometimes referred to as **polar regions** because they are around the North and South Poles. The North Pole is located in the Arctic and the South Pole is located in Antarctica. They are the coldest places on earth—frozen deserts covered in ice all year long. The North Pole is the farthest point north. When looking down at a globe of the earth, it is shown at the top. When you look down on a globe of the North Pole, the landmasses of North America, Europe, Asia, and even parts of Africa can be seen. The South Pole is the farthest point south. A map centered on the South Pole features the continent of Antarctica surrounded by ocean. Because it is over land instead of water, the Antarctic region is much colder than the Arctic. The closest continents visible from this vantage point are South America, Africa, and Australia.

Longitude and Latitude

Lines of latitude and longitude are imaginary lines that form a grid covering the whole globe. This grid, as shown in Figure 1.1.9, helps geographers find the location of places anywhere in the world. Lines of **latitude** run east to west around the globe. Lines of **longitude** run north to south, meeting at the poles. Taken together, latitude and longitude lines form a grid. Every place on earth has a unique position on this grid. Mogadishu, Somalia is located at 2°N latitude and 45°E longitude. New Orleans, Louisiana, is at 30°N and 90°W.

Key Note Terms

latitude – the angular distance north or south of the earth's equator, measured in degrees along a meridian, as on a map or globe

longitude – lines that run from the North Pole to the South Pole and are equal in length on a map or globe

Global Grid

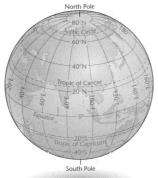

Parallels of Latitude

Meridians of Longitude

Figure 1.1.9:
The global grid.

Courtesy of Geosystems Global Corporation.

Key Note Terms

degree – a unit of latitude or longitude, equal to 1/360 of the globe

meridian – an imaginary circle on the earth's surface passing through the North and South poles; a line or parallel of longitude

parallel – lines that do not intersect

prime meridian – the line of longitude that passes through Greenwich, England, designated as zero degrees longitude, and from which longitude east and west is measured

equator – an imaginary line at 0 degrees latitude that circles the globe at its widest point halfway between the North Pole and South Pole

The concept of latitude and longitude has its origin in ancient times, nearly 2000 years before the earth could be photographed from space. The Ancient Greeks used observation and mathematics to determine that the earth was round and not flat. They then developed a method for locating places on the earth. They came up with a system to divide the globe into 360 segments, called **degrees**. The imaginary vertical lines used to divide these parts are the longitude lines or **meridians**. They run from the North Pole to the South Pole and are equal in length. The imaginary horizontal lines on the globe are the latitude or **parallel** lines. These lines are parallel to each other and form complete circles around the globe. The horizontal lines of latitude and the vertical lines of longitude are further broken down into degrees, minutes, and seconds so that any point on earth can be located using the two lines that meet at that point on a globe.

In 1884, the **prime meridian**, or the longitude line numbered 0 degrees, was established at an international conference. It is the starting point for measuring distances east and west around the globe. The prime meridian at 0 degrees and the 180th meridian or longitude line on the opposite side bisect the globe into eastern and western halves. Longitude lines east of the prime meridian are numbered 1 degree to 180 degrees east (E). This part of the earth is the Eastern Hemisphere. Longitude lines west of the prime meridian also numbered 1 degree to 180 degrees west (W) represent the Western Hemisphere. The prime meridian passes through the Royal Naval Observatory in Greenwich, a section of London, England.

The **equator**, or 0 degrees latitude, is an imaginary line that circles the globe at its widest point halfway between the North Pole and South Pole. The equator is the longest latitude line or parallel. Latitude is measured from 0 degrees to 90 degrees from the equator to the North Pole. This part of the earth from the equator to the North Pole is known as the Northern Hemisphere (Figure 1.1.10). Latitude is also measured from 0 degrees to 90 degrees from the equator to the South Pole. This part of the earth from the equator to the South Pole is known as the Southern Hemisphere. When any latitude line is given, it must be stated in north or south latitude.

Figure 1.1.10: The hemispheres.

Courtesy of MapQuest.com, Inc.

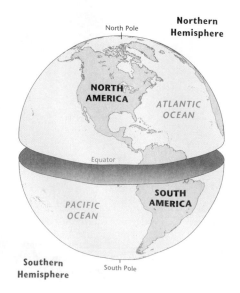

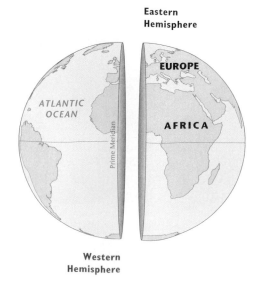

Conclusion

Understanding the world around you helps you to be a better citizen. You are not isolated, no matter where you live: in a small community, town, city or major metropolitan area. Your personal involvement and actions as a citizen can and will have a direct impact on the globe—the world around you and the world of tomorrow.

In the next lesson, you are introduced to maps. You will learn how to read and understand maps that will help you become more aware of the world around you. You will also learn how to orient a map using specific symbols that show you natural and manmade points.

Lesson Review

1. List the seven continents and four oceans on the globe.
2. What is the purpose of the longitude and latitude lines on a globe?
3. What do the North and South Poles represent?
4. Explain the difference between the equator and the prime meridian.

Lesson 2
Introduction to Maps

Key Terms

bar scale
contrast
elevation
intermittent
landforms
legend
man-made
marginal information
orient
prominent
relief
terrain
topographic maps

WHAT YOU WILL LEARN TO DO

- Use map reading skills

LINKED CORE ABILITIES

- Apply critical thinking techniques

SKILLS AND KNOWLEDGE YOU WILL GAIN ALONG THE WAY

- Identify symbols, colors, and features on standard road maps

- Identify locations on a city and state map

- Communicate directions to specified sites using a city and state map

- Define key words contained in this lesson

Introduction

Have you ever found yourself on the wrong road or in the wrong neighborhood? If you asked for directions in this situation, were you told, "Go right," or "Turn left"? After following these directions for a few blocks, the question arises, "Turn right . . .where?" These types of situations call for map reading skills.

Knowing how to read and understand maps are valuable skills that can strengthen your awareness of the world around you. Your effective use of maps requires a basic understanding of them, their scales, symbols, and colors. This lesson introduces you to this information and explains how to orient a map by matching man-made or natural features with map symbols.

Maps are in common use throughout the world today. For instance, when a family takes a vacation, a map is used to guide the driver from one city to another. The airline pilot and the sea captain use special charts or maps from which to navigate. Rarely do experienced navigators become lost because they apply their map reading abilities to read, understand, and use maps effectively.

Definition of a Map and Map Reading

A map is a line drawing of a portion of the earth's surface, drawn to scale as seen from above. Obviously any attempt to plot each feature to its exact shape and scale would result in a map too big to read. Therefore, maps are drawn "to scale" with each set measurement on the scale representing a set amount of the earth's surface.

In general, maps provide information about the existence and location of man-made and natural features; show distance, **elevation**, and different types of landforms; and depict man-made and natural features by the use of symbols, lines, colors, and forms or shapes.

There are many different types of maps. However, the most common types are:

- **City or state road maps**
- **Geographic maps/atlases**
- **Topographic maps**

City or state road maps, also known as tourist maps, provide information on street names, important buildings, route numbers, distance, transportation centers. In many cases, they include the location of recreational or historical areas, as well.

Geographic maps show an overall view of the mapped area in relation to climate, population, **relief**, vegetation, and hydrography (water features) (see Figure 1.2.1). An atlas is a collection of geographic maps of regions, countries, continents, or the world. These maps are generally not as accurate as city or state maps. And compared to **topographic maps**, their accuracy is significantly inferior, therefore, they should be used for general information only.

Figure 1.2.1:
A Geographical Map –
Mexico's Population
Distribution.

Courtesy of
MapQuest.com, Inc.

KEY

• One dot represents
200,000 people

Lambert Azimuthal Equal-Area Projection

0   200   400 mi

0   200   400 km

Key Note Terms

terrain – a region or
tract of land; the
character (or topog-
raphy) of a tract of
land

landform – a natural
or man-made fea-
ture on the earth's
surface

**marginal
information** –
instructions placed
around the outer
edge of a map

Topographic maps show **terrain** and **landforms** in a manner which can be measured. They also show the horizontal positions and elevations of these features.
Elevation on these maps is normally indicated by vertical contour lines. Topographic maps are the ones most commonly used in the military. Beginning with
the next lesson, you will examine topographic maps in detail and will use them
throughout the remainder of this unit so that you can begin to understand how
to read and use them.

Road Maps

You can compare a map to any piece of equipment—before you use it, you must
first read the instructions. Most mapmakers place the instructions on a map
(known as the **marginal information**) around the outer edge of a map. All maps
are not the same, so it is necessary to read the marginal information carefully
every time you use a different map (see Figure 1.2.2). The following discussion
describes and illustrates the most commonly used elements of marginal information that are found on road maps.

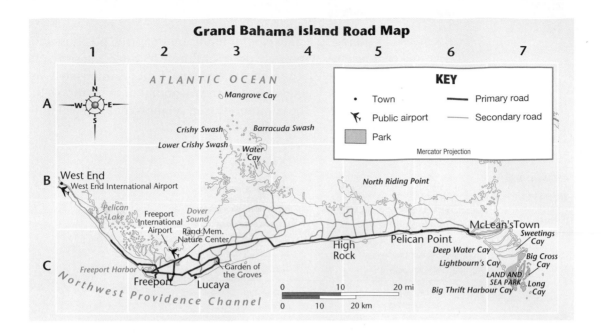

Grand Bahama Island Road Map

KEY
- • Town
- ✈ Public airport
- ▨ Park
- ▬▬ Primary road
- ─── Secondary road

Mercator Projection

Figure 1.2.2: A road map.

Courtesy of
MapQuest.com, Inc.

- **Sheet or Map Name.** Whenever possible, a map is named after the most **prominent** cultural or geographic feature in that area (for example, Orlando or the Official Transportation Map for the State of Florida). Although the most prominent feature on the map may be a state or other large geographical region (for example the Mid-Atlantic States), the map sheet normally contains numerous inserts of smaller sections in order to show them in more detail. These inserts can be found around the margin or on the reverse side of the map sheet.

- **Bar Scales.** **Bar scales** are special rulers used to measure ground distance on a map. Although these scales may vary with each road map, the most common units of measurement are miles and kilometers. Figure 1.2.3 shows an example of a scale used on the Official Transportation Map for the State of Florida.

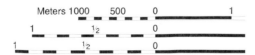

Key Note Terms

prominent – very noticeable or conspicuous; well-known

bar scale – a ruler used to measure actual ground distances by converting distances on a map

Figure 1.2.3: An example of a bar scale.

Courtesy of US Army JROTC.

- **Printing Note.** This note indicates the agency responsible for printing the map. The printing date determines when the map was printed, not when the information was obtained.

- **Legend.** The **legend** is part of the mapmaker's dictionary. It is a shorthand method of illustrating and identifying mapped features using symbols to show some of the more prominent features on the map. These symbols are not the same on every road map.

Key Note Term

legend – an explanatory description on a chart, map, or other illustration

Map Symbols

Because all features on a map cannot represent their true position and shape, mapmakers must use symbols to represent these features. These symbols are made to look as closely as possible to the actual features themselves as they are seen from above. The legend indicates the meanings of the symbols that are used on a map. A few of the commonly used symbols that you will find on road maps are identified in Figure 1.2.4.

Figure 1.2.4: Commonly used map symbols.

Courtesy of US Army JROTC.

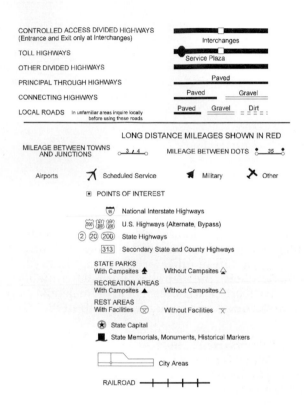

- **Roads.** Indicated by parallel or solid lines. Thickness and color of these symbols indicate the road size.

- **Interchanges.** Indicated by a heavy solid line for major access roads and parallel lines for intersecting secondary roads. Legends also illustrate full, partial, and no access at these interchanges.

- **Railroads.** Commonly shown by single or parallel lines with horizontal tick marks.

- **Buildings.** Symbols for buildings may vary from map to map according to the purpose of the map or building. Schools and churches are commonly represented by a solid square with a flag or cross affixed. Hospitals may be shown by a cross. Universities and colleges may sometimes have a special symbol as a point of interest.

- **Points of Interest.** Indicated by a special marking and its name; for example, a historical marker.

- **Airports.** Normally shown by a picture of an airplane.

- **Water Features.** Normally shown in blue and take the approximate shape of the feature.

- **Special Features.** Significant natural features (forests, recreational areas, national monuments, and so on), military reservations, or Indian reservations are normally highlighted with a specific color and do not have a standard shape. Many road maps also have a chart indicating the services that are available at the recreational areas and parks shown on the map.

You may also find the following symbols on road maps that can provide helpful information to you when using the map.

- **Route Markers.** Represented by a shield or some other shape containing the number of the road in its center. Although the map may show these route markers with white numbers and/or letters on a black shield or shape, the actual colors of the signs as seen on the highway are indicated in the previous bulleted list.

- **Interstate Highways.** There are a number of interstate highway types, and these are generally shown as:

  - **Principal Routes.** Red, white, and blue signs with one- or two-digit numbers. East-west routes have even numbers (I-4 or I-70), whereas north-south routes have odd numbers (I-5 or I-95).

  - **Loop or Belt Routes.** Red, white, and blue signs with three-digit numbers; the first number is always even (I-295). These routes circle or bypass major cities.

  - **Spur Routes.** Red, white, and blue signs with three-digit numbers; the first number is always odd (I-580). These routes lead into major cities.

  - **Business Routes.** Green signs marking routes from principal, loop, or belt highways that go to or through cities.

- **Boundary Symbols.** Shown as broken or **intermittent** lines that vary in pattern to denote different boundaries.

- **Mileage Markers.** Shown between towns and road junctions or between dots with the mileage indicated in red or black. State and regional maps also show long distance mileage between major cities by printing that information in red (with red directional arrows), and centering it between the two cities. An example of this long distance mileage indicator may appear as follows:

TAMPA

199 Miles

320 Kilometers

WEST PALM BEACH

- **Official Highway Mileages.** This chart shows the actual ground mileage between the major cities that are located on the map.

- **City/Street Names.** This information lists alphabetically (wherever space permits on the map—including on the reverse side of it—and printed adjacent to its corresponding feature) the names of cities on state and regional maps and the names of streets on city maps. Beside each city or street listing is a letter/number code (for example, D-9). Along the outer edge of the margin are letters ranging from "A" to "P" (or beyond) and numbers ranging from "1" to "15" (or beyond). Note that the letter "I" is usually omitted so as not to be mistaken for the number "1."

The following example shows how to locate features on a road map using this letter/number code.

Key Note Term

intermittent – alternately stopping and starting; coming at intervals

To find the feature at D-9, use a finger on one hand to locate the letter "D"—it should be close to the top left or top right edges of the map. Next, use a finger on your other hand to locate the number "9" across the top or bottom margin. Now, move both fingers in from the margins toward the map. Where they meet is the general location of the feature. Street names may still be hard to find on a cluttered map, but you have narrowed the search to a specific area.

- **Special Traffic Regulations/Traffic Control Devices.** This section contains some of the traffic regulations and/or signs (control devices) used within the state that may be different from other states within the region.

Map Colors

Key Note Terms

contrast – to show differences when compared

man-made – manufactured, created, or constructed by man, rather than formed by nature

Colors on a road map provide **contrast** to map features, making them easier to identify. Map symbols are usually printed in different colors with each color identifying a class of features. However, colors may vary from one map to another. When used differently, mapmakers indicate these colors and their uses in the marginal information.

The following describes the basic colors used on most road maps and the features they represent. Occasionally, mapmakers may use other colors to indicate special information.

- **Black.** Indicates the majority of **man-made** features: buildings or roads.
- **Blue.** Identifies water features: lakes, swamps, or rivers.
- **Brown.** Identifies elevation and relief features: mountain ranges.
- **Green.** Identifies vegetation: woods, grassland, brush, orchards, or vineyards.
- **Red.** Classifies man-made features: populated areas, main roads, special features, or boundaries on older maps.

Orienting a Map

Key Note Term

orient – to align or position oneself (or a map) in relationship to one's surroundings

Finding your way requires the ability to read and interpret a map, compare it to the features on the ground, and move to the desired location. One method of comparing your map to the ground is to **orient** it so that the map symbols fit the location of the features as they appear on the ground. A properly oriented map can also indicate direction; that is, after you have it correctly oriented to the ground, the top of it will usually point toward the north.

The following situation shows you how to orient a map without using a compass.

While participating in a bike rally, Barry traveled off the main road and became lost. He knew for certain he was lost when he came upon the main entrance to North Fork State Park on his right. Across from this entrance was a small bridge which crossed the North Fork River. Because Barry had a route map for this bike rally, he took the following steps to orient it.

1. **Barry determined his location using at least two known points. He chose to use the man-made features of the bridge and the park entrance and the natural feature of the river.**

2. **Next, he located these same features on his map. With the map in a horizontal position, he rotated it until the symbol for the river was pointed in the same direction as (or aligned with) the river in front of him.**

3. **Barry then checked to ensure that the park entrance was correctly aligned with its actual location. From where he was located, the park entrance was on the right side of the road. He checked to see if the map symbol for the park entrance was also on the right side of the road.**

With his map properly oriented, he realized what direction he had to take to rejoin the bike rally.

In many cases, orienting a map may mean turning it upside down or holding it with one of its edges pointing toward you. Holding a map like this may make it harder for you to read street names or other symbols, but it properly aligns the features on the ground with those on the map. After you know where you are (by using the two or more known points discussed in the above story), keep the map oriented until you are at your destination or in an area familiar to you.

The next time you are on a trip to a place where you have never been before, try this method. It works! You will be able to navigate your way to your destination much more easily.

Care of Maps

Because you may have to keep a map for a long time, exercise care when using it. Three important considerations in the care of maps are:

- **Properly refold it after each use**

- **Use a pencil if it becomes necessary to mark on it so that you can easily erase those marks**

- **Avoid spilling liquids on it**

Global Positioning System

The Global Positioning System (GPS) is a high-tech worldwide radio-navigation system formed from a network of 24 satellites and their ground stations. GPS provides more precise and efficient methods of surveying and mapmaking. Today,

GPS makes it possible to accomplish the same work in a fraction of the time. Mapping is the science of using GPS to pinpoint locations and then create maps of any location in the world, including both natural and man-made features.

Conclusion

Maps permit you to see an area of the earth's surface with the key features of that area properly positioned. They can take the guesswork out of traveling to new locations preventing wasted time and effort. Therefore, make the most of your trips—know how to read and understand your maps beforehand. Even the best maps are useless if you do not know how to properly use them.

Lesson Review

1. What information do maps provide?
2. Explain what a map's marginal information is.
3. What do the different colors on a map represent?
4. Describe how to orient a map without using a compass.

Lesson 3
Introduction to Topographic Maps

Key Terms

bench marks
declination
grid
grid north
grid zone
magnetic north
nautical miles
orienteering
statute miles
true north

WHAT YOU WILL LEARN TO DO

- Identify the characteristics of topographic maps

LINKED CORE ABILITIES

- Apply critical thinking techniques

SKILLS AND KNOWLEDGE YOU WILL GAIN ALONG THE WAY

- Differentiate between a topographical map and a standard road map
- Identify the symbols, colors, and features of a topographical map
- Define key words contained in this lesson

Introduction

This lesson presents an overview of topographic maps. It describes their characteristics and examines the marginal information, symbols, and colors used on them. The remainder of this chapter focuses on the use of topographic maps.

Compared to road maps, topographic maps show more detail of an area's natural features. Because of its detail, especially of terrain features, elevation, and relief, the military prefers this type of map.

After you have mastered the basics of map reading in this chapter, you will have the opportunity to demonstrate your knowledge of these skills during outdoor practical exercises. Whether you are practicing basic land navigation techniques, participating in **orienteering**, or performing land navigation at summer camp, knowing how to use topographic maps can help you in the following ways:

- **Finding your way if you become separated from a group**
- **Successfully, and safely, navigating a group, especially during cross-country movements**
- **Determining distances from one location to another**
- **Pinpointing locations in a given area**
- **Determining the type of terrain in which you or your unit must operate**
- **Planning trips or operations**

Interpreting a Topographic Map

A hiker poised at the start of an unfamiliar mountain trail needs a special kind of map tucked into his or her backpack: a topographic, or contour, map. This kind of map shows the changes in elevation that lie ahead—and how quickly these changes take place. Does the trail climb steeply for the next mile, or is the grade a slow and steady rise? Will there be serious climbing involved, or can the hiker cover the distance at an easy, arm-swinging pace? How far can the hiker expect to go in a single afternoon? A good topographic map can be used to answer all these questions and help ensure the success and safety of a hike.

Introducing Topographical Maps

Topographic maps are useful tools with many applications. Backpackers take them along when they set out on hiking, rock climbing, and camping trips; however, they are not the only people who use topographic maps. Engineers use them when deciding where to build highways and dams. Police and emergency medical personnel often consult topographic maps during search-and-rescue operations for people who are lost in the woods.

Figure 1.3.1: Topographical map of Tahiti.

Courtesy of Geosystems Global Corporation.

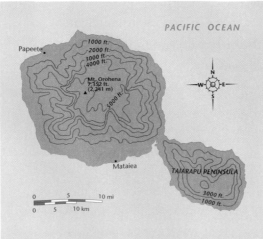

The topographic map in Figure 1.3.1 shows the Pacific island of Tahiti. Use the following steps to study and analyze the map.

1. **Understand what contour lines measure.** The lines on a topographic map are called contour lines. A contour line connects all points where elevation is equal. If you were to hike along one of the contour lines shown on this topographic map, you would always be at the same height above sea level. Notice that the contour lines are labeled with numbers that tell the elevation in feet along that contour line. Now use the map to answer the following questions:

   - What elevation does the coastline represent?

   - What is the highest point on Tahiti?

   - Are Papeete and Mataiea at about the same or different elevations?

2. **Interpret the relationships among contour lines.** When a series of contour lines is close together, it means that the elevation of the land is changing rapidly—in other words, the terrain is steep. On the other hand, contour lines spread wide apart indicate that the elevation is changing slowly and the land is relatively flat. Answer the following questions:

   - Is the island generally steeper near the top of Mt. Orohena or near the coast?

   - Where is the steepest part of the Taiarapu Peninsula?

3. **Put the data you have collected to use.** After you understand how to read a topographic map, you can use this skill to help plan a hike or a camping trip. Use the map to answer the following questions:

   - If you and a friend wanted to climb to the top of Mt. Orohena, how would you plot the most gradual ascent possible?

   - How would you plot a steeper climb?

Marginal Information

The marginal information for topographic maps varies significantly from that of road maps. One major difference is that the marginal information on topographic maps is more standardized than that on other maps. However, all topographic maps are not the same. Consequently, you must examine this information carefully before using each map. This lesson identifies ten items of marginal information that you will need to know when using a topographic map in the remainder of this unit. You will learn more about these items in subsequent lessons in this chapter.

The topographic map shown in Figure 1.3.2 is only an extract of how one actually appears; there are three major differences. The mapped area and bar scales are drawn to scale, but the extract represents only a small portion of the actual map.

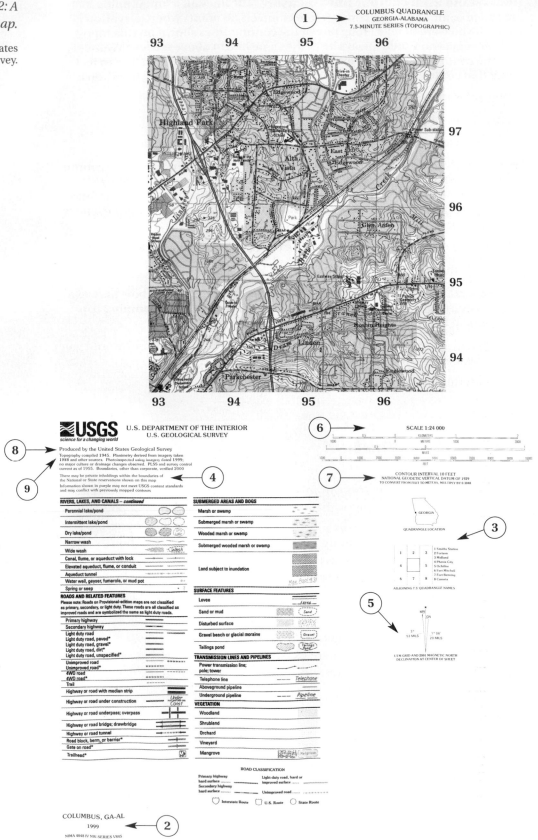

Figure 1.3.2: A topographic map.

Courtesy of the United States Geological Survey.

As you can see, this map has a detailed legend, which can be seen in more detail in Figure 1.3.3. The marginal information for this topographical map is as follows:

1. **Sheet Name.** You can locate the sheet name at the center of the top margin and in the lower left area of the map margin. As with road maps, mapmakers generally title a map after its prominent cultural or geographic feature.

2. **Sheet Number.** You can find the sheet number located in either the upper right or the lower left corners. Use it as a reference number for the map sheet.

3. **Adjoining Map Sheets Diagram.** Locate the adjoining (or adjacent) map sheets diagram in the right corner of the lower margin. This diagram contains nine squares; the center square is the map sheet at which you are looking. The remaining squares show the sheet numbers for those maps at the same scale that surround the area covered by the center square.

4. **Special Notes.** Special notes are statements of general information that relate to the mapped area; for example: the map is red-light readable (located in the lower right corner) or a lane is generally considered as being a minimum of 2.5 meters (located in the lower left corner).

5. **Declination Diagram.** Another item of information located in the lower right margin is the **declination** diagram. All you need to know at this time is that it indicates the direction and relationship of **true**, **magnetic**, and **grid north**.

6. **Scales.** Locate the graphic (bar) scales in the center of the lower margin of the map. Compare the differences between these scales and those found on road maps.

   Map scale is expressed as a representative fraction, which gives the ratio of map distance to ground distance. For example, the scale 1:50,000 indicates that one unit of measure on the map equals 50,000 units of the same measure on the ground.

   Most topographic maps have more than one scale, each using a different unit of measurement. The most common units of measurement are miles (**statute** and **nautical**), meters/kilometers, and yards.

   Mapmakers divide each scale into two parts: an extension scale and a primary scale. Use the primary scale, located to the right of the zero, to measure full units of measurement. Use the extension scale, located to the left of the zero, to measure tenths of a unit. Read the extension scale right to left from the zero and the primary scale left to right from the zero.

7. **Contour Interval Note.** The contour interval note also appears in the center of the lower margin. It represents the vertical distance between adjacent contour lines on the map.

8. **Unit Imprint.** You can find the unit imprint below the left corner of the mapped area. It identifies the agency that prepared and printed the map.

9. **Legend.** The legend appears below the unit imprint. It states the effective date of the road and other data and illustrates the symbols used on the map. Figure 1.3.3 shows another example of a legend.

10. **Grid Reference Box.** Some topographical maps also include a grid reference box. The **grid** reference box contains information for identifying the **grid zone** and the 100,000 meter square representing the area. It also provides instructions for giving grid references on the map. The next two sections present information on grid referencing systems and the usefulness of the grid reference box. Figure 1.4.11 shows an example of a grid reference box.

Key Note Term

declination – an angular difference between true north and either magnetic or grid north

true north – a line from any position on the earth's surface to the geographic north pole; symbolized by a line with a star at the apex

magnetic north – the direction to the north magnetic pole, as indicated by the north-seeking needle of a magnetic instrument

grid north – the direction of north that is established by using the vertical grid lines on a map

statute mile – a unit of measurement that is approximately 5,280 feet

nautical mile – a unit of measurement that is approximately 6,080 feet – which is one minute of latitude; it is slightly longer than a statute mile

grid – a pattern of intersecting parallel lines used to divide a map into small squares

grid zone – one of the 60 north-south divisions of the earth's surface between 84 degrees north latitude and 80 degrees south latitude, each six degrees wide

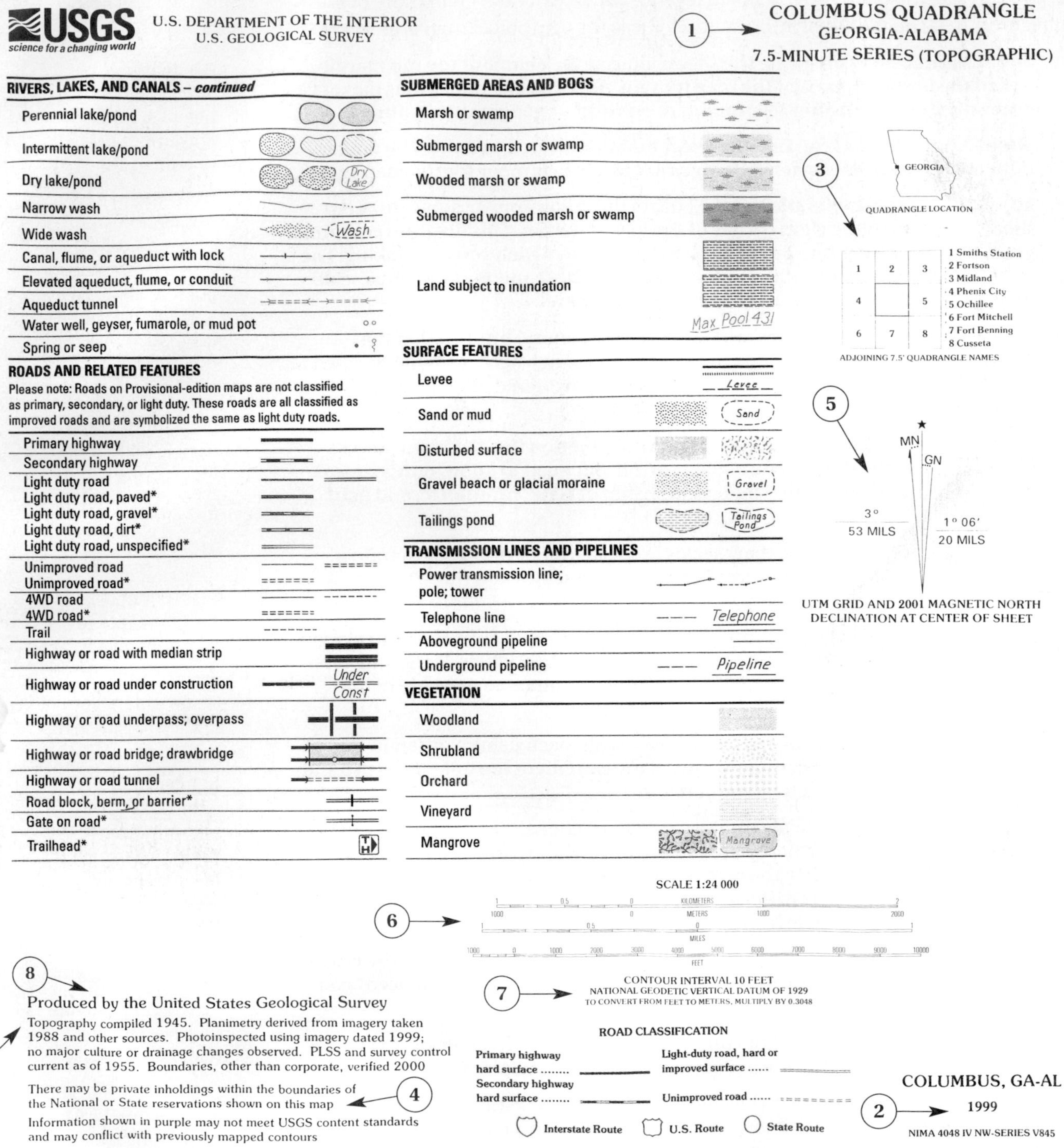

U.S. DEPARTMENT OF THE INTERIOR
U.S. GEOLOGICAL SURVEY

1 → **COLUMBUS QUADRANGLE**
GEORGIA-ALABAMA
7.5-MINUTE SERIES (TOPOGRAPHIC)

RIVERS, LAKES, AND CANALS – *continued*

Perennial lake/pond	
Intermittent lake/pond	
Dry lake/pond	*Dry Lake*
Narrow wash	
Wide wash	*Wash*
Canal, flume, or aqueduct with lock	
Elevated aqueduct, flume, or conduit	
Aqueduct tunnel	
Water well, geyser, fumarole, or mud pot	o o
Spring or seep	• ᵧ

ROADS AND RELATED FEATURES

Please note: Roads on Provisional-edition maps are not classified as primary, secondary, or light duty. These roads are all classified as improved roads and are symbolized the same as light duty roads.

Primary highway	
Secondary highway	
Light duty road	
Light duty road, paved*	
Light duty road, gravel*	
Light duty road, dirt*	
Light duty road, unspecified*	
Unimproved road	=======
Unimproved road*	=======
4WD road	
4WD road*	=======
Trail	- - - - - -
Highway or road with median strip	
Highway or road under construction	*Under Const*
Highway or road underpass; overpass	
Highway or road bridge; drawbridge	
Highway or road tunnel	
Road block, berm, or barrier*	
Gate on road*	
Trailhead*	[T H]

SUBMERGED AREAS AND BOGS

Marsh or swamp	
Submerged marsh or swamp	
Wooded marsh or swamp	
Submerged wooded marsh or swamp	
Land subject to inundation	*Max Pool 431*

SURFACE FEATURES

Levee	*Levee*
Sand or mud	*Sand*
Disturbed surface	
Gravel beach or glacial moraine	*Gravel*
Tailings pond	*Tailings Pond*

TRANSMISSION LINES AND PIPELINES

Power transmission line; pole; tower	
Telephone line	*Telephone*
Aboveground pipeline	
Underground pipeline	*Pipeline*

VEGETATION

Woodland	
Shrubland	
Orchard	
Vineyard	
Mangrove	*Mangrove*

3 →

GEORGIA

QUADRANGLE LOCATION

1	2	3
4		5
6	7	8

1 Smiths Station
2 Fortson
3 Midland
4 Phenix City
5 Ochillee
6 Fort Mitchell
7 Fort Benning
8 Cusseta

ADJOINING 7.5' QUADRANGLE NAMES

5 →

MN ★ GN

3°
53 MILS

1° 06'
20 MILS

UTM GRID AND 2001 MAGNETIC NORTH
DECLINATION AT CENTER OF SHEET

SCALE 1:24 000

6 →

CONTOUR INTERVAL 10 FEET
NATIONAL GEODETIC VERTICAL DATUM OF 1929
TO CONVERT FROM FEET TO METERS, MULTIPLY BY 0.3048

7 →

ROAD CLASSIFICATION

Primary highway hard surface	Light-duty road, hard or improved surface ......
Secondary highway hard surface	Unimproved road ...... =========

⬡ Interstate Route ▢ U.S. Route ◯ State Route

8 →

Produced by the United States Geological Survey

Topography compiled 1945. Planimetry derived from imagery taken 1988 and other sources. Photoinspected using imagery dated 1999; no major culture or drainage changes observed. PLSS and survey control current as of 1955. Boundaries, other than corporate, verified 2000

There may be private inholdings within the boundaries of the National or State reservations shown on this map ← 4

Information shown in purple may not meet USGS content standards and may conflict with previously mapped contours

9 →

COLUMBUS, GA-AL

2 → 1999

NIMA 4048 IV NW-SERIES V845

Figure 1.3.3: A topographic map legend.

Courtesy of the United States Geological Survey.

Map Symbols

As in the previous lesson on road maps, topographic maps use symbols to represent the position and shape of features as viewed from above. The legend explains the meanings for the symbols used on a topographic map.

Map symbols on topographic maps are generally in more detail than on other maps. For example, these maps include unimproved roads and trails, different gauges of railroad tracks, power lines, mines or quarries, **bench marks**, and spot elevations. However, the symbols are not always the same on every map. Always refer to the legend to avoid errors when reading a map.

Key Note Term

bench mark – a surveyor's mark made on rocks or other permanent objects to indicate known elevations

Map Colors

The five colors (black, blue, brown, green, and red) used for road maps and the features they represent are also used on topographic maps. In addition, topographic maps use two colors that are usually not found on other maps. These two colors are white, which identifies an area void of vegetation, and reddish-brown, which identifies man-made and relief features and elevation such as contour lines on red-light readable maps. These can be seen in Figure 1.3.4.

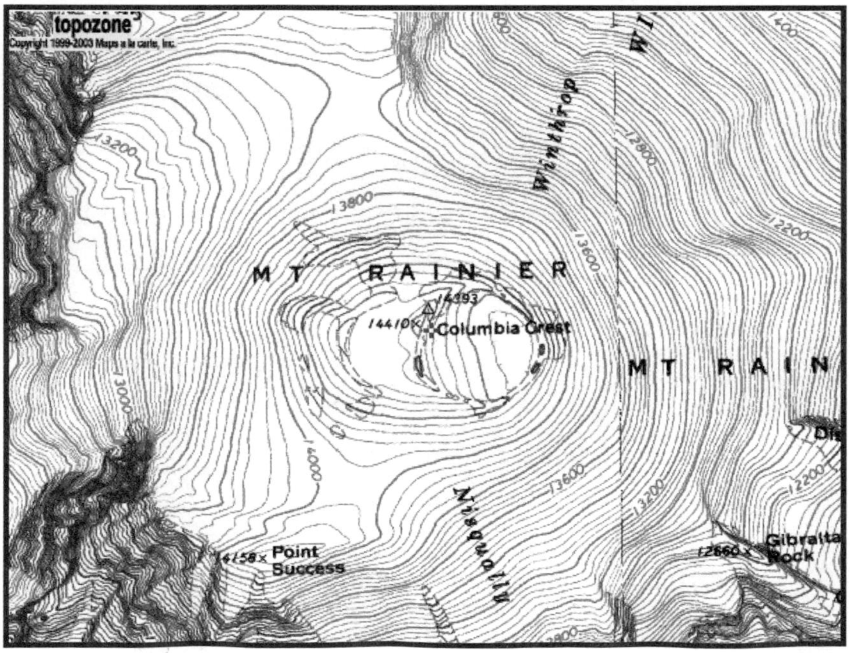

Figure 1.3.4: Topographical map of Crater Lake.

Courtesy of the United States Geological Survey.

> **Note**
>
> Brown also identifies relief features and may indicate elevation, or contour lines, on older maps. Refer to Figure 1.3.4 to see these colors on an actual topographic map of Mt. Rainier in Washington.

If other colors appear on a topographic map, the marginal information must contain an explanation of their use.

Conclusion

The topographic map is the one most commonly preferred by the military because of its detail in portraying terrain features, landforms, the horizontal positions of these features, and elevation/relief. Road maps and topographic maps differ in their marginal information, layout, and scales; however, your ability to read road maps will help you to read topographic maps as well.

In the next lesson, you will study a grid reference system. In the event a street address is not available to you, you can use the grid referencing system in conjunction with maps to help quickly and accurately pinpoint your location.

Lesson Review

1. **How is a topographical map different from a standard road map?**

2. **List three examples of symbols you might find on a topographical map that are not typically on standard road maps.**

3. **Identify the significance of the colors of a topographical map.**

4. **What do the contour lines on a topographical map tell you?**

Lesson 4
Grid Reference System

Key Terms

grid coordinate
grid lines
grid squares
meridians
military grid reference system
prime meridian
superimposed
Universal Transverse Mercator Grid System

WHAT YOU WILL LEARN TO DO

- Use the Grid Reference System to locate points anywhere in the world

LINKED CORE ABILITIES

- Apply critical thinking techniques

SKILLS AND KNOWLEDGE YOU WILL GAIN ALONG THE WAY

- Locate grid zones and grid segments using the Universal Transverse Mercator Grid System

- Determine the six-digit coordinate within 100 meters of given locations on a map

- Define key words contained in this lesson

Introduction

This lesson introduces you to the Universal Transverse Mercator Grid System and the military grid reference system. After you are familiar with these systems and how mapmakers divide the globe into north-south and east-west rings, you can better understand how to locate and identify points anywhere in the world.

From this very broad perspective, this lesson will then show you how to locate a point on a map to within 100 meters using a six-digit **grid coordinate**.

To keep from getting lost, you must know how to find your location. Street addresses may not always be available to you. Learning to use the grid referencing system in conjunction with maps will help you to quickly and accurately pinpoint your location.

Lines of Latitude and Longitude

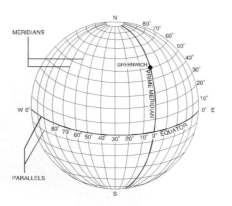

By drawing a set of east-west rings around the globe (parallel to the equator), and a set of north-south rings crossing the equator at right angles and converging at the poles, mapmakers can form a network of reference lines from which you can locate any point on the earth's surface (see Figure 1.4.1).

The distance of a point north or south of the equator is its latitude and the rings around the earth parallel to the equator are parallels of latitude, or simply parallels. Lines of latitude run east-west, but they are used to measure north-south distances. Starting with zero degrees at the equator, mapmakers number parallels to 90 degrees both north and south.

The second set of rings around the globe, that are at right angles to the lines of latitude and that pass through the poles are called **meridians** of longitude, or simply meridians. One meridian is the **prime meridian**, which runs through Greenwich, England. The distance east or west of the prime meridian to a point is known as its longitude. Lines of longitude run north-south, but they are used to measure east-west distances. Starting with zero degrees at the prime meridian, mapmakers number meridians to 180 degrees both east and west.

UTM Grid System

The U.S. military **superimposed** its grid reference system on the **Universal Transverse Mercator Grid System**, or UTM grid system. To better understand the military's grid reference system, you should have a basic knowledge of the UTM grid system.

Key Note Term

grid coordinate – a set of letters and numbers specifying the location of a point to the desired position within a 100,000 meter square

Key Note Term

meridian – an imaginary circle on the earth's surface passing through the North and South poles; a line or parallel of longitude

prime meridian – the line of longitude that passes through Greenwich, England, designated as zero degrees longitude, and from which longitude east and west is measured

superimpose – to place over or on top of something else

Universal Transverse Mercator Grid System – a grid system that has been designed to cover the part of the world between latitude 84 degrees north and latitude 80 degrees south, and, as its name implies, is imposed on the transverse Mercator projection

Figure 1.4.1: Meridians and parallels.

Courtesy of US Army JROTC.

The UTM grid system divides the surface of the earth into 60 north-south grid zones (each six degrees wide) like the one in Figure 1.4.2. Mapmakers number these zones from west to east, 1 through 60, starting at the 180 degree meridian. The grid zone in Figure 1.4.2 represents grid zone number 3.

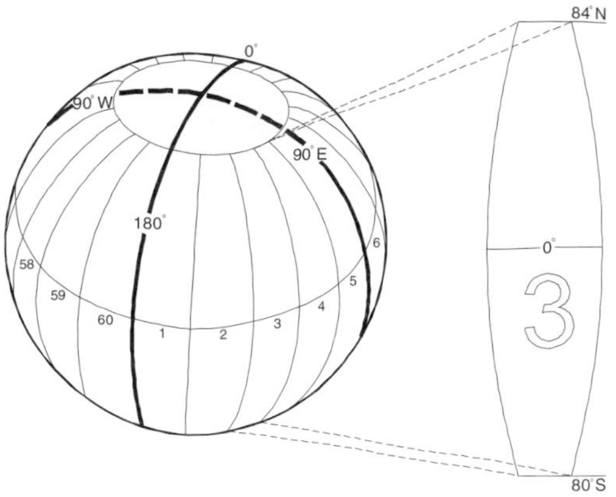

Figure 1.4.3 is this same grid zone, but now further divided into 20 north-south segments. Each grid segment has a letter for identification. Mapmakers use the letters "C" through "X" (omitting the letters "I" and "O") to identify these 20 grid segments. They do not use "I" and "O" because those letters can easily be mistaken for the numbers "1" and "0," respectively. Nineteen of these grid segments are eight degrees high and the one row at the extreme north is 12 degrees high. This combination of zone number and row letter constitutes the grid zone designation.

With this designator, you are now able to identify specific grids. For example, if you wanted to locate the first segment north of the equator, its grid zone designation would be 3N.

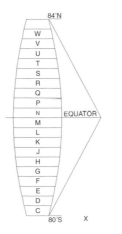

Figure 1.4.2: Grid Zones of the UTM Grid System.

Courtesy of US Army JROTC.

Figure 1.4.3: Grid Segments of the UTM Grid System.

Courtesy of US Army JROTC.

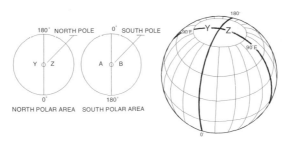

Figure 1.4.4: Polar Regions of the UTM Grid System.

Courtesy of US Army JROTC.

However, if you were to cut out 60 shapes identical to those in Figures 1.4.2 or 1.4.3, your globe would not be complete at either end. Each of these 60 grid zones lay between the 84 degrees north and the 80 degrees south lines of latitude. The polar regions would be missing. Therefore, to complete your globe, extend these grid lines to 90 degrees in both directions: 90 degrees north latitude is the North Pole and 90 degrees south latitude is the South Pole. Mapmakers use the remaining four letters, "A," "B," "Y," and "Z," to identify the polar regions as shown in Figure 1.4.4.

Military Grid Reference System

Superimposed on each grid zone segment are 100,000 meter squares. Each 100,000 meter square is assigned two identification letters (see Figure 1.4.5). The first letter is the column designation and the second letter is the row designation.

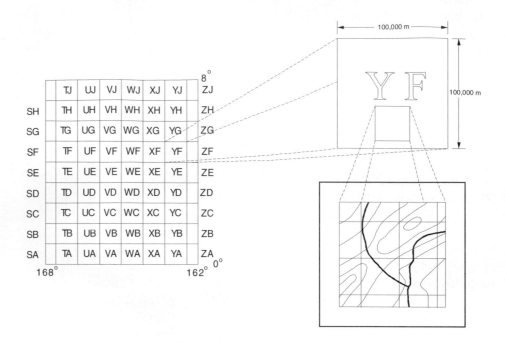

Each 100,000 meter square is then divided by parallel lines (or **grid lines**) that are 1,000 meters or 10,000 meters apart (depending on the scale of the map). These parallel lines come together at right angles to form 1,000 meter or 10,000 meter squares (called **grid squares**)—see Figure 1.4.6. These grid lines and grid squares are the lines that you see on a standard military topographic map. Mapmakers number grid lines along the outside edge of each topographic map for easy reference. Using the two 100,000 meter square identification letters in conjunction with these numbers, you can identify each grid square accurately, without any two grid squares having the same grid number (or grid coordinate).

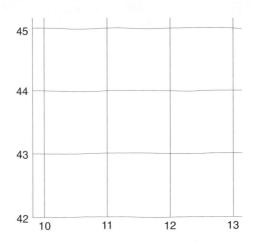

Locating a Point Using the Military Grid Reference System

Whenever you read a grid coordinate, you always read right first, then up. This is one of the cardinal rules in map reading. Based on this rule, you can determine locations on a map using grid coordinates. The number of digits in a grid coordinate represents the degree of precision to which you can locate and measure a point on a map—the more digits, the more precise the measurement. For example, a four-digit grid coordinate locates a point to within 1,000 meters, a six-digit grid coordinate to within 100 meters, and an eight-digit grid coordinate to within ten meters.

You write grid coordinates as one continuous alphanumeric symbol without spaces, parentheses, dashes, or decimal points. Further, grid coordinates must always contain an even number of digits, both letters and numbers. To determine grid coordinates without using a protractor, the reader simply refers to the grid lines numbered along the margin of any map. The following example shows how to form a four-digit grid coordinate.

Suppose you want to locate Spot Elevation 450 in Figure 1.4.7 to the nearest 1,000 meters. Use the following steps to find this specific location:

Figure 1.4.7:
Determining a four-digit
grid coordinate.

Courtesy of US Army JROTC.

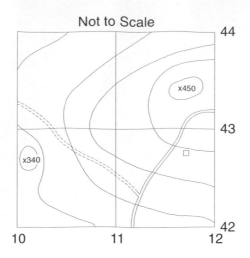

1. **Identify the 100,000 meter square identification letters for the map you are using. You can find this identification in the Grid Reference Box located at the bottom center of the lower margin of a topographic map. For this example, continue to use the "YF" identifier from Figure 1.4.5.**

> ### Note
>
> The next two steps would normally be to break down the 100,000 meter square into 10 equal 10,000 meter grid squares, then to further break down one of those into 10 equal 1,000 meter grid squares. However, you can omit these steps because this example already has 1,000 meter grid squares.

2. **Identify the 1,000 meter grid square in which the spot elevation is located. To do this, remember the first cardinal rule of map reading: read right, then up. When reading a map right and up, each north-south grid line increases in value from west to east, and each east-west grid line increases in value from south to north.**

2. **Read right. You will see that the last north-south grid line before reaching the grid square containing Spot Elevation 450 is 11.**

3. **Read up. Note that the last east-west grid line before reaching the grid square containing Spot Elevation 450 is 43.**

4. **Combine these steps by writing the 100,000 meter square identifier (YF) and the coordinates of the 1,000 meter grid square (11 and 43) as one continuous symbol. Thus, you would write this grid coordinate as YF1143. You have now correctly located a point on the map (Spot Elevation 450) to the nearest 1,000 meters and written a four-digit coordinate.**

Locating a Point Using Six-Digit Grid Coordinates

To locate a point to within 100 meters, follow the procedures in the previous section, and add one more step. In this step, you must divide the 1,000 meter grid square into tenths, or 100 meter increments. Figure 1.4.8 shows what a 1,000 meter grid square would look like if you divided it into 100 meter segments.

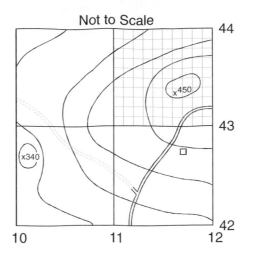

Figure 1.4.8:
Determining a six-digit
grid coordinate.

Courtesy of US Army JROTC.

Suppose you now want to again locate Spot Elevation 450, but this time to within 100 meters. First, read right. Spot Elevation 450 is approximately six-tenths into the grid square. The right reading then is the value of the last north-south grid line before reaching this grid square, or 11, plus a 6 for the six-tenths. This value is read as 116.

By reading up, you can see that Spot Elevation 450 is approximately four-tenths of the way up into the grid square. Therefore, the up reading is the value of the last east-west grid line before reaching this grid square, or 43, and a 4 for the four-tenths. This value is read as 434.

Combining both of these numbers and the 100,000 meter square identifier labels the location as YF116434 for Spot Evaluation 450. You have now used one method to locate a point to the nearest 100 meters by using a six-digit grid coordinate.

Using a Coordinate Scale

Another way to locate a point to within 100 meters is to make use of a coordinate scale. The following is the correct way to use a coordinate scale. To explain this procedure, once again find the six-digit grid coordinate for Spot Elevation 450.

The coordinate scale used by the Army is the one shown in Figure 1.4.9. Note that in the center, it has three different scales: 1:100,000 meters, 1:50,000 meters, and 1:25,000 meters (or 1:250,000 meters).

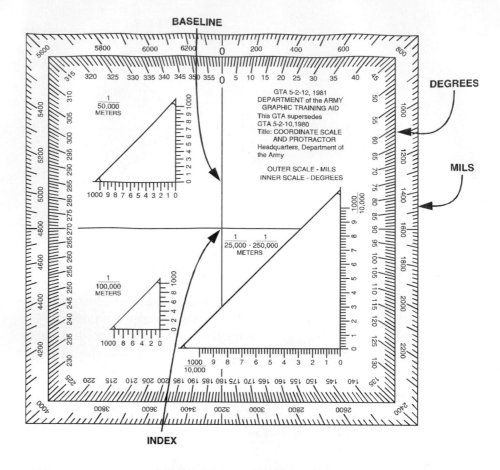

First, check to ensure that you are using the correct scale.

> **Note**
>
> If you obtained a coordinate scale from the JROTC instructor staff, use the 1:25,000 scale for Figures 1.4.9 and 1.4.10.

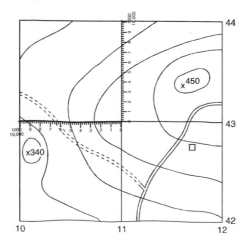

Place the horizontal scale parallel to and directly on top of grid line 43 with the "0 mark" at the lower left corner of grid square YF1143 (see Figure 1.4.9).

Keeping the horizontal scale on top of the 43 grid line, slide the scale to the right into the grid square until the vertical scale intersects the center of mass of Spot Elevation 450 (see Figure 1.4.10).

Now, reading left from the "0 mark," you can see that Spot Elevation 450 lies almost directly on the six-tenths indicator. Therefore, you would read this number as 116.

Reading up, you can see that Spot Elevation 450 lies midway between the three and four mark on the coordinate scale. By applying the above rounding-off rule, round up to read this number as 434. Next, combine both sets of numbers and add the 100,000 meter square identifier to give you the location of YF116434. You have now correctly located a point to the nearest 100 meters by using a coordinate scale.

Grid Reference Box

The grid reference box found on topographic map sheets contains step-by-step instructions for using the grid and military grid reference systems. Mapmakers divide the grid reference box into two parts (see Figure 1.4.11).

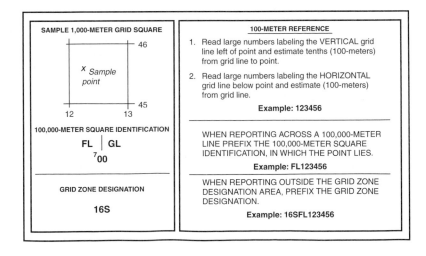

Figure 1.4.11: A grid reference box.

Recreated by Pearson Custom Publishing.

The left portion identifies the grid zone designation and the 100,000 meter square identifier. If the map sheet falls in more than one 100,000 meter square, the number of the grid line that separates these squares and the 100,000 meter square identifications are given. The right portion briefly explains how to find and write a six-digit coordinate.

Conclusion

Being successful at map reading requires a thorough understanding of many basic concepts. This lesson presented several precise systems of finding locations on maps. Your ability to use these systems and to locate four-and six-digit grid coordinates can increase your confidence in identifying your location.

"Contours and Landforms," the following lesson, will help you improve your map reading skills by introducing you to contour lines and intervals. It also explains and illustrates the 10 types of natural and man-made terrain features as well as their corresponding contour lines.

Lesson Review

1. What is the purpose of the Universal Transverse Mercator Grid System?

2. What do the six-digit coordinates on a map tell you?

3. How are the polar regions on the globe identified in the UTM Grid System?

4. How are grid coordinates written?

Lesson 5
Contours and Landforms

Key Terms

concave
concentric
convex
cut
depression
draw
fill
hachures
marginal
mean sea level
ridge
ridgeline
saddle
sinkhole
spur

WHAT YOU WILL LEARN TO DO

• Use terrain features to orient a map and determine location

LINKED CORE ABILITIES

• Apply critical thinking techniques

SKILLS AND KNOWLEDGE YOU WILL GAIN ALONG THE WAY

• Differentiate between elevation and relief

• Recognize the three types of contour lines on a map

• Calculate the elevation of points on a map

• Recognize the ten terrain features

• Define key words contained in this lesson

You can estimate or determine the elevation of a point on a map by following these steps:

1. **Determine the contour interval and the unit of measurement (feet, meters, or yards) from the marginal information.**

2. **Find the numbered index contour line nearest your point.**

3. **Count the number of intermediate contour lines to your point. If you are increasing elevation, add the contour interval to the nearest index contour line. If you are decreasing elevation, subtract the contour interval from the nearest index contour line.**

For example, the point you want to locate is on the second intermediate contour line above the 300 meter index contour line (see Point A on Figure 1.5.2). Note the contour interval for this example is 20 meters. Since your point is closer to the 300 meter index contour line, start there and for each one of the intermediate contour lines that you cross or arrive at to reach your point, add 20 meters to the value of the 300-meter index line. Thus, the elevation of Point A is 340 meters. Notice that your elevation has increased.

Figure 1.5.2: Using intermediate contour lines to calculate elevation.

Courtesy of US Army JROTC.

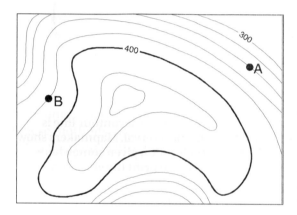

However, let's say that your point (Point B) is now located on the intermediate contour line immediately below the 400 meter index contour line. Below means downhill, or at a lower elevation. Therefore, for the one intermediate contour line that you arrive at to reach this point, subtract 20 meters from the value of the 400 meter index line. The elevation of Point B is 380 meters.

To determine the elevation of the top of an unmarked hill, add one-half the contour interval to the elevation of the last (highest) contour line around the hill. In our example, the last contour line before the hilltop is an intermediate contour line at an elevation of 440 meters. Add one-half the contour interval, or 10 meters, to the value of this intermediate contour line. The elevation of the hilltop is 450 meters.

There may be times when you must estimate the elevation between contour lines. For example, for a point half-way between contour lines, estimate the elevation to one-half the contour interval. For points less than one-forth the distance between the lines, use the same elevation as the nearest line. Remember, if the desired point is on a contour line, its elevation is that of the contour line.

To estimate the elevation to the bottom of a **depression**, subtract one-half the contour interval from the value of the lowest contour line before the depression. In Figure 1.5.3 (with the contour interval still at 20 meters), the lowest contour line before the depression is 240 meters, which is also the elevation at the edge of the depression. Because 10 meters is one-half the contour interval, the bottom of this depression is 230 meters. The tick marks on the contour line forming a depression always point to lower elevations.

Key Note Term

marginal information – instructions placed around the outer edge of a map

Key Note Term

depression – a sunken or low place in the ground

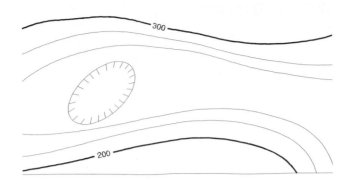

In addition to contour lines, mapmakers use bench marks and spot elevations to indicate points of known elevation on a map. Bench marks (abbreviated BM) are the more accurate of the two. Mapmakers show a bench mark with a black "X" (such as BMx214) with the center of its elevation given in feet, meters, or yards above sea level. Mapmakers show spot elevations with a brown "X" to mark road junctions, hilltops, or other prominent terrain features.

Landforms

In addition to the map symbols introduced earlier in this unit, mapmakers use symbols to represent natural land formations of the earth's surface. They position them on a map so that the center of the symbol remains in its true location. These symbols closely resemble the actual features when viewed from above.

No matter where you live, there are hills, valleys, streams, or other landforms in your area. The relief of an area is the illustration of these shapes as depicted on a map. For example, the relief of Denver would be different from that of Salt Lake City.

Most maps depict up to a total of 10 different natural or man-made landforms or terrain features. All terrain features result from landmasses known as mountains or ridgelines. A **ridgeline** is a line of high ground, usually with changes in elevation along its top and low ground on all sides, from which mapmakers classify the 10 terrain features (Figure 1.5.4).

Key Note Term

ridgeline – a line of high ground, usually with changes in elevation along its top

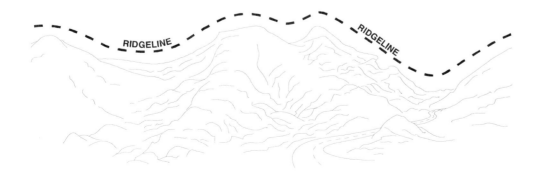

Figure 1.5.4: Ridgeline.

Courtesy of US Army JROTC.

Terrain Features

The 10 natural or man-made terrain features fall into three categories: major features, minor features, and supplementary features. There are five major features, two minor features, and three supplementary features.

The five major terrain features are hill, saddle, valley, ridge, and depression.

Hill

A hill is an area of high ground (see Figure 1.5.5). When you are located on a hilltop, the ground slopes down in all directions. Maps will show a hill with a regular closed contour line, or a series of **concentric** closed contour lines. The inside of the smallest closed circle is the hilltop. The more contour lines, the higher the hill.

Key Note Term

concentric – having a common center

Figure 1.5.5: Hill.

Courtesy of US Army JROTC.

Saddle

A **saddle** is a dip or low point between two areas of higher ground (see Figure 1.5.6). It is not necessarily the lower ground between two hilltops; it may simply be a dip or break along a level ridge or crest. If you were in a saddle, there would be high ground in two opposite directions and lower ground in the other two directions. Maps will show a saddle with the contour lines forming an hourglass or a figure-eight-shaped feature.

Key Note Term

saddle – a low point between two areas of higher ground

Figure 1.5.6: Saddle.

Courtesy of US Army JROTC.

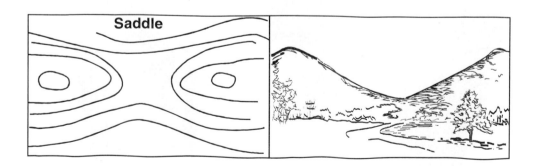

Valley

A valley is a stretched-out groove in the land, usually formed by streams or rivers (see Figure 1.5.7). A valley begins with high ground on three sides, and usually has a course of running water through it, which always flows from higher to lower ground. If you were standing in a valley, there would be high ground in two opposite directions and a gradual slope in the other two directions. Contour lines forming a valley are either "U-shaped" or "V-shaped." To determine the direction water is flowing, look at the contour lines. The closed end of the "U" or "V" always points upstream or toward the high ground.

Figure 1.5.7: Valley.

Courtesy of US Army JROTC.

Ridge

A ridge is a sloping line of high ground (see Figure 1.5.8). If you were standing in the center of a ridge, you would normally have low ground in three directions and high ground in one direction.

Key Note Term

ridge – a sloping line of high ground

Figure 1.5.8: Ridge.

Courtesy of US Army JROTC.

If you cross a ridge at right angles, you climb steeply to the crest, and then descend steeply to the base. When you move along the path of the ridge, depending on your location, there may be either a barely noticeable slope or a very obvious incline. Contour lines forming a ridge tend to be "U-shaped" or "V-shaped." Notice that the closed end of the contour line points away from high ground.

Depression

A depression is a low point in the ground, or a **sinkhole**, surrounded by higher ground in all directions (see Figure 1.5.9). Maps will show depressions by closed contour lines that have tick marks pointing toward the low ground. The closer the contour lines, the deeper the depression.

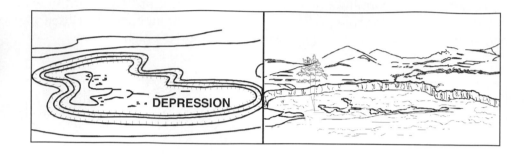

Minor Terrain Features

Along with the terrain features mentioned in the previous sections, there are three minor terrain features. These are **draw**, **spur** and cliff.

Draw

A draw is a less developed stream course than a valley (see Figure 1.5.10). There is no level ground. If you were standing in a draw, the ground would slope up in three directions and down in the other. A draw is sometimes considered to be the initial formation of a valley. Maps will show a draw as a series of successive "U-shaped" or "V-shaped" contour lines that point uphill or upstream.

Spur

A spur is a short, continuous sloping line of high ground, normally jutting out from the side of a ridge (see Figure 1.5.11). It is often formed by two parallel streams cutting draws down the side of a ridge. The ground will slope down in three directions and up in one. Maps will show a spur as a series of successive "U-shaped" or "V-shaped" contour lines that point in a downhill direction.

Figure 1.5.11: Spur.

Courtesy of US Army JROTC.

Cliff

A cliff is a vertical or near vertical slope that is an abrupt change of the land formation (see Figure 1.5.12). Maps show the contour lines for cliffs as being very close together, and in some cases, touching each other.

Figure 1.5.12: Cliff.

Courtesy of US Army JROTC.

Note

Although, as a general rule, a regular contour line is never broken, there are two exceptions when illustrating a cliff or a very steep slope. A contour line may be broken or may converge. Also, a contour line may be broken for the purpose of printing the elevation number.

Supplementary Terrain Features

In the final category, the two supplementary terrain features are cut, and fill.

Cut and Fill

Cuts and **fills** are man-made features resulting from the cutting through of high areas and the filling in of low areas to form a level bed for a road or railroad track (see Figure 1.5.13). Maps will show cuts when they are at least 10 feet high. Mapmakers draw the contour lines along the length of the cut. They also use tick marks to extend from the cut line to the roadbed, if the map scale permits this level of detail.

Key Note Terms

cut – a man-made feature resulting from the removal of high ground, usually to form a level area for roads or railroad tracks

fill – a man-made feature resulting from raising a low area, usually to form a level area for roads or railroad tracks

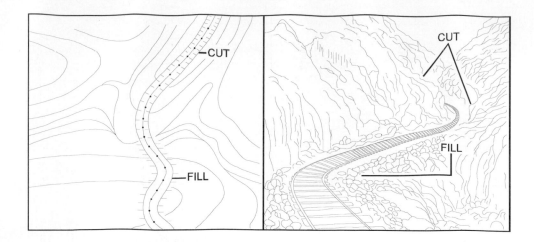

Figure 1.5.13: Cut and fill.

Courtesy of US Army JROTC.

As with cuts, maps will show fills when they are at least 10 feet high. Mapmakers draw the contour lines along the fill line for the length of the filled area and use tick marks to point toward the lower ground.

Your hand can help you visualize eight of the terrain features mentioned above (see Figure 1.5.14). You can demonstrate all but cuts and fills.

Figure 1.5.14: Using your hand to demonstrate terrain features.

Courtesy of US Army JROTC.

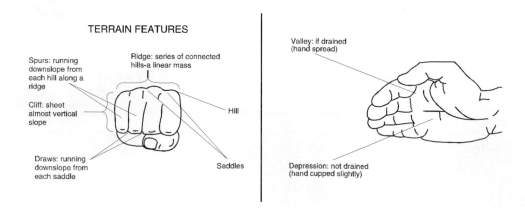

TERRAIN FEATURES

Spurs: running downslope from each hill along a ridge

Ridge: series of connected hills-a linear mass

Cliff: sheet almost vertical slope

Hill

Draws: running downslope from each saddle

Saddles

Valley: if drained (hand spread)

Depression: not drained (hand cupped slightly)

Types of Slopes

The rate of the rise or fall of the ground is known as its slope. You can determine slope by studying the contour lines on a map—the closer the contour lines, the steeper the slope; the farther apart the contour lines, the gentler the slope. The four types of slopes are gentle, steep, **concave**, and **convex**. Figure 1.5.15 gives an example of each slope.

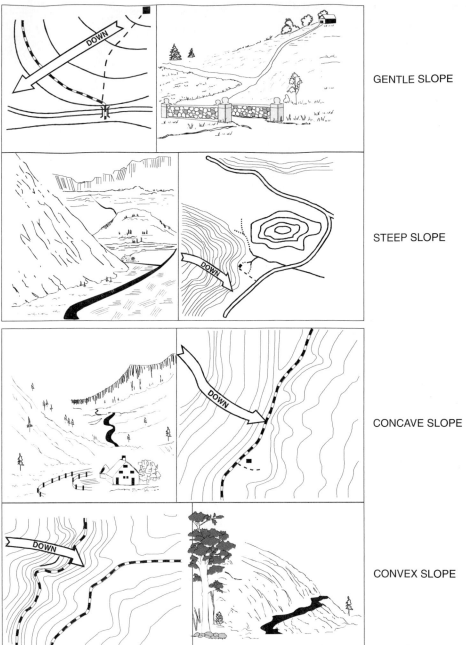

Figure 1.5.15: The four types of slopes.

Courtesy of US Army JROTC.

GENTLE SLOPE

STEEP SLOPE

CONCAVE SLOPE

CONVEX SLOPE

Maps show the contour lines for concave slopes as being closely spaced at the top of the feature and widely spaced at the bottom. Contour lines for convex slopes are just the opposite.

Conclusion

This lesson presented two fundamental concepts of land navigation: understanding elevation and relief and recognizing terrain features.

Practice using these concepts. Study the contours and landforms within your region. When traveling, look for differences in terrain and elevation. Become successful in applying your map-reading skills so that you will always be able to answer the question, "Where am I?"

In the next lesson, you will combine your location-finding skills with the art of determining distance and direction to those locations.

Lesson Review

1. What is the difference between elevation and relief?
2. What are the three types of contour lines on a map?
3. How do you estimate the elevation of points on a map?
4. List the 10 terrain features.

Chapter 1

Lesson Review

Lesson 6
Determining Distance

Key Terms

center of mass
nautical miles
representative fraction
statute miles

WHAT YOU WILL LEARN TO DO

* Measure distance using maps

LINKED CORE ABILITIES

* Apply critical thinking techniques

SKILLS AND KNOWLEDGE YOU WILL GAIN ALONG THE WAY

* Demonstrate how to measure straight-line distance on a topographic map using the scales on that map and procedures for calculating distances that exceed those scales

* Demonstrate how to measure curved-line distance on a topographic map using the scales on that map and procedures for calculating distances that exceed those scales

* Identify the factors that may affect one's pace

* Describe how to determine distance on the ground using estimation and the factors that can cause underestimation or overestimation

* Define key words contained in this lesson

Introduction

Navigating from one point to another with the use of a map and compass involves the ability to apply simple map-reading skills. Previous lessons discussed how to plot locations on a map. In these next lesson, you learn how to determine distance and direction to those locations, both on the map and on the ground. You also learn how to convert a grid azimuth on a map to a magnetic azimuth on the ground and vice versa. When you have successfully completed the next three lessons, you will know "how to get there."

Determining Distance

As you know, a map is a scaled graphic drawing of a portion of the earth's surface. The scale of the map allows the user to convert distance on it to distance on the ground or vice versa. The ability to determine distance on a map, as well as on the earth's surface, is an important factor in plotting a distant location and determining how to get there.

There are two methods of determining distance on a map using the scales found in the marginal information.

- **Mapmakers express a map scale as a representative fraction, which gives the ratio of map distance to ground distance. For example, the scale 1:50,000 indicates that one unit of measure on the map equals 50,000 units of the same measure on the ground. The most common units of measurement are miles, meters, and yards.**

- **Mapmakers divide the graphic (bar) scale into two parts: an extension scale and a primary scale. Use the primary scale, located to the right of the zero, to measure full units; use the extension scale, located to the left of the zero, to measure tenths of a unit. Read the extension scale right to left from the zero and the primary scale left to right from the zero (see Figure 1.6.1).**

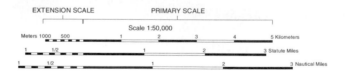

Most road maps indicate distance in miles along primary roads between towns, road junctions, or dots. However, this is not the case with topographic maps. When using a topographic map, you must determine the distance between two points because it is not given. To accomplish this, you must first measure the map distance, then convert that measurement to actual ground distance. Using the bar scales is the best way to perform this task.

Measuring Straight-Line Distance

To determine a straight-line distance between two points on a map, lay a straight-edged piece of paper on the map so that the edge of the paper touches both points and extends past them. Make a mark on the edge of the paper at the **center of mass** for each point (see Figure 1.6.2).

Figure 1.6.1: The bar scale: primary scale and extension scale.

Courtesy of US Army JROTC.

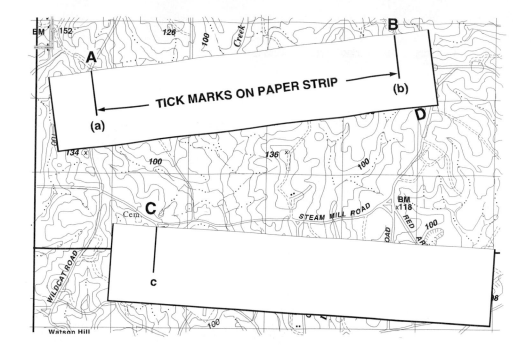

Figure 1.6.2:
Step 1: Measuring
straight-line distance.

Courtesy of US Army JROTC.

To convert the map distance to ground distance, move the paper down to the graphic bar scale, and align the right mark (b) with a printed number on the primary scale so that the left mark (a) is in the extension scale (see Figure 1.6.3).

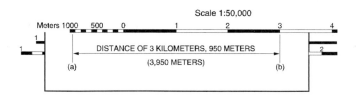

Figure 1.6.3:
Step 2: Measuring
straight-line distance.

Courtesy of US Army JROTC.

In this example, we aligned the right mark (b) with the 3,000-meter mark on the primary scale; thus, the distance is at least 3,000 meters.

Now, to determine the distance between those two points to the nearest 10 meters, look at the extension scale. Because mapmakers number the extension scale with zero at the right and increasing to the left, always read this scale from right to left. Notice that each alternating shaded and clear rectangle is equal to 100 meters. To determine the distance from the zero to mark (a):

1. **Count the number of whole shaded and clear 100 meter rectangles. In our example, there are nine of them, representing 900 meters.**

2. **Mentally divide the distance inside the rectangle containing mark (a) into tenths (or 10-meter intervals)—see Figure 1.6.4. Since mark (a) is approximately half the distance of that rectangle, or five-tenths, you would add another 50 meters to the total in the first step.**

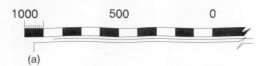

1000   500   0

(a)

Complete your calculations by adding the distance of 3,000 meters (determined using the primary scale) to the 950 meters (determined using the extension scale) the total distance between points (a) and (b) is 3,950 meters.

Measuring Curved Lines

To measure a distance along a winding road, stream, or any other curved line, you must first decide on which side of the feature to take your measurement. Never measure from side to side or down the middle. Start by making a mark on the straight-edged paper at the beginning point's center of mass. Move the edge of this paper along the curve, making marks at short straight distances on both the paper and the map as you proceed.

For accurate results, after placing a mark on both the paper and map, proceed to the next straight portion of this distance by pivoting the paper until the edge of the paper and area you are measuring are aligned. Use your pencil to hold the straight-edged paper in place while pivoting. Continue in this manner until you reach the center of mass at the ending point; then place the paper on the desired bar scale and read the distance between the beginning and ending marks.

In the next example, you measure the road distance between two points once again, by marking the beginning point (c) on the straight-edged paper (see Figure 1.6.2). Next, place marks on both the straight edge piece of paper and the map for each straight portion of road between points (c) and (d). Pivot the straight-edged paper as you make the marks on the paper and map until you reach point (d)—see Figure 1.6.5.

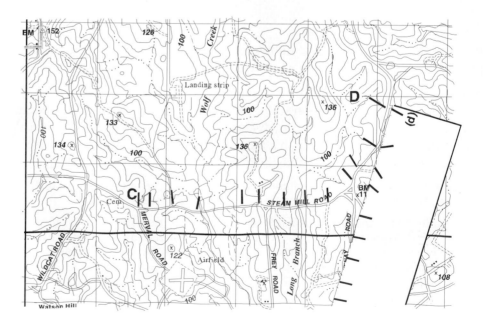

Place the straight-edged paper on the correct bar scale. Using only the beginning and ending marks (ignoring the ones in between), calculate the total distance. You can now use the same method as in the previous example. Notice in Figure 1.6.6 that point (d) falls on the 4,000 meter mark on the primary scale and point (c) is closest to the 550 meter reading on the extension scale. Thus, the road distance between points (c) and (d) is 4,550 meters.

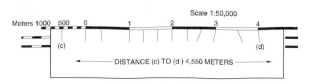

Calculating Distance That Exceeds the Scale

There may be times when the distance you measure on the edge of the paper exceeds the graphic scale, as in Figure 1.6.7. When this happens, there is a procedure you can follow to measure this distance. The first step is to align the right mark (b) with the last printed number on the primary scale, in this case—5 kilometers.

When you include the 1000 meters in the extension scale, you can see that the distance from point (a) to (b) is more than 6,000 meters (or 6 kilometers). To determine the exact distance to the nearest 10 meters, place another mark (c) on the edge of the paper at the end of the extension scale. Remember that the distance from point (b) to (c) is 6,000 meters.

Slide the paper to the right to align mark (c) with zero; then measure the distance between marks (a) and (c). Because the distance between marks (a) and (c) is 420 meters, the total ground distance between start and finish points is 6,420 meters (see Figure 1.6.8).

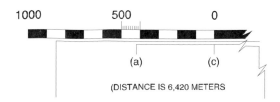

Calculating Distance to a Point off the Map

To determine distance to a point off the map, measure the distance (straight-line or curved-line) from the start point to the edge of the map. Check to see if the marginal information gives the road distance from the edge of the map to the point you

statute mile – a unit of measurement that is approximately 5,280 feet (it is commonly referred to as a "mile")

nautical mile – a unit of measurement that is approximately 6,080 feet, which is one minute of latitude; it is slightly longer than a statute mile

want. Oftentimes, maps will give distances to towns, highways, or junctions off the map. Then, add the distance measured on the map to the distance given in the marginal information. Ensure that the unit of measure is the same. When measuring distance in **statute** or **nautical miles**, round it off to the nearest one-tenth of a mile.

Note

Distance measured on a map does not take into consideration the rise and fall of the land. All distances measured by using the map and graphic scales are flat distances. Therefore, the distance measured on a map will increase when actually measured on the ground. You must take this into consideration when navigating across country.

Other Methods of Determining Distance

When navigating, you may encounter circumstances where you are unable to determine distance using your map or where you are without a map. It is therefore essential to learn alternative methods by which you can accurately pace out or estimate distances on the ground.

Pace Count

One method used to measure ground distance is the pace count. A pace is equal to one natural step, about 30 inches long. To accurately use a pace count, you must know how many paces it takes you to walk 100 meters. To determine this, you must walk an accurately measured course and count the number of paces (steps) it takes. The pace course must be on terrain similar to that over which you will be walking. It will not help you very much to walk a course on flat terrain and then try to use that pace count on hilly terrain. Additionally, you may have to adjust your pace count because of the following conditions:

- **Slopes.** Your pace will lengthen on a down-slope and shorten on an upgrade.
- **Winds.** A head wind shortens the pace and a tail wind increases it.
- **Surfaces.** Sand, gravel, mud, snow, and similar surfaces tend to shorten your pace.
- **Elements.** Snow, rain, or ice may cause you to reduce the length of your pace.
- **Clothing.** Excess clothing and shoes with poor traction can also affect the pace length.
- **Visibility.** Poor visibility, such as fog, rain, or darkness, can shorten your pace.

There are several methods to keep track of the distance you travel when using a pace count. Some of the most common methods are:

- **Put a pebble in your pocket every time you have walked 100 meters according to your pace count**
- **Tie knots in a string (one for every 100 meters)**
- **Put marks in a notebook (one for every 100 meters)**

Never try to remember the count; always use one of these methods, or design your own.

Estimation

Another method is to use estimation. To effectively use this method, you must be able to visualize a distance of 100 meters on the ground. For distances up to 500 meters, determine the number of 100 meter increments between the two objects you wish to measure. Beyond 500 meters, select a point halfway to the objects and determine the number of 100 meter increments to the halfway point, then double it to find the distance to the objects (see Figure 1.6.9).

Figure 1.6.9:
Using estimation to determine distance.

Courtesy of US Army JROTC.

Conclusion

This lesson described several methods for determining distance and presented them in their order of accuracy. The most accurate method is to use a map scale and to convert the map distance (straight-line or curved-line) to ground distance; however, other ways of determining distance on the ground are by pacing and estimation. Estimation is the least accurate means of determining distance.

The next lesson in this chapter covers how to determine direction. Direction plays a very important part in getting from one place to another and without being able to determine direction, you can't get from point A to point B as easily and accurately.

Lesson Review

1. Describe how to measure straight-line distance on a topographic map using the map scale.

2. Describe how to measure curved-line distance on a topographic map using the map scale.

3. List and explain the factors that may affect one's pace.

4. Describe how to determine distance on the ground using estimation and the factors that can cause underestimation or overestimation.

Lesson 7
Determining Direction

Key Terms

azimuth
back azimuth
degree
grid azimuth
grid north
magnetic azimuth
magnetic north
true north

WHAT YOU WILL LEARN TO DO

- Calculate direction on topographic maps

LINKED CORE ABILITIES

- Communicate using verbal, non-verbal, visual, and written techniques

- Apply critical thinking techniques

SKILLS AND KNOWLEDGE YOU WILL GAIN ALONG THE WAY

- Define the three base directions

- Identify the symbols that represent direction on a topographic map

- Demonstrate how to determine and measure a magnetic azimuth

- Demonstrate how to determine, measure, and plot a grid azimuth

- Demonstrate how to determine a back azimuth

- Define key words contained in this lesson

Introduction

In the last lesson, you learned how to determine the distance between two points. After you have determined this distance, you have part of the information you need to get where you are going. To reach your destination, however, you still need to know what direction to travel.

Directions play an important role in everyday life. People oftentimes express them as right, left, straight ahead, and so forth; but then the question arises, "to the right of what?" To answer that question, this section first defines different types of azimuths and three different types of north. It then explains how to determine grid and magnetic azimuths using a protractor and compass.

Expressing Directions

Direction is typically expressed as a unit of angular measure. The most common unit of measure is the **degree**. There are 360 degrees in a circle. Each degree is subdivided into 60 minutes and each minute into 60 seconds.

To express direction as a unit of angular measure, there must be a starting point (or zero measurement) and a point of reference. These two points designate the base direction or reference line. There are three base directions—**true north**, **magnetic north**, and **grid north**—but you will only be using magnetic and grid north in this lesson.

- **True north is a line from any point on the earth's surface to the north pole. All lines of longitude are true north lines. Mapmakers normally represent true north in the marginal information with a star, as shown in Figure 1.7.1.**

- **Magnetic north is the direction to the north magnetic pole, as shown by the north-seeking needle of a compass or other magnetic instrument. Mapmakers usually illustrate magnetic north in the marginal information by a line ending with a half arrow-head, as shown in Figure 1.7.1.**

- **Grid north is the north that mapmakers establish with the vertical grid lines on a map. They usually illustrate it by placing the letters "GN" on a vertical line in the marginal information, as shown in Figure 1.7.1.**

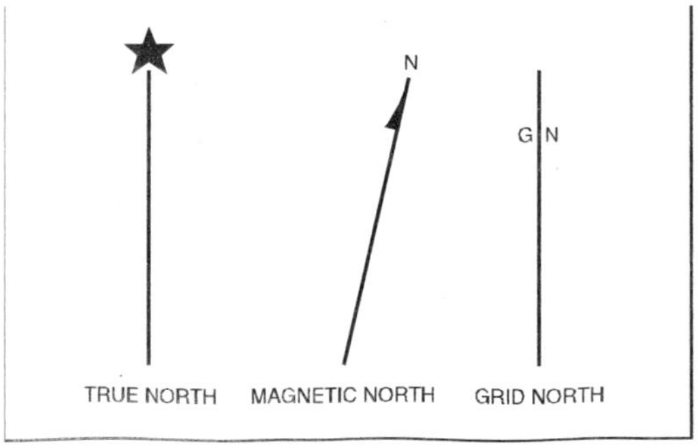

TRUE NORTH   MAGNETIC NORTH   GRID NORTH

Figure 1.7.1: The three norths.

Courtesy of US Army JROTC.

Azimuths

An **azimuth** is defined as a horizontal angle measured clockwise from a base direction. The azimuth is the most common military method to express direction. When using an azimuth, the point from which the azimuth originates is the center of an imaginary circle (see Figure 1.7.2).

Key Note Terms

degree – a unit of latitude or longitude, equal to 1/360 of the globe

true north – a line from any position on the earth's surface to the geographic north pole; symbolized by a line with a star at the apex

magnetic north – the direction to the north magnetic pole, as indicated by the north-seeking needle of a magnetic instrument

grid north – the direction of north that is established by using the vertical grid lines on a map

Key Note Term

azimuth – a horizontal angle usually measured clockwise in degrees from a north base line (direction)

Figure 1.7.2: The circle used to determine an azimuth.

Courtesy of US Army JROTC.

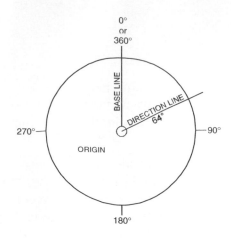

Key Note Terms

back azimuth – the opposite direction of an azimuth obtained by adding 180 degrees to or subtracting 180 degrees from an azimuth

magnetic azimuth – a direction that is expressed as the angular difference between magnetic north and a line of direction

grid azimuth – the angle measured between grid north and a straight line plotted between two points on a map

There are three distinct ways to express an azimuth: **back azimuth**, **magnetic azimuth**, and **grid azimuth**. Following the definition of these azimuths, the remainder of this lesson explains how to measure magnetic and grid azimuths.

A back azimuth is the opposite direction of an azimuth. It is just like doing an "about face." To obtain a back azimuth from an azimuth, *add* 180 degrees if the azimuth is 180 degrees or less; or *subtract* 180 degrees if the azimuth is 180 degrees or more (see Figure 1.7.3). The back azimuth of 180 degrees may be stated as 0 degrees or as 360 degrees.

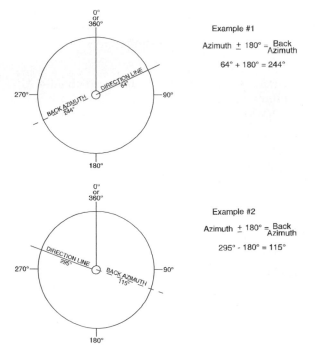

A magnetic azimuth is a direction expressed as the angular difference between magnetic north and the direction line (see Figure 1.7.4). You can determine a magnetic azimuth using a compass or other magnetic instrument (such as surveying equipment).

A grid azimuth is the angle measured between grid north and a straight line plotted between two points on a map (see points "a" and "b" in Figure 1.7.4). You would use a protractor to measure this angle.

Figure 1.7.3: Calculating a back azimuth.

Courtesy of US Army JROTC.

Types of Compasses

You determine a magnetic azimuth with the use of a compass. Two of the most common types of compasses are the magnetic lensatic compass and the silva compass.

The Magnetic Lensatic Compass

The magnetic lensatic compass (see Figure 1.7.5), used by the military, is the most common and simplest instrument for measuring direction. It has three major parts: cover, base, and lens.

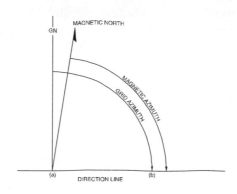

Figure 1.7.4: Magnetic and grid azimuths.

Courtesy of US Army JROTC.

Figure 1.7.5: The magnetic lensatic compass.

Courtesy of US Army JROTC.

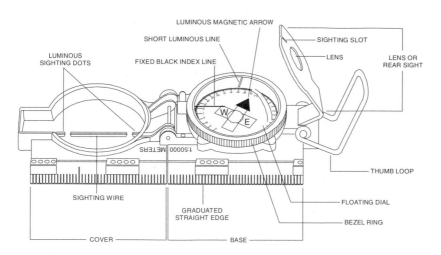

The cover protects the floating dial. It contains the sighting wire (front sight) and two luminous sighting slots or dots used for night navigation. The base contains several movable parts, including the floating dial, the bezel ring, and the thumb loop.

The floating dial is mounted on a pivot so it can rotate freely when you hold the compass level. Printed on the dial in luminous figures are an arrow and the letters E and W or E, W, and S. The arrow always points to magnetic north and the letters fall at East (90 degrees), South (180 degrees), and/or West (270 degrees). There are two scales. The outer denotes mils and the inner scale (normally in red) denotes degrees. Encasing the floating dial is a glass containing a fixed black index line.

The bezel ring is a ratchet device that clicks when turned. It contains 120 clicks when rotated fully. Each click is equal to 3 degrees. A short luminous line used in conjunction with the north-seeking arrow is contained in the glass face of the bezel ring.

The base also contains the thumb loop.

You use the lens to read the dial. The rear sight also serves as a lock and clamps the dial when closed. You must open the rear sight more than 45 degrees to allow the dial to float freely. There is also a rear-sight slot used for sighting on objects. Use this with the front sight sighting wire.

The Silva Compass

The Silva Polaris (Type 7) precision compass (see Figure 1.7.6) is also one of the most accurate compasses on the market today. Some high schools prefer it over the military issued, magnetic lensatic compass due to its cost and availability. The Silva compass is easy to use, especially with its hand-contoured base plate. It is typically available at certain discount department stores for just under $10. Figure 1.7.6 shows the Silva Polaris (Type 7) compass along with its eight features.

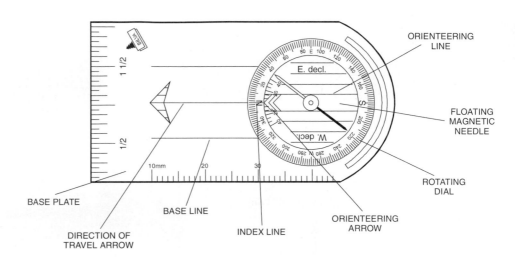

The floating needle is mounted on a pivot so that it can rotate freely when you hold the compass level. It settles within four seconds, always pointing to magnetic north. Printed distinctly on the rotating dial are the letters N and S, to represent 0/360 degrees and 180 degrees, respectively. The dial is graduated at two degree intervals, marked at 20 degree intervals, and contains the letters E (at 90 degrees) and W (at 270 degrees).

The base plate contains two rulers (one measured in inches and the other in millimeters). It also has a 40-degree east and west declination scale inside the area of the floating dial.

Measuring a Magnetic Azimuth

The following steps explain how to determine a magnetic azimuth using the centerhold technique (see Figure 1.7.7). This method is the fastest and easiest way to measure a magnetic azimuth. There is also a compass-to-cheek technique as well as ways for presetting a compass; however, those procedures will not be covered in this unit.

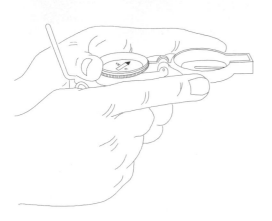

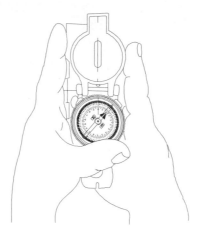

Figure 1.7.7:
The centerhold technique
is used to determine a
magnetic azimuth.

Courtesy of US Army JROTC.

These six steps are for the magnetic lensatic compass.

1. **Open the compass to its fullest so that the cover forms a straightedge with the base.**

2. **Move the lens (rear sight) to the rearmost position, allowing the dial to float freely.**

3. **Place your thumb through the thumb loop, form a steady base with your third and fourth fingers, and extend your index finger along the side of the compass. Place the thumb of the other hand between the lens (rear sight) and the bezel ring. Extend the index finger along the remaining side of the compass, and the remaining fingers around the fingers of the other hand.**

4. **Pull your elbows firmly into your sides. This action places the compass between your chin and waist.**

5. **To measure an azimuth, simply turn your entire body toward the object, pointing the compass cover (zero or index mark) directly at the object.**

6. **After you are pointing at the object, look down and read the azimuth from beneath the fixed black index line. Figure 1.7.8 shows a magnetic azimuth of 320 degrees.**

For the Silva compass, modify step 3 to hold it either completely in one hand (with the curved end toward the back of the palm) or with both hands (as shown in Figure 1.7.7, but disregarding the information on thumb loop and rear sight).

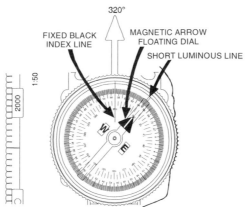

320°

FIXED BLACK INDEX LINE   MAGNETIC ARROW FLOATING DIAL

SHORT LUMINOUS LINE

Figure 1.7.8: Using the
centerhold technique to
determine a magnetic
azimuth of 320 degrees.

Courtesy of US Army JROTC.

Note

Ensure that you are away from power lines, vehicles, or other metal objects when using a compass because these objects will affect its accuracy.

Some compasses may have a 1:25,000 scale; you can still use this scale with a 1:50,000 scale map, but you must halve the values read.

Using Protractors

You determine a grid azimuth with the use of a protractor. There are several types of protractors: full circle, half circle, square, or rectangular. All of them divide the circle into units of angular measure, and each has a scale around the outer edge and an index mark. The index is the center of the protractor circle from which you measure all directions.

On the military protractor, you read the inner of two scales because it is graduated into degrees—from 0 to 360 degrees. Each tick mark on the degree scale represents one degree. The base line of this protractor is a line from 0 degrees to 180 degrees. Where the base line intersects the horizontal line, between 90 degrees and 270 degrees, is the index or center of the protractor.

When using the protractor, the base line is always oriented parallel to a north-south grid line. The 0- or 360-degree mark is toward the top or north on the map, and the 90-degree mark is to the right. Steps for determining and plotting grid azimuths are explained in the following section.

Measuring a Grid Azimuth

The following steps explain how to measure a grid azimuth using a map and protractor (see Figure 1.7.9).

Figure 1.7.9: Using a protractor to measure a grid azimuth.

Courtesy of the United States Geological Survey, modified by Pearson Custom Publishing.

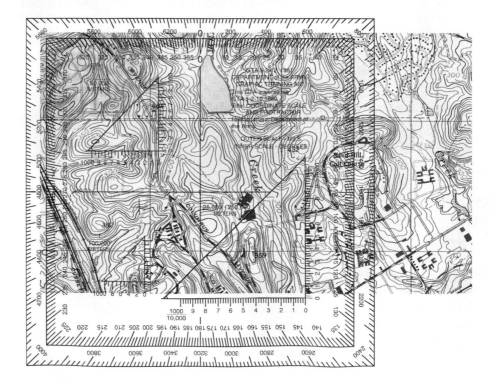

1. Draw a line connecting the two points (A and B on Figure 1.7.9).

2. Place the index of the protractor at the point where the drawn line crosses a vertical (north-south) grid line.

3. Keep the index at that point and align the 0–180 degree line of the protractor on the vertical grid line.

4. Read the value of the angle from the scale. This value is the grid azimuth from point A to point B, or 68 degrees in our example.

Plotting a Grid Azimuth

Use the following steps to plot an azimuth from a known point on a map (see Figure 1.7.10). For this example, you will *not* have to convert the azimuth from magnetic to grid.

1. Place the protractor on the map with the index mark at the center of mass of the known point and the 0–180 degree base line parallel to a north-south grid line. (Use BM 145 on State Route 103.)

2. Make a mark on the map at the desired azimuth. (Use an azimuth of 210 degrees.)

3. Remove the protractor and draw a line connecting the known point and the mark on the map. This is the grid direction line or grid azimuth.

> **Note**
>
> Distance has no effect on azimuths.

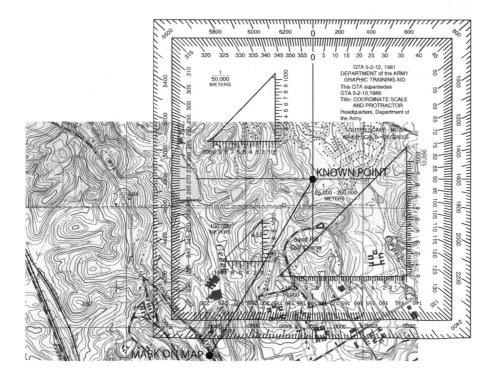

Figure 1.7.10: Using a protractor to plot a grid azimuth.

Courtesy of the United States Geological Survey, modified by Pearson Custom Publishing.

> ### Proceed with Caution!
>
> When measuring azimuths on a map, remember that you are measuring from a starting point to an ending point. If you make a mistake and you take the reading from the ending point, the grid azimuth will be opposite, thus causing you to go in the wrong direction.

Conclusion

Regardless of where you live, you need a way of expressing direction that is accurate and has a common unit of measure. Simply expressing, "to the right of that_._._._," may not be sufficient. The use of azimuths, compasses, protractors, and maps will improve the accuracy of your directions.

Lesson Review

1. Define and describe the three base directions.
2. Describe how to determine and measure a magnetic azimuth.
3. Describe how to determine, measure, and plot a grid azimuth.
4. Explain how to calculate a back azimuth.

Lesson 8
Converting the Grid-Magnetic Angle

Key Terms

arc
declination
grid convergence
Grid-Magnetic (G-M) Angle

WHAT YOU WILL LEARN TO DO

• Use a compass and grid to locate a position on a topographical map

LINKED CORE ABILITIES

• Communicate using verbal, non-verbal, visual, and written techniques

• Apply critical thinking techniques

SKILLS AND KNOWLEDGE YOU WILL GAIN ALONG THE WAY

• Use the declination diagram to convert grid azimuths to magnetic azimuths

• Use the declination diagram to convert magnetic azimuths to grid azimuths

• Convert a magnetic azimuth when the G-M Angle is greater

• Define key words contained in this lesson

Key Note Terms

declination – an angular difference between true north and either magnetic north or grid north

Grid-Magnetic Angle – angular difference in direction between grid north and magnetic north; it is measured east or west from grid north

Introduction

In this section, you learn how to use the **declination** diagram to convert grid azimuths to magnetic azimuths and vice versa. Converting the **Grid-Magnetic Angle** (G-M Angle) is one of the most difficult tasks to understand in map reading; therefore, this lesson presents simple step-by-step procedures for converting the G-M Angle.

The Declination Diagram

Mapmakers place the declination diagram in the lower margin of most topographic maps.

Declination is the angular difference between true north and either magnetic or grid north. There are two declinations, a magnetic declination and a grid declination. The declination diagram shows the angular relationship, represented by prongs, between the three norths (see Figure 1.8.1). However, the position of the three prongs in relation to each other varies according to the declination data for each map.

Figure 1.8.1:
A declination diagram.

Courtesy of US Army JROTC.

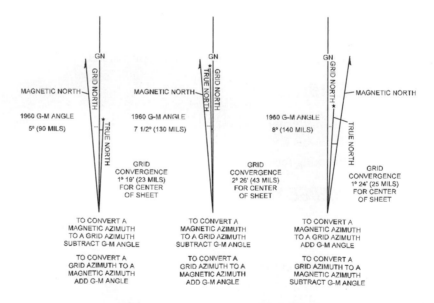

Furthermore, mapmakers usually do not plot the angles between the prongs exactly to scale. Although you can obtain the position of the norths in relation to each other from the diagram, you should not measure the numerical value from it. For example, if the amount of declination from grid north to magnetic north is one degree, the **arc** shown on the diagram only represents the direction of the declination and the diagram may exaggerate its value. If measured, the declination may have an actual value of five degrees.

Key Note Term

arc – anything shaped like a curve, bow or arch; a curved line

The Grid-Magnetic (G-M) Angle

The Grid-Magnetic Angle, or the G-M Angle, is the angular size that exists between grid north and magnetic north in the year that mapmakers prepared the angular size. It is an arc, indicated by a dashed line, that connects the grid-north and magnetic-north prongs. Maps express this value to the nearest one-half (1/2) degree with mil equivalents shown to the nearest 10 mils. The G-M Angle is important in map reading because it helps a user to apply direction to an object that is on a map to its actual direction on the ground and vice versa.

Grid Convergence

The **grid convergence** is an arc indicated by a dashed line connecting the prongs for true north and grid north. The value of the angle for the center of the sheet is given to the nearest full minute (of degrees) with its equivalent to the nearest mil. Mapmakers show these data in the form of a grid-convergence note.

Conversion

There is an angular difference between the grid north and the magnetic north caused by the attraction of the earth's magnetic field (found in Northern Canada). Because all compasses point toward magnetic north, the location of this magnetic field does not match exactly with the grid-north lines on the maps; therefore, a conversion from magnetic to grid, or vice versa, is needed.

Conversion with Notes

If the declination diagram on a map provides conversion notes explaining the use of the G-M Angle, simply refer to them. One note gives instructions for converting a magnetic azimuth to a grid azimuth. The other shows how to convert a grid azimuth to a magnetic azimuth. The conversion (to add or subtract) depends on the direction of the magnetic-north prong relative to the grid-north prong.

Conversion without Notes

Some maps, however, do not contain these declination conversion notes. Thus, it is necessary to convert from one type of declination to another. A magnetic compass gives a magnetic azimuth, but in order to plot this line on a map with grid lines, you must change the magnetic azimuth value to a grid azimuth value. Therefore, you must use the declination diagram for these conversions. A rule to follow when solving such problems is "starting from the reference line, *always* measure the angle to the azimuth line in a clockwise direction." With this rule in mind, you can now solve the problem using the following steps (see Figure 1.8.2).

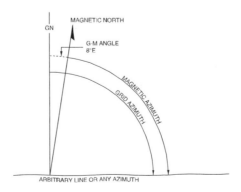

Figure 1.8.2: Converting without notes.

Courtesy of US Army JROTC.

1. Draw a vertical, or grid-north, line (prong). Always align this line with the vertical lines on the map.

2. From the base of the grid-north line, draw a direction line (or an azimuth line) at roughly a right angle from north, regardless of the actual value of the azimuth in degrees.

3. Examine the declination diagram on the map and determine the direction of the magnetic north (right-left or east-west) relative to that of the grid-north prong. Draw a magnetic prong from the base of the grid-north line in the desired direction.

4. Determine the value of the G-M Angle by drawing an arc from the grid prong to the magnetic prong and placing the value of the G-M Angle above the arc.

5. Complete the diagram by drawing an arc from each reference line to the vertical line you first drew. A glance at the completed diagram shows whether the given or desired azimuth is greater, and thus whether you must add or subtract the known difference between the two azimuths.

6. The inclusion of the true-north prong in relationship to the conversion is of little importance.

Applications of the G-M Angle Conversion

For the remainder of this lesson, you learn how to apply this conversion technique when you have an east G-M Angle, a west G-M Angle, and when the G-M Angle is greater than the magnetic or grid azimuth.

The first application is to convert an east magnetic azimuth to a grid azimuth.

Working with an East G-M Angle

To plot a magnetic azimuth of 210 degrees on a map, you must convert it to a grid azimuth. To do so, follow these steps:

1. **Determine the declination in degrees. In this example, it is 12 degrees east (see Figure 1.8.3).**

Figure 1.8.3: Converting an east magnetic azimuth to a grid azimuth.

Courtesy of US Army JROTC.

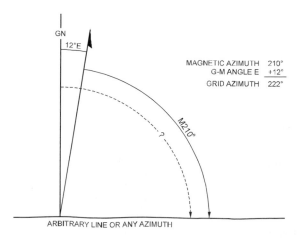

MAGNETIC AZIMUTH 210°
G-M ANGLE E +12°
GRID AZIMUTH 222°

2. **Because the arc from magnetic north to the azimuth line is shorter than the arc from grid north to the azimuth line, you must add the G-M Angle. This yields a grid azimuth of 222 degrees.**

To use a magnetic azimuth in the field with a compass when you have a grid azimuth of 303 degrees, you must convert it to a magnetic azimuth.

The second application is to convert an east grid azimuth to a magnetic azimuth.

1. **Determine the declination in degrees. In this example, it is 10 degrees east (see Figure 1.8.4).**

2. **Because the arc from grid north to the azimuth line is longer than the arc from magnetic north to the azimuth line, you must subtract the G-M Angle. This yields a magnetic azimuth of 293 degrees.**

The third application will be to convert to a magnetic azimuth when the G-M Angle is greater (see Figure 1.8.5).

In converting a grid azimuth to a magnetic azimuth, when the G-M Angle is greater than the grid azimuth, first do the following:

1. **Add 360 degrees to the grid azimuth. In this example, the grid azimuth is 2 degrees (refer to Figure 1.8.5). You can now convert the grid azimuth to a magnetic azimuth because the grid azimuth is larger than the G-M angle.**

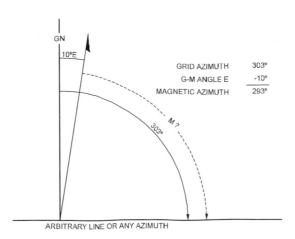

GRID AZIMUTH	303°
G-M ANGLE E	-10°
MAGNETIC AZIMUTH	293°

Figure 1.8.4: Converting an east grid azimuth to a magnetic azimuth.

Courtesy of US Army JROTC.

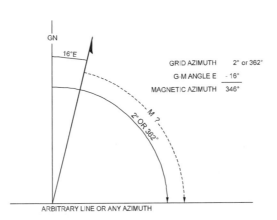

GRID AZIMUTH	2° or 362°
G-M ANGLE E	- 16°
MAGNETIC AZIMUTH	346°

Figure 1.8.5: Converting to a magnetic azimuth when the G-M Angle is greater.

Courtesy of US Army JROTC.

Note

Because there are no negative azimuths on the azimuth circle, 0 degrees is the same as 360 degrees; therefore, 2 degrees [in this example] is the same as 362 degrees. This is because 2 degrees and 362 degrees are located at the same point on the azimuth circle.

2. **This procedure is the same as Step 2 in the last example. Because the grid north arc of 362 degrees is longer than the arc from magnetic north to the azimuth line, you must subtract the G-M Angle. This yields a magnetic azimuth of 346 degrees.**

Working with a West G-M Angle

The fourth application is to convert a west magnetic azimuth to a grid azimuth. To plot a magnetic azimuth of 65 degrees on a map, you must convert it to a grid azimuth.

1. **Determine the declination in degrees. In this example, it is 8 degrees west (see Figure 1.8.6).**

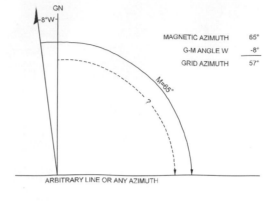

Figure 1.8.6: Converting a west magnetic azimuth to a grid azimuth.

Courtesy of US Army JROTC.

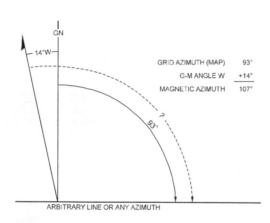

Figure 1.8.7: Converting a west grid azimuth to a magnetic azimuth.

Courtesy of US Army JROTC.

2. Because the arc from magnetic north to the azimuth line is longer than the arc from grid north to the azimuth line, you must subtract the G-M Angle, giving you a grid azimuth of 57 degrees.

To use a magnetic azimuth in the field with a compass when you have a grid azimuth of 93 degrees, you must convert it to a magnetic azimuth.

The fifth application is to convert a west grid azimuth to a magnetic azimuth.

1. Determine the declination in degrees. In this example, it is 14 degrees west (see Figure 1.8.7).

2. Because the arc from grid north to the azimuth line is shorter than the arc from magnetic north to the azimuth line, you must add the G-M Angle. This yields a magnetic azimuth of 107 degrees.

The final application is to convert to a grid azimuth when the G-M Angle is greater. In converting a magnetic azimuth to a grid azimuth, when the G-M angle is greater than the magnetic azimuth, first do the following:

1. Add 360 degrees to the magnetic azimuth. In this example, the magnetic azimuth is 5 degrees (see Figure 1.8.8). You can now convert the magnetic azimuth to a grid azimuth because the magnetic azimuth is larger than the G-M Angle.

Note

Because there are no negative azimuths on the azimuth circle, 0 degrees is the same as 360 degrees; therefore, 5 degrees (in this example) is the same as 365 degrees. This is because 5 degrees and 365 degrees are located at the same point on the azimuth circle.

2. Because the magnetic north arc of 365 degrees is longer than the arc from grid north to the azimuth line, you must subtract the G-M angle. This yields a grid azimuth of 353 degrees.

Each time you convert a G-M Angle, construct a G-M Angle diagram that shows the required azimuths. The construction of a diagram takes the guesswork out of converting azimuths when the map does not give any conversion notes.

Converting the G-M Angle requires practice. Become familiar with the proper procedures to follow whether there is an east or west G-M Angle, or the G-M Angle is greater than your grid or magnetic azimuth.

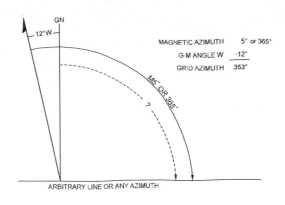

MAGNETIC AZIMUTH   5° or 365°
G-M ANGLE W   -12°
GRID AZIMUTH   353°

Figure 1.8.8: Converting to a grid azimuth when the G-M Angle is greater.

Courtesy of US Army JROTC.

Conclusion

This lesson presented map reading skills that you can use not only in later map reading instruction, but also in many practical ways. It discussed how to determine distance and direction (with a protractor and a compass) between two points. It also investigated how to convert the Grid-Magnetic Angle using a grid azimuth from a map or a magnetic azimuth from a compass. Mastering these skills will help you to navigate more effectively when the challenge arises.

The next lesson introduces you to how you determine location. This will give you the skills needed to be able to precisely determine your location, or the location where you need to be.

Lesson Review

1. What does the declination diagram on a map indicate?

2. Explain how to convert grid azimuths to magnetic azimuths.

3. Explain how to convert magnetic azimuths to grid azimuths

4. You are given a 13 degree westerly declination. From your location you see a radio tower on a magnetic azimuth of 275 degrees. What azimuth will you use to locate the radio tower on your map?

Lesson 9
Determining Location

Key Terms

field-expedient
intersection
polar coordinates
resection

WHAT YOU WILL LEARN TO DO

- Apply map reading and land navigation skills to determine location

LINKED CORE ABILITIES

- Communicate using verbal, non-verbal, visual, and written techniques

- Apply critical thinking techniques

SKILLS AND KNOWLEDGE YOU WILL GAIN ALONG THE WAY

- Describe the procedure for locating an unknown point on a topographic map by intersection

- Describe the procedure for locating unknown position on a topographic map by resection

- Identify procedures for locating or plotting an unknown point on a topographic map using polar coordinates

- Identify procedures for determining direction using field-expedient methods

- Define key words contained in this lesson

Introduction

Sometimes it is not enough to know how to locate a point to within 1,000 or 100 meters, or to estimate the location of a distant point on the ground. There may be times when you have to determine your location, or a distant point, even more accurately. Or, perhaps you will need to use certain known locations as reference points. This lesson will help you to accomplish these tasks.

In this chapter, you have encountered most of the basic map reading skills. However, skills such as determining an eight-digit grid coordinate and locating an unknown point using polar coordinates, intersection, and resection will help you to more accurately locate and plot points on a map. This lesson examines those skills and gives you an opportunity to practice them. You also learn how to determine direction using a **field-expedient** method.

Key Note Term

field-expedient – adapting to a particular situation by using available materials and/or resources

Determining an Eight-Digit Grid Coordinate

To determine an eight-digit coordinate, you must use a coordinate scale. Keep in mind that there are 100 meters between each 100-meter mark (number) on the coordinate scale, with a short tick mark to indicate 50 meters between each 100-meter mark. To locate spot elevation (SE) 450 in Figure 1.9.1 to within 10 meters, use the following procedures:

1. **Recall that you must first identify the 1,000 meter grid square in which the spot elevation is located. To do this, remember the first cardinal rule of map reading: read right, then up. When reading a map right and up, each north-south grid line increases in value from west to east, and each east-west grid line increases in value from south to north.**

   - **By reading right, the last north-south grid line before reaching the grid square containing SE 450 is 11.**

   - **By reading up, the last east-west grid line before reaching the grid square containing SE 450 is 43.**

   - **By adding the 100,000 meter square identifier (YF), YF1143 locates SE 450 to the nearest 1,000 meters.**

2. **Place the coordinate scale parallel to and directly on top of grid line 43 with the "0 mark" at the lower left corner of grid square YF1143 (see Figure 1.9.2).**

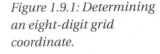

Figure 1.9.1: Determining an eight-digit grid coordinate.

Courtesy of US Army JROTC.

Figure 1.9.2: Placing the coordinate scale.

Courtesy of US Army JROTC.

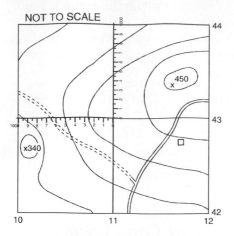

3. **Keeping the horizontal scale on top of the 43 grid line, slide the scale to the right into the grid square until the vertical scale intersects the center of mass of SE 450 (see Figure 1.9.3).**

Figure 1.9.3: Slide the scale to the right.

Courtesy of US Army JROTC.

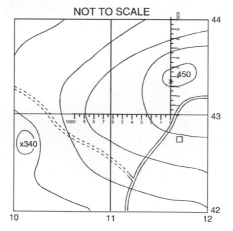

4. **Reading from the "0 mark," the right reading shows that SE 450 lies between the 600 and 650 meter mark by approximately 30 meters.**

Note

You determine that it is approximately 30 meters by estimating how many 10s SE 450 is beyond the 600-meter mark. In this case, there are three, which gives you the third and fourth digits of the coordinate. Thus, the center of mass of SE 450 is 630 meters into the grid square and you would read this number as 1163.

5. **Reading up, you can see that SE 450 lies midway between the 300 and 400 meter marks, or 350 meters into the grid square; therefore, the up reading is 4335.**

6. **By combining both sets of numbers and adding the 100,000 meter square identifier, the location of SE 450 is YF11634335. You have now correctly located a point to the nearest 10 meters.**

To trace the degree of accuracy of an eight-digit grid coordinate from 1,000 to 10 meters, you can break it down as follows:

1. The underlined numbers in YF<u>11</u>63<u>43</u>35 represent the 1,000 meter grid square and they locate the point to within 1,000 meters.

2. The third and seventh digits of YF11<u>6</u>34<u>3</u>35 denote 600 and 300 meters and locate the point to within 100 meters.

3. The fourth and eighth digits of YF116<u>3</u>433<u>5</u> denote 30 and 50 meters and locate the point to within 10 meters.

Intersection

You can use **intersection** to locate an unknown point by determining where the azimuths from two (preferably three) known positions on the ground intersect. There are two ways to determine intersection—the map and compass method, and the straightedge method.

Map and Compass Method

The first way to find an unknown point by intersection is with a map and compass. Follow these steps and examine Figure 1.9.4.

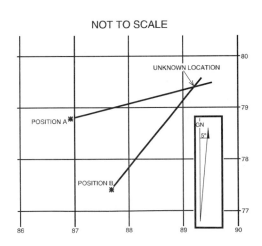

NOT TO SCALE

Figure 1.9.4: Using intersection: the map and compass method.

Courtesy of US Army JROTC

1. **Orient the map using the compass.**

> **Note**
>
> The best way to orient a map is to use a compass.

2. **Determine the Grid-Magnetic angle (G-M angle) of the map you are using. In this example, the G-M angle is 5 degrees east.**

3. **Locate and mark your first known position (Point A) on the map.**

4. **Measure the magnetic azimuth to the unknown point from Point A using a compass. In this example, the magnetic azimuth is 71 degrees.**

5. Convert the magnetic azimuth to a grid azimuth. In this example, 71 degrees plus 5 degrees equals a 76-degree grid azimuth.

6. Place the coordinate scale on the map, ensuring that the zero-degree indicator is at the top and the index point is directly over the center of mass of Point A. Place a tick mark at 76 degrees on the map. Draw a line from Point A along this grid azimuth.

7. Move to Point B (the second known point) and locate it on the map; then, repeat steps 4, 5, and 6. For this example: (1) The magnetic azimuth in step 4 from Point B to the unknown point is 35 degrees. (2) Convert this to a grid azimuth using the formula 35 + 5 = 40. (3) Place a tick mark at 40 degrees on the map and draw a line along that grid azimuth.

8. The location of the unknown position is where the lines cross on the map. Determine the eight-digit grid coordinate for this position.

Straightedge Method

The second way to locate an unknown point by intersection is by using a straightedge. Follow these steps and examine Figure 1.9.5.

Figure 1.9.5: Using intersection: the straightedge method.

Courtesy of US Army JROTC.

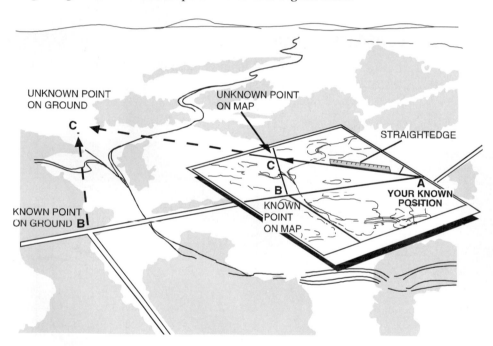

1. Orient the map (on a flat surface) to the ground by terrain association.

2. Locate and mark your known position on the map (Point A).

3. Place a straightedge on the map with one end at your position (Point A) as a pivot point. Rotate the straightedge until the unknown point (C) is sighted along the edge.

4. Draw a line along the straightedge.

5. Repeat steps 3 and 4 with the second known position (Point B) and check for accuracy. The intersection of these lines on the map is the location of the unknown point (C).

6. Determine the six- or eight-digit grid coordinate (depending upon the desired degree of accuracy) for the unknown point.

Resection

You can use **resection** to locate your unknown position on a map by determining the grid azimuth to at least two well-defined locations on the map. For greater accuracy, the desired method of resection would be to use three well-defined locations. There are three ways you can use resection: the map and compass method, modified resection, and the straightedge method.

Map and Compass Method

The first way to find your unknown location by resection is with a map and compass. Follow these steps and examine Figure 1.9.6.

1. **Orient the map using the compass.**

2. **Determine the Grid-Magnetic Angle (G-M Angle) of the map you are using. In this example, the G-M Angle is 3 degrees east.**

3. **Identify two or three known locations on the ground. Mark them on the map, such as Hilltop 408 and the control tower.**

4. **Measure the magnetic azimuth to one of the known positions from your location using a compass. In this example, the magnetic azimuth to Hilltop 408 is 312 degrees.**

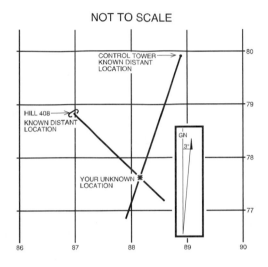

NOT TO SCALE

5. **Convert the magnetic azimuth to a grid azimuth. In this example, 312 degrees plus 3 degrees equals a 315-degree grid azimuth.**

6. **Convert the grid azimuth to a back azimuth by adding or subtracting 180 degrees. In this example, 315 degrees minus 180 degrees equals a 135-degree back azimuth.**

7. **Place the coordinate scale on the map, ensuring that the zero-degree indicator is at the top and the index point is directly over the center of mass of the known point. Place a tick mark at 135 degrees. Draw a line on the map from the known position back toward your unknown location.**

8. **Repeat steps 4, 5, 6, and 7 for the second known position (the control tower). For this example:**

   a. **The magnetic azimuth to the control tower is 15 degrees.**

   b. **Convert this to a grid azimuth: 15 + 3 = 18.**

   c. **Convert this to a back azimuth: 18 + 180 = 198.**

   d. **Place a tick mark at 198 degrees on the map and draw a line back toward your unknown location.**

9. **The intersection of these two lines is your location. Determine the eight-digit grid coordinate for your position.**

Key Note Term

resection – the method of locating your unknown position by determining where the back azimuths from two or three well-defined locations on a map meet

Figure 1.9.6: Using resection: the map and compass method.

Courtesy of US Army JROTC.

Straightedge Method

Another way to locate your unknown position by resection is by using a straightedge. Follow these steps and examine Figure 1.9.7.

Figure 1.9.7: Using resection: the straightedge method.

Courtesy of US Army JROTC.

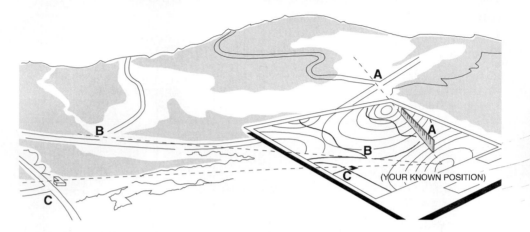

1. **Orient the map (on a flat surface) to the ground by terrain association.**

2. **Locate at least two known distant locations or prominent features on the ground and mark them on the map (Points A, B, and C).**

3. **Place a straightedge on the map pointing toward one of the known points (Point A). Rotate the straightedge until the known point on the map is aligned with the same known point on the ground.**

4. **Draw a line along the straightedge away from the known point on the ground toward your position.**

5. **Repeat steps 3 and 4 using the other known points (Points B and C).**

6. **The intersection of these lines on the map is your location.**

7. **Determine the six- or eight-digit grid coordinate (depending upon the desired degree of accuracy) for your location.**

Key Note Term

polar coordinates – a method of locating or plotting an unknown position from a known point by giving a direction and distance along that direction line

Polar Coordinates

You can use **polar coordinates** to locate or plot an unknown point from a known location by giving a direction and a distance along the direction line. Three elements must be present to use polar coordinates: a known location on the map, an azimuth (grid or magnetic), and a distance (normally in meters). There are two ways that you can use polar coordinates—the map and compass method, and the protractor method.

Map and Compass Method

Use the following steps and examine Figure 1.9.8 for the map and compass method.

1. **Orient the map using a compass.**

2. **Determine the Grid-Magnetic Angle (G-M Angle) of the map you are using. In this example, the G-M Angle is 0 degrees.**

3. **Identify the known location on the ground and mark it on the map. In this example, the known location is the water tank in grid square FL4526.**

4. **Measure the magnetic azimuth to the unknown point (a building in grid square FL4729) from the known location using a compass. In this example, the magnetic azimuth to building is 24 degrees.**

5. **Convert the magnetic azimuth to a grid azimuth. In this example, 24 degrees plus 0 degrees equals a 24-degree grid azimuth.**

6. **Place a coordinate scale on the map, ensuring that the zero-degree indicator is at the top and the index point is directly over the center of mass of the known point.**

7. **Place a tick mark at 24 degrees.**

8. **Draw a line on the map from the known location along this grid azimuth until it intersects the building.**

9. **Determine the distance to the unknown position. Using a straightedge and the procedure for measuring straight line distance, you determine the distance to the building in grid square FL4729 to be 3,600 meters.**

Protractor Method

The second way to locate or plot an unknown point from a known location using polar coordinates is the protractor method. Follow these steps and examine Figure 1.9.8.

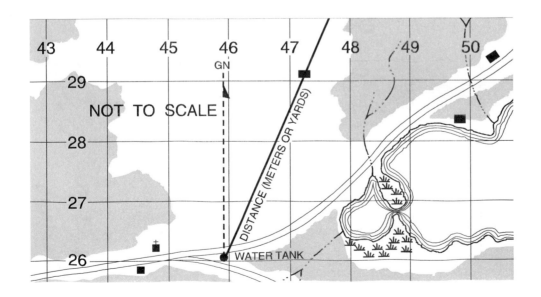

Figure 1.9.8: Using polar coordinates.

Courtesy of US Army JROTC.

1. Determine the location of a known point on the map to within 100 or 10 meters. In this example, the known location is the water tank at grid coordinates FL45952610.

2. Measure a grid azimuth to the desired location or destination (the building in grid square FL4729). By using your protractor, you determine the grid azimuth to be 24 degrees to the building.

3. Determine the distance as you did in step 9 of the map and compass method.

Determine Direction Using Field-Expedient Methods

Sometimes a compass is not available and you must determine your location by using the materials and resources available to you. There are several methods you can use to determine direction by using the sun and the stars. These include the shadow-tip method and the watch method.

Shadow-Tip Method

The following steps show you how to use the shadow-tip method to determine direction and/or orient a map without a compass.

Figure 1.9.9:
The shadow-tip method.

Courtesy of US Army JROTC.

FIRST
SHADOW-TIP
MARK

1. Place a stick or branch at least 12 inches long vertically into the ground at a fairly level spot where the sun will cast a distinct shadow. Mark the shadow tip on the ground with a small stone, twig, or other means. See Figure 1.9.9.

Note

If the tip of the shadow is difficult to find, tap the end of the stick; the movement of the shadow will help you locate it.

2. Wait 10 to 15 minutes until the shadow moves a few inches. Mark the new position of the shadow tip in the same way as the first. See Figure 1.9.10.

3. **Draw a straight line through the two marks to obtain an east-west line. Extend this line past the second mark (refer to Figure 1.9.10).**

4. **Determine which is the east end of the line and which is the west end using these tips: the sun rises in the east and sets in the west; the shadow tip moves in the opposite direction, and; the first shadow tip mark is always west, and the second mark is always east.**

5. **To find north and south, draw a line at a right angle to the east-west line at any point (see Figure 1.9.11). From this north-south line, you can now orient your map and determine the direction you want.**

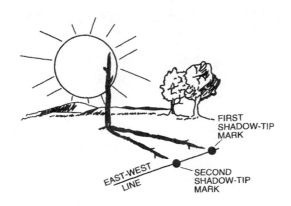

Figure 1.9.10: Mark the new location.

Courtesy of US Army JROTC.

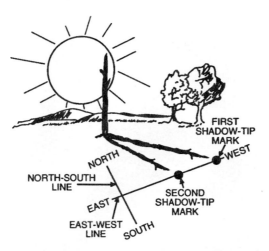

Figure 1.9.11: Determining north and south.

Courtesy of US Army JROTC.

Watch Method

You can also use a watch to determine the approximate true north or true south; however, this method can result in errors, especially in the lower latitudes, and may cause circling.

In the northern hemisphere, point the hour hand toward the sun. Find a north-south line midway between the hour hand and 12:00 o'clock, standard time. If on daylight saving time, find the line between the hour hand and 1:00 p.m. If you have any doubt as to which end of the line is north, remember that the sun is in the east before noon and is in the west after noon (see #1, Figure 1.9.12).

In the southern hemisphere, point the 12:00 o'clock dial toward the sun, and halfway between 12:00 o'clock and the hour hand will be a north-south line. If on daylight saving time, the line will lie midway between the hour hand and 1:00 p.m. (see #2, Figure 1.9.12).

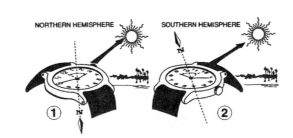

Figure 1.9.12: The watch method.

Courtesy of US Army JROTC.

Global Positioning System

The Global Positioning System (GPS) is a high-tech worldwide radio-navigation system formed from a network of 24 satellites (see Figure 1.9.13) and their ground stations. GPS is the first system to pinpoint such a precise location for any point on the globe, during any kind of weather. This system utilizes these satellites to calculate positions down to a matter of meters. As a matter of fact, use of advanced forms of GPS can pinpoint locations down to a centimeter. GPS receivers have become more economical and, therefore, accessible in recent times. Uses of the GPS system include: air navigation, mapping, pinpointing locations, and navigating routes for cars and boats.

Figure 1.9.13: A global positioning satellite.

Courtesy of
Photo Researchers.

A GPS receiver uses the travel time of radio signals to measure distance. The satellites are closely monitored so that their exact location is always known. Any delays created by the radio signals traveling through the atmosphere are corrected.

Conclusion

In this chapter, you discovered how to determine a point on a map to within 10 meters using an eight digit coordinate; locate an unknown point using intersection, resection, and polar coordinates; and determine direction using two field-expedient methods.

By using these skills in conjunction with the other map reading skills that we have presented in the previous lessons, you should be capable of finding your way regardless of the situation. You may even have the opportunity to test your skills on an orienteering course (as explained in the next chapter) or on another form of a land navigation course.

The next lesson covers orienteering, a skill that began as part of military training, but has become a popular competitive event.

Lesson Review

1. Describe the procedure for locating an unknown point on a topographic map by intersection.

2. Describe the procedure for locating an unknown position on a topographic map by resection.

3. How do you locate an unknown point on a topographic map using polar coordinates?

4. Describe two ways of determining direction using field-expedient methods.

Chapter 1

Lesson Review

Lesson 10
Orienteering

Key Terms

aiming off
attack point
control points
orienteering
steering mark

WHAT YOU WILL LEARN TO DO

- Relate map-reading skills to orienteering

Linked Core Abilities

- Communicate using verbal, non-verbal, visual, and written techniques

- Apply critical thinking techniques

SKILLS AND KNOWLEDGE YOU WILL GAIN ALONG THE WAY

- Explain orienteering and how it originated

- Differentiate between six types of orienteering courses

- Explain the five-step process to determine direction of travel

- Demonstrate five movement techniques used in orienteering

- Identify the control areas and safety aspects used in orienteering

- Define key words contained in this lesson

Introduction

This lesson introduces you to **orienteering**, its techniques and terminology, as well as the various types of orienteering courses. In addition, many of the map reading and land navigation skills practiced in previous lessons are applied.

Orienteering began in Scandinavia in the 1800s, primarily as a military event and as part of military training. By 1919 it had become a competitive sport in Sweden. In the early 1930s, the sport received a boost with the invention of an improved compass. Bjorn Kjellstrom, one of the inventors of that compass, introduced orienteering to the United States in 1946.

Orienteering is for all ages and degrees of fitness and skill. It provides the suspense and excitement of a treasure hunt. The object is to locate **control points** (see Figure 1.10.1) by using a map and compass to navigate the terrain.

Organizers of an orienteering event will give each participant a topographic map with various control points circled see Figure 1.10.2). Each control point has a corresponding flag marker on the ground and a special punch which organizers use to mark the scorecard. Competitive orienteering involves running from point to point. It is more demanding than road running, not only because of the terrain, but because the participant must make decisions, and keep track of the distances covered. Courses may be as long as 10 kilometers.

Key Note Terms

orienteering – a competitive form of land navigation in which each participant uses a map and compass to navigate between check points

control point – a trapezoid-shaped marker (usually orange, red, or white) used to mark features on a orienteering course, usually with clipper or control punch attached to mark a control card as proof of arrival

Figure 1.10.1: Orienteering control points.

Courtesy of US Army JROTC.

Figure 1.10.2: Topographic orienteering map.

Courtesy of Quantico Orienteering Club.

Although orienteering challenges both the mind and the body, the competitor's ability to think under pressure and make wise decisions is sometimes more important than speed or endurance. The person just starting out in orienteering should concentrate more on refining map reading and land navigation skills than on running between the control points.

Types of Orienteering Courses

There are different types of orienteering events that range from individual courses, to a relay event, to night competition. All types of orienteering courses are interesting and challenging, but they vary in their degree of difficulty. The best location for an orienteering course is one that is easily identifiable on both a map and the actual terrain. It should also be accessible from several routes. Listed below are some of the most common orienteering events/courses.

Route Orienteering

This form of orienteering can be used by beginners to the sport as well as for advanced competition. In route orienteering, a master (or advanced competitor) walks a route while beginners trace the actual route walked on the ground using their maps. Beginners circle the location of the different control points found along the walked route. When they finish, organizers analyze and compare the maps. For beginners, time is not a factor in this event.

Another variation of route orienteering involves a course laid out with markers for the competitor to follow. Because the route is indicated with flags or markers, there is no master map. The winner of the event is the competitor who successfully traces the route and accurately plots the most control points.

Figure 1.10.3: Line orienteering.

Courtesy of US Army JROTC.

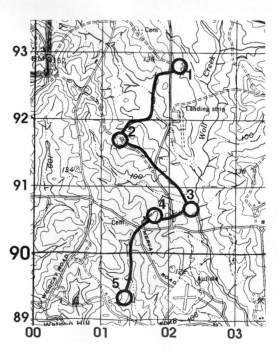

Line Orienteering

In line orienteering, competitors trace on their maps a preselected route from a master map that has at least five control points. The object is to walk the route shown on the map, circling the control points on the map as competitors locate them on the ground. See Figure 1.10.3.

Chapter 1   Map Skills

Cross-Country Orienteering

Cross-country (or free-point orienteering) is the most common type of orienteering competition. It is considered to be the most competitive and intriguing form of orienteering. In this event, all competitors must visit the same control points in the same order. With the normal one-minute starting interval, it becomes a contest of route choice and physical skill. The competitor with the fastest time is the winner.

The length and difficulty of the course is determined by the skill of the competitors. There are usually 6 to 12 control markers on the course in varying degrees of difficulty and distances apart so that there are no easy, direct routes. The course may be closed-in with the start and finish located at the same position (see Figure 1.10.4) or the start and finish may be at different locations.

Organizers mark each point in order on a master map. They give competitors a clue list that describes each control point with an 8-digit grid coordinate, a two-letter control code, and a clue describing the terrain in the location of the marker. Competitors must indicate on their score cards proof of visiting each control marker. This is usually done with a special stamp or punch.

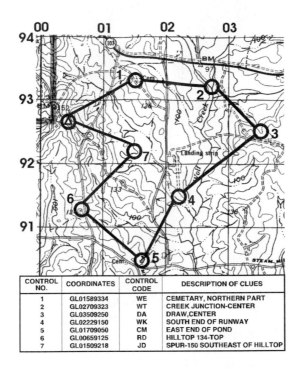

Figure 1.10.4: Cross-country orienteering.

Courtesy of US Army JROTC.

CONTROL NO.	COORDINATES	CONTROL CODE	DESCRIPTION OF CLUES
1	GL01589334	WE	CEMETARY, NORTHERN PART
2	GL02709323	WT	CREEK JUNCTION-CENTER
3	GL03509250	DA	DRAW,CENTER
4	GL02229150	WK	SOUTH END OF RUNWAY
5	GL01709050	CM	EAST END OF POND
6	GL00659125	RD	HILLTOP 134-TOP
7	GL01509218	JD	SPUR-150 SOUTHEAST OF HILLTOP

Score Orienteering

In this event, the area chosen for the competition has many control points. The control points near the start/finish point (usually identical in this event) have a low point value, while those more distant or more difficult to locate have a high point value. The competitor must locate as many control markers as possible within the specified time (usually 90 minutes).

As with a cross-country event, organizers give each competitor a map and an event card. The card lists all the control points with their different values.

Organizers design the course (see Figure 1.10.5) so that there are more control points than a competitor can possibly visit in the allotted time. Therefore, competitors must plan and choose their route between control points carefully. Points are awarded for each control point visited and deducted for exceeding the specified time; however, there is no reward for returning early with time still available to find more points. The good competitor must be able to coordinate time and distance with the ability to land navigate while running the course. The competitor with the highest point score is the winner.

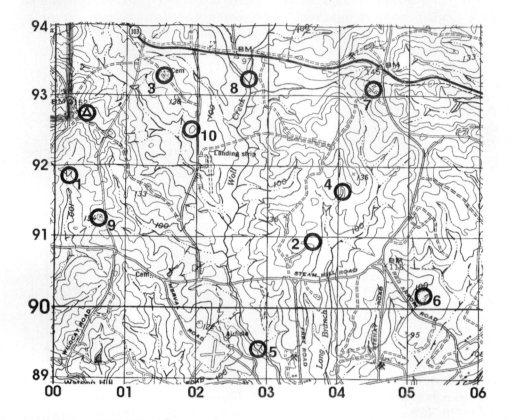

Figure 1.10.5: Score orienteering.

Courtesy of US Army JROTC.

Relay Orienteering

This type of orienteering is a popular team sport. Each member of the team runs a free-point or line orienteering leg of one to two miles. No person runs more than one leg. The competition may be held using a master map for the entire course or one for each leg.

In the case of a master map for the entire course, the first team member copies down all legs of the course. After completing the first leg, he or she hands the map to the next runner, who completes the next leg of the course. The team repeats this process until all members have run their portion of the course.

In the case of a master map for each leg, the first trainee goes to a master map that has only the first location on it. When that person completes the first leg, he or she gives the map to the next person, who goes to a different master map and copies the second portion of the course. This continues until all members of the team have completed their legs.

Night Orienteering

Night orienteering is a free-point or score event occurring in the evening. The main differences between a night conducted free-point or score and one conducted during the day are:

- Control points are marked by a light that is visible from 30 to 50 meters in all directions
- Control points are located no more than 400 to 800 meters apart
- The event is run over less difficult terrain
- The signal used to indicate the conclusion of the event or an emergency is a vehicle horn or a flare

Controlling Your Movement

A sound knowledge of the basics of map reading will help you immensely as an orienteering event competitor. Additional skills such as accurate compass reading, good decision making, and using the terrain are critical as well. The beginner-level orienteer should learn the following techniques.

Determining Direction of Travel

After you have plotted the course's control points, you must determine how to get to the first and other control points. The basic compass technique used in orienteering to determine direction of travel consists of five steps:

1. **Lay the map on a flat surface and orient it to magnetic north by placing the edge of the compass along a north-south grid line. Rotate the map and compass until the north arrow is under the black hairline.**

2. **Keeping the map oriented, move the compass in such a way that one side of the compass touches your location and your destination. The compass is now pointing in the direction of travel.**

3. **Rotate the bezel ring until the luminous line is pointing to grid north on the map. The luminous line should be over the north arrow (if the map is still oriented) and it should be parallel to the north-south grid line.**

4. **Lift the compass off the map and correct for magnetic declination. If the declination is west, rotate the bezel ring counterclockwise; if east, then rotate it clockwise.**

5. **Holding the compass in front of you, rotate your body until the north arrow lies under the luminous line. The direction of travel is now indicated by the black hairline.**

Route Selection

As mentioned at the beginning of this lesson, orienteering develops many skills besides map reading. An important one is decision making. Route selection is where competitors must make decisions. Which is the fastest way from point A to point B? Is it over or around a hill? Is it going cross country or using a road or trail? Except for those instances when organizers mark or specify the route in advance, wise route selection is important.

A good orienteering course will have some elevation obstacles. These obstacles will force you to decide if it is faster to go the most direct route over it or to take a longer detour around it. A simple formula to convert height into comparable flat distance is: 25 feet of elevation equals 100 meters on a flat surface. For example, suppose the straight line distance to point B is 500 meters with a 50 foot high hill en route. The energy you would expend would be equivalent to running 500 meters plus an additional 200 meters for going over the hill. If the detour around the hill equals a total of 680 meters, it may be easier to go around it, depending upon the type of terrain you encounter.

The type of terrain and vegetation that you encounter has a major impact on your pace. You must know your pace count through several types of terrain. In addition, you must know your pace when trotting and running, both when you are fresh and when you are tired. Although pacing will vary from individual to individual, Figure 1.10.6 may be useful to a beginner. These figures apply during daylight, when the runner is fresh and on flat terrain. The numbers represent paces or each time the left foot strikes the ground.

	SMALL	MEDIUM	TALL
	(less than 5'8")		(over 6' tall)
Road/Path	42	40	47
Light Vegetation	45	43	40
Open Forest	50	46	43
Dense Forest	55	50	46

Movement Techniques

In addition to knowing where the control points are and where you are at all times, you must also know the best route for getting to the next control point. The shortest route may not be the fastest, and it may not pay to travel between two points as fast as possible if you tire yourself out in the process.

Note

Remember, you can locate your position on a map using terrain features, a back azimuth, or resection.

There are several techniques available to aid you in moving from one control point to another. They include the following:

- **Direct line.** This method involves establishing a compass bearing between your location and the destination; then, follow the compass bearing until you reach the point. A variation of this technique is to establish a compass bearing that you will follow for a specific distance at which time you establish a new bearing. Repeat this process until you reach the final destination.

- **Steering marks.** A **steering mark** is a prominent object or terrain feature on the ground that you can see and that is in the general direction of travel. Such objects as a lone tree or building are good examples of steering marks. One of the advantages of this technique is that once you reach the steering mark, you can reorient yourself before continuing.

- **Aiming off.** The **aiming off** technique is valuable when your destination lies along a linear terrain feature such as a road or stream. Due to errors in compass or map reading, you may reach a linear feature and not know whether your objective lies to the right or the left. Furthermore, each degree that you

Chapter 1 Map Skills

are offset to the right or left will move the aim-off point from the destination 17 meters to the right or left for each 100 meters traveled. For example, if the number of degrees offset is 10 and the distance traveled is 100 meters, then your location is 170 meters to the left of the objective (10 degrees offset X 17 meters per 100 meters traveled = 170).

> **Note**
>
> A proven technique to prevent this from occurring is to deliberately aim to one side of the destination; then, when you reach the linear feature, you will know in which direction to turn.

- **Attack points.** When using the **attack points** technique, you select a prominent terrain feature, such as a hilltop or road junction, near your destination. You may use any technique to arrive at this point. After there, you can reorient yourself, and then make a final short approach to it. The purpose of this technique is to minimize the distance you have to travel on the final approach. This in turn limits any errors in compass work or pacing you might make in locating the destination. The difference between an attack point and a steering mark is that you select an attack point from a map.

- **Geographic orientation.** This technique involves keeping the map oriented as you travel and remembering what terrain features you will encounter en route to the next control point. For example, if you decide to follow a road to reach the next control point, you should orient the map as you stop and make turns along the road.

Using Figure 1.10.7, assume that you want to travel from your position at "A" to control point 4. One route that you could take would be to use the north-south intermittent stream bed. Pass the first two east-west intermittent stream junctions that you encounter and take the eastern fork at the third junction. Follow that intermittent stream and draw to the road junction (which you can call an attack point). From the road junction, shoot an azimuth of 77 degrees to the control point.

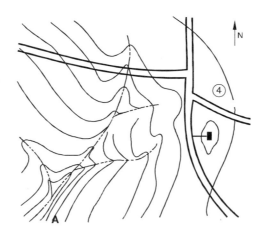

Figure 1.10.7: Use terrain features to plot a route.

Courtesy of US Army JROTC.

Clothing and Equipment

When planning to participate in an orienteering event, you should wear and take the proper clothing and equipment.

Choose the clothing to wear depending on the type of vegetation and terrain you will encounter on the course. For example, in bushy terrain, you should wear a long-sleeve shirt and long pants to protect against cuts and scratches. For those who want to pursue orienteering as a sport, consider purchasing light nylon racing suits. These are full-length suits (usually fluorescent) with long sleeves and pouches in the front to carry maps, compasses, and so on.

Hiking shoes or boots are excellent for orienteering because of their durability and the ankle support they provide. High-top sneakers also provide excellent ankle support. Cross-country running shoes are good because they are light-weight and have better traction in mud, but they do not normally support the ankles.

Although a standard military lensatic compass is very good for orienteering, its one disadvantage is the time required for the needle to stabilize prior to lining up an azimuth. Those who desire to pursue orienteering as a sport may want to acquire an induction dampened or liquid-filled compass.

The map is probably the most important item the participant carries. The most common map used in orienteering is a topographic map with a 1:50,000 scale; however, competitors prefer a 1:25,000 scale because it is easier to read and it shows features in greater detail. Try to use multi-colored maps if they are available. After a competitor outlines the course details and copies the key terrain features from color-coded master maps, his/her own maps should be covered with a clear, plastic-like material such as a document protector to prevent these marks from smearing and/or becoming unreadable.

Organization of the Course

At every orienteering event, there are a few basic elements that you will encounter. These are essential to the efficient and safe operation of the event, and are covered in the following sections.

Officials

Most events often use the same officials at both the start and finish, although their functions are different at each end. At the start, these officials include:

- **Course organizer.** Briefs competitors in the assembly area, issues event cards and maps, and calls competitors forward to start individually (or in groups if it is a group event).

- **Recorder.** Records the competitor's name and start time on recorder's sheet, checks the competitor's name and start number on the event card, and issues any last-minute instructions.

- **Timer.** Controls the master clock and releases the competitors across the start line at their start time (usually at one-minute intervals) to the master map area.

At the finish, the officials include:

- **Timer.** Records the finish time of each competitor on his or her event card and passes the card to the recorder.

- **Recorder.** Records competitor's finish times on the recorder's sheet and tallies final score based on time and correctness of control points visited.

- **Course organizer.** Verifies correctness of names, finish times, and final score. Posts competitors' positions on a results board and accounts for all participants at the end of the event.

More officials and/or assistants may be used; however, the three listed here are the minimum required to run the competition.

Control Areas

In many orienteering events, there are at least three control areas. They are:

- **Assembly area. Here participants register and receive instructions, maps, event cards, and start numbers. They may also change into their orienteering clothes if facilities are available, study their maps, and fill out their event cards. Sanitation facilities are normally available in this area.**
- **Start (Start/Finish). At the start, each competitor reports to the recorder and timer to be logged in and released. Oftentimes, the start and finish are at the same location.**
- **Master map area. There are three to five master maps 20 to 50 meters from the start. When the participants arrive at this area, they must mark all the course's control points on their maps. Having done this, competitors must decide on the route they will follow. Experienced competitors will take the time to orient their map and carefully plot the route before rushing off.**

Control Cards

Organizers make the event card as small as possible so that competitors can easily carry it in a pocket. It contains the following items: name, start number, start time, finish time, total time, place, and spaces for marking the control points visited. It may also contain a listing of descriptive clues. Figure 1.10.8 is a sample event card for the most common type of an orienteering course.

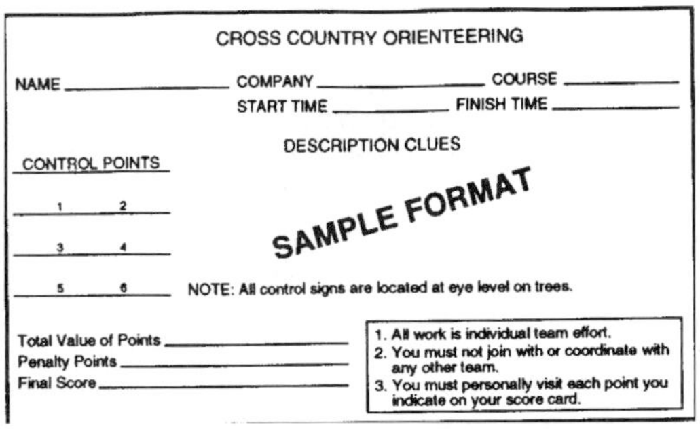
CROSS COUNTRY ORIENTEERING

NAME ______ COMPANY ______ COURSE ______

START TIME ______ FINISH TIME ______

DESCRIPTION CLUES

CONTROL POINTS

1 ______ 2 ______

3 ______ 4 ______

5 ______ 6 ______

SAMPLE FORMAT

NOTE: All control signs are located at eye level on trees.

Total Value of Points ______

Penalty Points ______

Final Score ______

1. All work is individual team effort.
2. You must not join with or coordinate with any other team.
3. You must personally visit each point you indicate on your score card.

Figure 1.10.8: A typical control card.

Courtesy of US Army JROTC.

Clue Description Cards

Organizers prepare these cards with the master maps after the course is set. They contain the descriptive clues for each control point, control code, grid coordinate references, returning time for competitors, removal times for each location, and panic azimuth. Organizers keep the clue description cards and the master maps confidential until the competitors start the event.

Scoring

Organizers score the cross-country or free event by the competitor's time alone. Competitors must visit all control points; failure to visit one results in a disqualification. In this event, the fastest time wins. A variation that organizers often use for beginners is to have a "not-later-than" return time at the finish and to add minutes on to their final time for the number of minutes late and for the number of control points not located.

The score event requires the participant to collect as many points as possible within the time limit. Organizers deduct points for extra time spent on the course—usually one point for every 10 seconds over the time limit.

Safety

The following items and provisions are required to ensure that an orienteering course runs as safely as possible. Furthermore, the course organizer ensure that all participants receive a detailed safety briefing that covers the following key information.

- **First aid.** Ensure that a first aid kit is available at the start and finish. One of the officials should be trained in first aid, or a qualified medical person should be at the event.

- **Control points.** Locate all control points where the safety of the competitors is not endangered by hazardous terrain or other conditions.

- **Safety lane.** Designate a location, usually linear, on the course where competitors may go if injured, fatigued, or lost. A good course will usually have a well-defined boundary as a safety lane; then competitors can set a panic azimuth on their compass and follow it until they reach the boundary.

- **Finish time.** All orienteering events must have a final return time. At this time, organizers should sound a loud siren or horn and all competitors must report to the finish line, even if they have not completed the course.

- **Search and rescue procedures.** If all competitors have not returned by the end of the competition, the officials should drive along the boundaries of the course to pick up the missing people.

Give orienteering a try!

Interest in orienteering within the United States has grown rapidly over the years. Orienteering is conducted under the guidelines of the United States Orienteering Federation, which presently has approximately 70 clubs affiliated with it. For more information, check out the International Orienteering Federation's website at http://www.orienteering.org/.

Conclusion

Orienteering is a form of land navigation where the terms, symbols, and techniques are different from military land navigation. Although an expert military map reader/land navigator is by no means ready to complete a civilian orienteering event, military experience and training in navigating on the ground and reading maps (as well as physical training and decision-making) will help you to become a good orienteering competitor. Several orienteering practices and a complete familiarization with the map reading skills presented in previous lessons will help you to gradually become competitive in this exciting and challenging sport.

Air navigation is discussed in the next lesson. You will learn about flight execution, and see the differences and similarities between getting there by land or by air.

Lesson Review

1. What is orienteering and how did it originate?
2. List the six types of orienteering courses.
3. Explain the five-step process to determine direction of travel.
4. Describe the five movement techniques used in orienteering.

Lesson 11
Air Navigation

Key Terms

altimeter
cultural features
Greenwich Mean Time
hydrographic features
linear features
nautical mile
pilotage
preflight
meridian
statute mile

WHAT YOU WILL LEARN TO DO

- Plan an air flight

LINKED CORE ABILITIES

- Communicate using verbal, non-verbal, visual, and written techniques

- Apply critical thinking techniques

SKILLS AND KNOWLEDGE YOU WILL GAIN ALONG THE WAY

- Compare common units of measure for distance in air and road travel

- Contrast aeronautical charts and topographic maps

- Compare aeronautical symbols with topographical map symbols

- Identify types of aeronautical charts, scales, and characteristics

- Distinguish among the time zones

- Identify appropriate charts for planning a flight route

- Define key words contained in this lesson

Introduction

For centuries, people dreamed of flying like birds. They told stories of flying beings and designed flying contraptions that remained earthbound. In 1903, the Wright brothers made human flight a reality, and today air flight is a common occurrence. Aircraft are used to transport cargo as well as people. People "fly" for recreation as well as business. Travel by air brings almost every part of the world physically within your reach in far less time than travel by car, train, or boat.

This lesson gives you a glimpse into the world of flight by teaching you about air navigation and flight execution. It boosts your map reading skills and points out the differences between getting there on the ground and flying there in the air.

As you discovered in previous Map Reading lessons, when you travel on foot, you have to consider the terrain. Where is the best place to cross a stream? Do you walk over a hill or around it? How long will it take to get there if the ground level keeps rising and falling? Likewise, travel by car depends on the roads leading to your destination, which in turn maneuver around natural and man-made features. Very rarely can you travel in a straight line on the ground from your departure point to your destination.

Air travel, however, is different. Without the limitations of terrain, you determine your heading and fly in a straight line from point A to point B. Of course, as with ground navigation, you must plan your trip carefully; and once in the air, you must follow your route and keep alert. You may be free from terrain difficulties in the sky, but flying comes with its own set of rules.

Air Navigation Charts

Imagine that you live in Alexander City, Alabama, and during spring break you want to attend a race at the Talladega International Speedway in Talladega, Alabama. You have your private pilot's license and an available airplane. Before you can begin planning your trip, you need to find the proper map. The information found on topographic and road maps, such as trail markers, building symbols, highway route numbers, and points of interest, will be of little help when flying at 6,000 feet.

Also, road or topographic maps do not depict information about radio aids and tall towers. You need a map designed for air navigation, specifically an aeronautical chart that will show landmarks to aid you in navigating to Talladega.

> **Note**
>
> You can use the words "chart" and "map" interchangeably, but most professional navigators refer to maps as charts.

Chart Scales

Not all aeronautical charts are the same. The pilot of a light aircraft flies low enough to navigate by landmarks identifiable from the air. An airline pilot, however, is only near enough to the ground to navigate by landmarks on takeoffs and landings. Therefore, the light plane pilot and the airline pilot need to use different charts with different scales.

Remember, when it comes to charts, covering a large area means using a small scale, while covering a small area means using a large scale. Because you are flying within the state of Alabama, you will use a large scale chart that shows more detail of a small area. An airline pilot crossing the U.S. would use a small scale chart covering a large area.

As discussed in previous Map Reading lessons, the scale of a chart may be given as a representative fraction. For example, 1:500,000 indicates that one unit on a chart equals 500,000 units of the same measure on the ground. The most common unit of measure for distance in air navigation is the **nautical mile**.

To understand the size of a nautical mile, recall that you can divide each degree of latitude and longitude into 60 minutes. A nautical mile is one minute of latitude or approximately 6,080 feet—slightly larger than the **statute mile** used in road travel in the U.S., which is 5,280 feet. Since a nautical mile is one minute of latitude, there are an even 60 nautical miles in one degree of latitude. This makes navigating long distances with the nautical mile easier than with the statute mile.

Jet Navigation Chart (JNC)

The Jet Navigation Chart (JN) has a scale of 1:2,000,000 or one inch to 27.4 nautical miles. Pilots flying long-range, high-speed aircraft use the JN which details **hydrographic** and **cultural features** identifiable from high altitudes.

Operational Navigation Chart (ONC)

The Operational Navigation Chart (ONC) has a scale of 1:1,000,000 or one inch to 13.7 nautical miles. Because it covers less area on a single chart than the JN, it shows more detail of hydrographic and cultural features. Pilots flying higher-speed aircraft use the ONC for medium- and some low-level navigation.

Sectional Aeronautical Chart

The sectional aeronautical chart has a scale of 1:500,000. It is the largest scale of the three charts discussed here, and therefore shows even more detail of hydrographic and cultural features. It provides excellent ground details for visual ground-chart orientation and depicts navigation aids and air facilities. The sectional aeronautical chart is the basic aeronautical chart of the U.S., and because of its scale and detail, is the chart you choose for your flight.

Because sectional aeronautical charts cover small areas, there are 37 that make up the continental U.S. You must choose which one to use. In Figure 1.11.1, you can see that the Atlanta Sectional covers Alabama and is the appropriate chart

Key Note Terms

nautical mile – a unit of measurement that is approximately 6,080 feet – which is one minute of latitude; it is slightly longer than a statute mile

statute mile – a unit of measurement that is approximately 5,280 feet (it is commonly referred to as a "mile")

hydrographic feature – an ocean, coast line, lake, river, stream, swamp or reef portrayed by tinting or blank spaces on a map

cultural feature – a manmade feature depicted on maps; for example, a road, railroad, dam, bridge, etc.

for your trip. It gives enough details of the ground for you to navigate using visual landmarks from Alexander City to Talladega. This type of landmark flying, called **pilotage**, is the basic method of light plane navigation in good weather.

Key Note Term

pilotage – "landmark flying" using charts that give enough details of points on the ground for navigating

Figure 1.11.1: U.S. sectional aeronautical chart.

Courtesy of US Army JROTC.

Preflight

There are several responsibilities to tend to before any flight. Because these occur before your actual flight, they are generally referred to as **preflight**. As with any hike or road trip you undertake, how well you plan, or preflight, will directly affect how successful and enjoyable your flight is. Preflight activities include:

Key Note Term

preflight – includes planning a flight and making a check of your aircraft

- **Choosing and studying the appropriate charts**
- **Planning your flight route**
- **Checking the weather**
- **Inspecting the aircraft**
- **Filing a flight plan**

Studying the Appropriate Charts

As discussed in previous Map Reading lessons, around the edge of a map are marginal (title) information, relief data, and other symbols that make up the legend. This is also true of aeronautical charts. Check the title information on your chart first, noting that you have the right sectional and, most importantly, that the chart is not obsolete. Never use an obsolete chart for flying! Running into a new tower not plotted on an old chart can ruin a trip.

Next, familiarize yourself with the aeronautical symbols used on the chart. In Figure 1.11.2, note the examples of symbols you may not find on a topographic or road map.

Figure 1.11.2: Typical aeronautical chart symbols.

Courtesy of US Army JROTC.

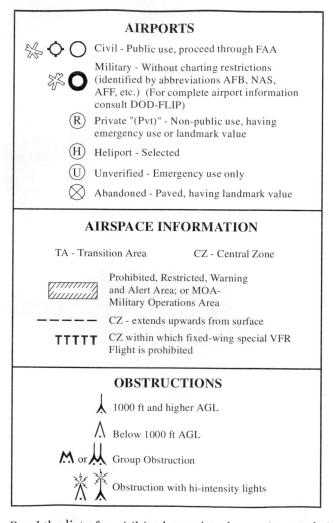

AIRPORTS

Civil - Public use, proceed through FAA

Military - Without charting restrictions (identified by abbreviations AFB, NAS, AFF, etc.) (For complete airport information consult DOD-FLIP)

ⓡ Private "(Pvt)" - Non-public use, having emergency use or landmark value

Ⓗ Heliport - Selected

Ⓤ Unverified - Emergency use only

⊗ Abandoned - Paved, having landmark value

AIRSPACE INFORMATION

TA - Transition Area   CZ - Central Zone

Prohibited, Restricted, Warning and Alert Area; or MOA- Military Operations Area

– – – – – CZ - extends upwards from surface

T T T T T CZ within which fixed-wing special VFR Flight is prohibited

OBSTRUCTIONS

1000 ft and higher AGL

Below 1000 ft AGL

M or Group Obstruction

Obstruction with hi-intensity lights

Read the list of prohibited, restricted, warning, and alert areas included on your chart. This list explains restrictions that apply to designated areas and who is responsible for the areas. For example, altitude is restricted to 5,000 feet over Anniston Army Depot, Alabama, from 0700 to 1800 Monday through Friday under the authority of the CO, Anniston Army Depot. If your flight path crosses any of those areas, make note of what altitude to maintain, adjust your flight path to avoid the areas, or contact the appropriate authority for permission to fly over.

Finally, familiarize yourself with other pertinent information on the chart, such as radio frequencies along your route of flight.

Planning Your Flight Route

Planning a route includes the four elements of navigation: position, direction, distance, and time. Refer to the appropriate part of the Atlanta Sectional Chart (Figure 1.11.3) as you read about planning your route and follow the steps to planning your route.

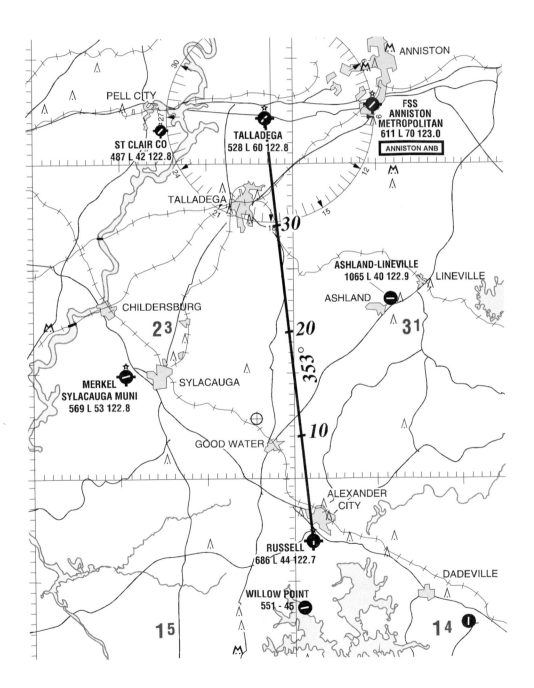

Figure 1.11.3: A subsection of the Atlanta Sectional Chart.

Courtesy of US Army JROTC.

1. **Position** is a point that you can identify. In this case, you locate the positions of your departure and destination points, specifically Russell Airfield outside Alexander City and Talladega Airport north of Talladega.

2. **Direction** is the position of one point in relation to another without reference to the distance in between them. On your chart, you draw a line between Russell Field and Talladega Airport; then figure direction using an air navigation plotter (Figure 1.11.4). The plotter consists of a protractor with direction scales and a straight edge. Using this tool, you figure your course from Russell Field to Talladega Airport is 353 degrees.

Figure 1.11.4: Air navigation plotter.

Courtesy of US Army JROTC.

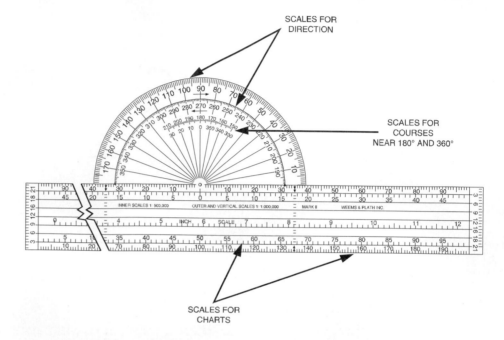

3. **Distance** is the space between two points measured by the length of the line joining them. You determine distance for your flight by using the scales on the air navigation plotter, or using the graphic or bar scales on your chart. If using the chart scale, you note ten-mile increments from the scale on a piece of paper; then place the paper along your route. Transfer the ten-mile increments to your chart marking each increment with the mileage. Your straight-line distance is 40 miles.

4. **Time** is an elapsed interval. Your aircraft cruises at 120 mph or 2 miles per minute. To determine your flight time enroute, divide 40 miles by 2 miles per minute and you get 20 minutes. Add a few minutes for climbing and reaching cruising speed, and your flight time from Russell Field to Talladega Airport is about 25 minutes.

As you plan your route, familiarize yourself with the locations of other airports or airfields in case you need to make an emergency landing. Look for alternate routes. Identify **linear features** that you can follow. Pinpoint landmarks along your route against which you can cross-check your position.

Key Note Term

linear feature – a straight road, railroad, power line, and so on, which can be followed from the air

Checking the Weather

After planning your flight route, call the Federal Aviation Administration (FAA) Flight Service Station (FSS) or the National Weather Service (NWS) for a preflight weather briefing tailored to your specific flight. Your local phone directory lists FSS and NWS telephone numbers in the U.S. Government section. You will receive current reports and forecasts for departure, enroute, and destination weather, as well as winds at flying altitude and pilot weather reports. For the day you plan to fly to Talladega, you learn that the forecasted weather is good. Winds will be light so they will not affect your flying time.

Checking the Aircraft

You are familiar with your chart, you have studied your route, and you have clear skies. You proceed to your aircraft and perform preflight checks. Everything is in order.

Filing a Flight Plan

The FAA does not require you to file a flight plan when you travel in good visibility. Understand, however, that the FAA highly recommends a flight plan for all flights regardless of visibility. It lets the proper authorities know your intentions in case of an emergency or if you are overdue at your destination. A flight plan contains your name and address, aircraft description, airspeed, departure and destination points, cruising altitude, and departure and arrival times.

Recording time on your flight plan in this situation is straightforward—you are only flying a short distance north of your present position. However, if you fly far enough east or west of your position, recording time becomes a factor. Unlike ground travel, especially on foot, you travel faster and farther when flying. Therefore crossing time zones becomes a concern.

Before the establishment of time zones in 1883, every city and town had their own time, which led to much confusion. An international convention designated that the prime **meridian**, or 0 degrees longitude, pass through the Royal Observatory at Greenwich, England. This established Greenwich Mean Time, the time of day at any given moment in Greenwich, England.

Because the earth rotates 360 degrees in 24 hours, you can divide the equator into 360 degrees or 24 hours. Each hour represents 15 degrees of longitude, and every 15 degrees of longitude, measured from the prime meridian, represents a time zone. Certain populated areas that are divided into two time zones have kept the time of one or the other zone to avoid confusion. You can see this in Figure 1.11.5.

Key Note Terms

meridian – an imaginary circle on the earth's surface passing through the north and south poles; a line in parallel of longitude

Greenwich Mean Time – the time of day at any given moment at Greenwich, England; also known as "Z" or "ZULU" time, in accordance with the international phonetic alphabet

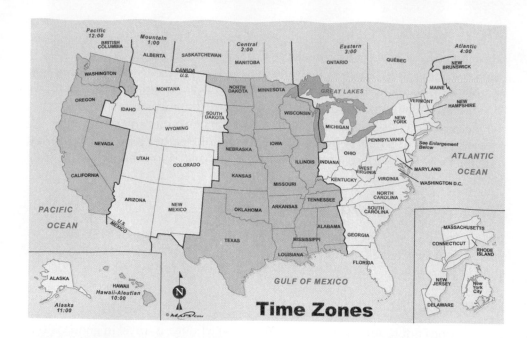

As a pilot, you have several options when giving your Estimated Time of Arrival (ETA) on a flight plan. For example, if you were to fly from Alabama east into Georgia, intending to arrive at 10 o'clock in the morning your time, you could give 1000 as your ETA and indicate that it is Central Standard Time (CST). Or, because you know that Georgia is in the Eastern Standard Time (EST) zone and it is one hour later there, you could give your ETA as 1100 EST. Another commonly used way to indicate your arrival time would be to use Greenwich Mean Time (GMT) or ZULU time. In this case, you would give your ETA as 1600 GMT or ZULU.

The Flight

Key Note Term

altimeter – an instrument in an aircraft that measures altitude, the distance above the horizon

With your preflight complete and your departure time at hand, you takeoff on your flight. As in orienteering, the compass on board your aircraft indicates your direction. Similar to the speedometer in your car, the airspeed indicator informs you of your speed. Unique to flight, the **altimeter** measures your aircraft's altitude. Throughout your trip, check your instruments to ensure you are on track with your planned direction, speed, and altitude.

The Global Positioning System (GPS) is a high-tech worldwide radio-navigation system formed from a network of 24 satellites and their ground stations. GPS provides precise air navigation and landing systems. This technology makes flying safer, and more efficient. GPS provides the most direct air route for pilots, which saves time and fuel. In addition, the accuracy offered by GPS allows planes to fly closer together on more direct routes. This in turn means that more aircraft can occupy airspace. The benefits of time and fuel efficiency are wide-ranging.

Fly Safe

Whether you are hiking, driving, or flying, getting lost or caught in bad weather is no fun and may even put you in an unsafe situation. Proper execution of your predetermined route requires your complete attention, especially when you are in the air. Running out of gas in your car is an inconvenience; running out of fuel in the air can be life threatening. Likewise, traveling at night or in bad weather on the ground requires caution, but you should never fly at night or in bad weather if you are not night-qualified or instrument-certified. If you find yourself running low on fuel, or darkness or bad weather is approaching, do not hesitate to land at the nearest suitable airfield.

After you learn the basics of pilotage, it is not too complicated to get from here to there in the air. Just pay attention, maintain course and keep track of elapsed time. Along your route, follow the landmarks that you noted on your chart during preflight. Cross-check your position using the features below. First note that you fly directly over Alexander City after takeoff. Because you are flying two miles per minute or ten miles per five minutes, make sure you are on schedule by checking the time against the ten-mile increments marked along your route. For example, within about five minutes into your flight, check that the little town of Good Water is off to your left. Then, as you pass Talladega on your left at the 30-mile marker, check that you are 15 or 20 minutes into your flight. Continue your trip in this fashion, and you will be landing safely as planned.

Conclusion

In a plane, you can travel much farther and faster than you can on the ground; and from the air, your perspective broadens as miles of the earth unfold beneath you. Through this lesson you have become familiar with air navigation charts, preflight, and flight execution. Whether you become a pilot someday or simply travel as an airline passenger, having a basic understanding of air navigation will be helpful in our fast-paced, ever-moving world.

This ends the lessons on map skills. In the following chapter, "Exploring the World," you will have the opportunity to learn about each continent that makes up our planet. These continents include North America, South America, Europe, Asia, Africa, Australia, and Antarctica.

Lesson Review

1. **Define the common units of measure for distance in air and road travel.**
2. **What are the key differences between aeronautical charts and topographic maps?**
3. **List some aeronautical symbols that you might not find on a topographical map.**
4. **What charts do you need when planning a flight route?**

Exploring the World

LESSONS

Chapter 2

Lesson 1
Before You Get Started

Key Terms

automation
Christian
ethnicity
Hinduism
ideological
Islamic
Judaism
per capita
spatial
tectonic plates

WHAT YOU WILL LEARN TO DO

- Show how geographic characteristics interact to form unique cultures

LINKED CORE ABILITIES

- Communicate using verbal, non-verbal, visual, and written techniques
- Apply critical thinking techniques

SKILLS AND KNOWLEDGE YOU WILL GAIN ALONG THE WAY

- Define geography
- Identify specialties in the geography field
- Explain the concept of regions
- Identify the continents and oceans
- Examine basic world climates and the major factors affecting them
- Summarize the physical and political characteristics of Antarctica
- Define key words contained in this lesson

Chapter 2

Introduction

In today's world, news about places around the globe comes into your home daily through television, radio, newspaper, and the Internet. Much of this news has political, economic, and social implications for the U.S. In order to better understand these events, their origin and their importance, you must learn more about the location of each event. Studying the characteristics of those places, including both their physical and human aspects, will greatly enhance your insight into these events.

This chapter provides you with a basic overview of world geography from important physical features, natural resources, and climates to political boundaries and other human characteristics that make up the world's diverse landscape. Knowing where places are in relation to each other as well as their differences and similarities furnish the background information you need to interpret world events. To be an informed citizen of a leading world power and a knowledgeable participant in our global environment, you must possess a broad understanding of the physical world and its human dimensions.

This lesson investigates the subject of geography and approaches to studying different parts of the world. It explains the approach taken in this text and the basic concepts you should know as you read this chapter.

Defining Geography

Geography is the study of the earth and life on it. It brings together both the physical and human dimensions of the planet, combining earth science (studying the physical makeup or landscape of the environment) with social science (studying humans and their activities within the environment). For this reason, geography encompasses a broad range of subjects and a multitude of specialties within the field. The four specialties—physical, cultural, economic, and political—pertain to the aspects of geography that are discussed in later lessons. Taken together, they provide you with a **spatial** perspective of how places and people are organized on the earth, as well as the characteristics of those places and people.

Physical Geography

Physical geography focuses on terrain features, climate, soil, vegetation, and natural resources such as water supplies and mineral deposits. The following are examples of how the information gathered in the study of physical geography can be applied:

- **Studying terrain features and determining what forces have created them—for example, mountains and volcanoes created by the movement of tectonic plates—can guide predictions on how natural forces will continue to shape the physical landscape in the future.**

- Studying the impact that climate has on an area helps explain the way people live in that area—for example, the types of crops grown, houses built, and clothes worn all vary depending upon whether an area is wet or dry, hot or cold, and so on.

- Studying the type of soil, vegetation, and natural resources in an area helps explain the way people make a living there. Economies and standards of living in many areas depend in part on what is supplied naturally to the people in an area—such as rivers to transport goods, coastlines for fishing, and rich soil for agriculture.

- Studying the makeup and importance of natural habitats can be used environmentally to understand the effects of while trying to minimize human impacts on those habitats.

Cultural Geography

Cultural geography focuses on the characteristics of different groups of people, their distribution throughout the world, their relationship to each other, and the historical developments that resulted in their characteristics and distribution. Understanding the influences of human characteristics, such as culture, language, religion, **ethnicity**, political beliefs, and standards of living can provide insight into the way different groups of people dress, eat, work, form relationships, support political leaders and governments, treat their environment and other people, and so on.

Religion and Daily Life

The following two examples demonstrate how religion can impact daily life and certain situations.

Many businesses close on the day of worship associated with the predominant religion of the region—such as Sunday in **Christian** areas and Friday in **Islamic** areas. Knowing this type of information is important when traveling or doing business in different parts of the world. Will a bank be open when you need to exchange money? If you need to call a branch of a company in another country, what days should you call?

Islam and **Judaism** forbid eating pork. Therefore, in many predominantly Islamic or Jewish areas of the world, pork is not consumed. **Hinduism** forbids killing cows, which are considered sacred; therefore, in predominantly Hindu areas, beef is not consumed. When marketing internationally, a U.S. company that produces pork or beef products would need to know about these religious beliefs and the locations of these religious groups around the world.

Studying the cultural geography of an area can also provide background into why conflicts occur in different parts of the world. Many conflicts arise from ethnic, **ideological**, and religious differences between distinct groups within a country or in bordering countries. Knowing the location and population of the different groups within a region and their level of toleration for each other can aid in understanding trouble spots around the world. Perhaps, too, this knowledge can help predict and even prevent conflicts.

Key Note Terms

ethnicity – of or relating to large groups of people classified by racial, national, religious, linguistic or cultural origin, or by background

Christian – relating to a religion based on the life and teachings of Jesus Christ, who followers of the religion believe to be the Son of God

Islamic – relating to Islam, a religious faith that includes belief in only one God, (Allah, which is Arabic for God), Mohammed as his prophet, and the Koran as the word of God; followers of Islam are known as Muslims

Judaism – the religion of the Jewish people developed among ancient Hebrews and characterized by belief in only one God and the eventual coming of a Messiah to rule Israel and the world

Hinduism – the chief religion of India characterized by individual worship rather than congregational, devotion to many gods, belief in reincarnation, and the caste system (inherited social rank with strict rules governing each class of people)

ideological – pertaining to the way an individual, group or culture thinks about economic, political or social concepts

Key Note Term

automation — controlled operation of equipment or a system by mechanical or electronic devices that take the place of human labor

Economic Geography

Economic geography focuses on how people make a living in different parts of the world and the distribution of types of economic activities throughout the world (see Figure 2.1.1). Types of economic activities include agriculture (raising crops and livestock), mining, lumbering, fishing, manufacturing (processing raw materials into machinery, vehicles, chemicals, textiles, paper products, food products, and so on), services (activities that do not produce a product but provide a service like banking, retail, education, tourism, and so on), and high-technology industries involved in information collection and processing (such as computer and software development, telecommunications, simulation, and **automation**).

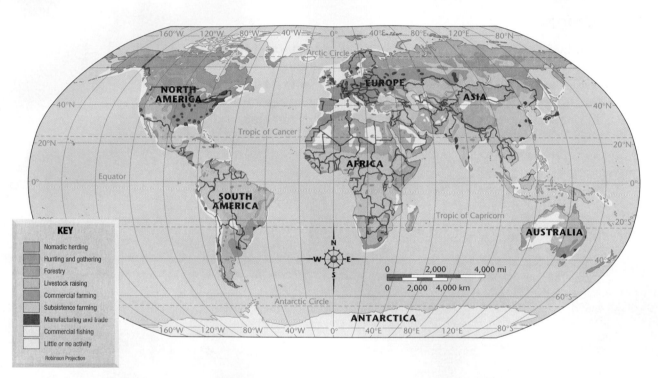

KEY

- Nomadic herding
- Hunting and gathering
- Forestry
- Livestock raising
- Commercial farming
- Subsistence farming
- Manufacturing and trade
- Commercial fishing
- Little or no activity

Robinson Projection

Figure 2.1.1: The World: Economic activity.

Courtesy of GeoSystems Global Corporation.

Interpreting an Economic Activity Map

An economic activity map uses a color-coded key to communicate basic information about a given region. This type of thematic map allows us to compare data in a general way. It is easy to see, for example, that far more land in Africa is used for subsistence farming than in Europe. However, precise measurements in square miles are not shown on this map.

Use the following steps to read and analyze the world map shown in Figure 2.1.1.

1. **Identify the variety of economic activities shown. Economic activity can range from gathering nuts and berries to manufacturing cars and trucks on an assembly line. Use the key to answer the following questions:**

   (a) What appears to be the major economic activity in Australia?

   (b) What appears to be the major economic activity in the northernmost region of Asia?

   (c) Where are the manufacturing and trade centers in South America?

2. **Look for relationships among the data. Use the map to look for patterns. Answer the following questions:**

   (a) Does more manufacturing and trade take place in countries in the northern hemisphere or in the southern hemisphere?

   (b) How does the amount of land used for commercial farming in the United States compare with the amount used in Australia?

   (c) In South America is more area used for commercial fishing or for subsistence farming?

Studying the economic activities of an area can explain its wealth and the standard of living of its people. For example, an area that grows a crop and also has the capability to manufacture it into a food product for export will generally be wealthier than an area without manufacturing capability for its raw materials. In general, areas involved in technologically-advanced industries are the wealthiest, while areas in which people rely on subsistence farming (growing the minimum required to keep a group or family alive) are the poorest. Understanding the economies of different parts of the world is important in dealing with and trying to lessen economic inequalities. It is also important as investments in businesses and trade relationships are made worldwide.

Political Geography

Political geography focuses on the political behavior of countries. It examines boundaries established by countries on land, claims by countries to parts of the oceans, relationships between different countries, differences in the government and administration of countries, and the causes of countries remaining intact or dissolving. Having a basic understanding of political geography is important as these countries conduct foreign relations and involve themselves in situations around the globe.

What Is a Region?

When studying geography, the Earth is often separated into regions. Regions are places grouped together because they possess one or more common characteristics. As with the various geographic specialties, characteristics used to categorize places into regions are physical (location, landscape, climate) and human (cultural, economic, political).

Depending upon the characteristic, a place can belong to many regions. Venezuela, for example, is considered South American (located on the continent of South America), Caribbean (having a coastline on the Caribbean Sea), Latin American (people from Middle and South America whose native speech is one of the Romance languages—French, Portuguese, and Spanish), and developing (characterized by low **per capita** income and less technological development due to social and economic conditions). Even Venezuela itself can be considered a region, since its boundaries enclose a specific political area.

Often, geography is discussed in terms of countries or continents because they are familiar concepts. This text follows that pattern. In each of the following six lessons, a different continent is investigated.

> **Key Note Term**
>
> **per capita** – per person

Each lesson explores important physical terrain features for the continent and shows political boundaries of the countries within the continent. Cultural, economic and, in some cases, further physical information is provided for each country or for groups of countries considered regions within the continent.

Remember that geography is a way of organizing information spatially, so that you can picture physical locations and relate the distribution of certain characteristics across those locations. Therefore, as you read through the text, note similar characteristics between countries or areas on different continents. Then visualize a world map with areas containing a specific characteristic: where are the mountainous regions on Earth . . . desert regions . . . English-speaking areas . . . Islamic areas . . . underdeveloped areas, and so on? While the text takes the continent/country approach, it also provides you with information to put in global perspective the distribution of many other physical and human characteristics around the world. The next section provides an example of associating a physical characteristic (different climates) spatially across all continents.

Basic Concepts

Figure 2.1.2 shows the locations of the continents (minus Antarctica) and the oceans of the world. Everything above the Equator (0° latitude) lies in the Northern Hemisphere, and everything below it lies in the Southern Hemisphere. Everything to the right of the Prime Meridian (0° longitude) lies in the Eastern Hemisphere, and everything to the left of it lies in the Western Hemisphere.

The Tropics of Cancer and Capricorn parallel the Equator at about 23.5° north and south, respectively. The Tropic of Cancer marks the farthest point north at which the sun can be seen directly overhead at noon. The sun reaches its vertical position over this tropic on about June 21. This means that on that day, the Tropic of Cancer is the latitude closest to the sun. The Tropic of Capricorn marks the farthest point south that the sun can be seen directly overhead at noon. The sun reaches its vertical position over this tropic on about December 21. This means that on that day, the Tropic of Capricorn is the latitude closest to the sun.

For this reason, seasons in the Northern Hemisphere are opposite the seasons in the Southern Hemisphere. While people living north of the Equator are experiencing summer weather from June to September, people living south of the Equator are experiencing winter weather. Likewise, the Northern Hemisphere's winter runs from December to March, during the Southern Hemisphere's summer.

The Arctic Circle (about 66° N latitude) and the Antarctic Circle (about 66° S latitude) are centered on the North and South Poles, respectively. They mark the northern and southern regions in which there is at least one day when the sun never sets and one day when it never rises. For example, when the sun is overhead at the Tropic of Cancer, the North Pole is tilted toward the sun, and the Arctic Circle experiences 24 hours of daylight. The Antarctic Circle, however, experiences 24 hours of darkness because the South Pole is tilted away from the sun. The opposite occurs when the sun is overhead at the Tropic of Capricorn,

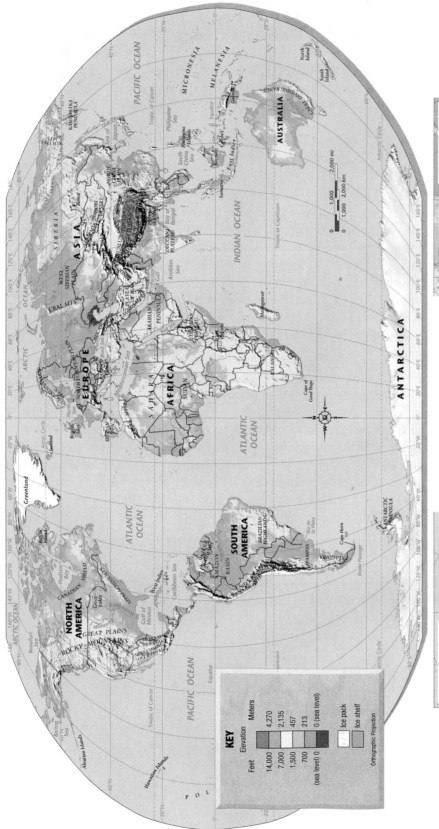

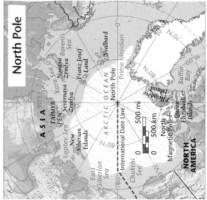

North Pole

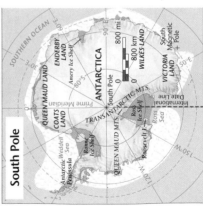

South Pole

with the Arctic Circle in darkness for 24 hours and the Antarctic Circle in sunlight for 24 hours.

The details of this discussion have been offered as an accurate explanation for why latitudes have such importance. However, the basic concepts that you should understand from this discussion are that the areas of the Earth between the Tropics of Cancer and Capricorn are closest to the sun. Conversely the areas of the Earth inside the Arctic and Antarctic Circles are the most distant from the sun.

Climate

Several factors affect climate such as elevation and proximity to large bodies of water. Yet the most important factor affecting climate is exposure to the sun, or solar radiation, which, as demonstrated in the previous discussion, is determined by latitude. The Equator at 0° latitude receives the most solar radiation, while the poles at 90° North and South latitude receive the least. Using the Equator, Tropics of Cancer and Capricorn, and the Arctic and Antarctic Circles as guides is a good way to develop a general perspective of basic world climates and the vegetation that grows naturally in an area due to climate.

Between the Tropics of Cancer and Capricorn, tropical climates exist, characterized by hot temperatures throughout the year. Areas along the Equator get plenty of rain all year and the corresponding vegetation is tropical forest (jungle and rain forest). Figure 2.1.3 shows the island of Java, near the equator. Moving away from the Equator are drought-resistant, tropical grasslands (savanna), particularly in South America, Africa, and Australia, with distinct wet and dry seasons. Moving still farther from the Equator to areas crossed by the Tropics of Cancer and Capricorn are deserts and semi-deserts that get little or no rainfall. Exceptions include each continent's eastern coasts, which continue to get regular rainfall and have more tropical vegetation.

Figure 2.1.3: Equatorial climate in Java (Indonesia).

Courtesy of National Geographic Society.

Between the Tropic of Cancer and the Arctic Circle as well as between the Tropic of Capricorn and the Antarctic Circle are areas of temperate (moderate) climate that have four seasons. Of course, areas located closer to the Arctic and Antarctic Circles (see Figure 2.1.4) have cooler summers and colder winters than most areas located closer to the tropics. Within this temperate zone, much of Asia, Australia, and western North America receive little rainfall, but coastlines, eastern North America, and Europe receive plenty of rainfall. Temperate forests cover much of this area in the Northern Hemisphere, with temperate grasslands (prairies) on the interiors of continents, and deserts and semi-deserts in southwestern Asia and parts of central Asia.

Figure 2.1.4: Arctic climate in Siberia (Russia).

Courtesy of National Geographic Society.

Within the Arctic and Antarctic Circles is a polar climate marked by year-round cold weather and little moisture except in the form of snow. Most of the land is covered by tundra, a treeless, marshy plain of mosses on top of permanently frozen subsoil. Much of the water is frozen; in fact, the Arctic Ocean, in which the North Pole is located, is permanently frozen except around its edges.

Generally, people populate areas that have a temperate climate, fertile soil, and adequate rainfall for agriculture. The more populated areas of the planet are southeastern North America, Europe, and south and Southeastern Asia. Desert areas and polar areas have few, if any, inhabitants.

Antarctica

Antarctica (see Figure 2.1.5), the fifth largest continent, surrounds the South Pole and is the coldest, iciest piece of land on Earth. During the summer months (November to January) temperatures are usually no warmer than 0°F, and during the winter months (May to July) the average temperature is 270°F. The area is then in continual darkness, and there are dangerous blizzards.

Figure 2.1.5: Antarctica.

Courtesy of GeoSystems Global Corporation.

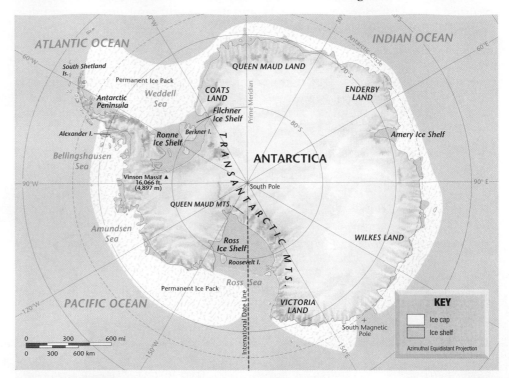

Antarctica's terrain is comprised of about 98 percent thick continental ice sheet and 2 percent barren rock, with average elevations between 2,000 and 4,000 meters. It has a few ice-free coastal areas including parts of southern Victoria Land, Wilkes Land, and the Antarctic Peninsula area. Glaciers form ice shelves along about half of the coastline, and floating ice shelves constitute 11 percent of the area of the continent. Few plants and animals can survive its frigid conditions, and it remains the only large landmass on earth without permanent human settlements. The ice and the cold actually prevented anyone from setting foot on the continent until 1895.

Despite the harsh landscape of the continent, several countries have claimed parts of Antarctica because of its rich supply of natural resources (see Figure 2.1.6). Minerals and fuels lie beneath its surface, and large schools of fish inhabit its waters. Only Marie Byrd Land remains unclaimed. Antarctica is also very valuable for scientific research. Many countries have set up seasonal and year-round research stations there. In 1961, 12 countries ratified the Antarctic Treaty. This treaty provided for the peaceful use of the continent and the sharing of scientific research. It also prohibits military activities, nuclear explosions, and disposal of radioactive waste on the continent. The treaty was renewed in 1989, including a ban on mineral extraction and mining for 50 years.

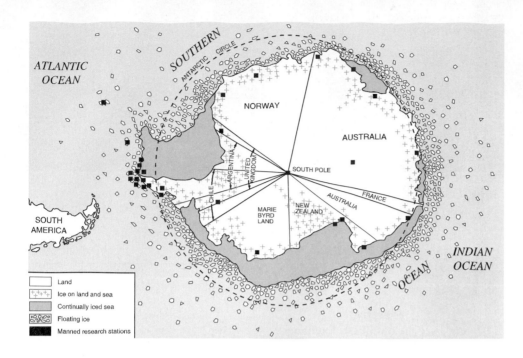

Figure 2.1.5: The claimed lands of Antarctica.

Courtesy of US Army JROTC.

Conclusion

Geography looks at both the physical and human landscapes of our planet. It encompasses a broad range of topics, including the specialties of physical, cultural, economic, and political geography. The following lessons discuss these four aspects of geography using the familiar concepts of continents and countries as a framework. As similar characteristics between places worldwide are revealed throughout this text, visualize the distribution of those characteristics across the globe. Possessing the skills to organize information in this spatial way and to understand both the physical and human landscapes of our planet is essential to being a geographically informed person in our global environment.

Lesson Review

1. Define the term "geography."
2. What are the four specialties in the geography field?
3. What are the major factors affecting the climate of an area?
4. Summarize the physical and political characteristics of Antarctica.

Lesson 2
North America—From Tundra to Tropics

Chapter 2

Key Terms

Catholic
cay
collective
Columbian Exchange
commonwealth
continental divide
coral
cordillera
dominion
drainage basin
fragmented state
hurricane
hydroelectric power
isthmus
literacy
plural state
postindustrial
prairie
Protestant
semiautonomous
standard of living
tributaries
tundra

WHAT YOU WILL LEARN TO DO

- Explore the unique geographic characteristics of North America

LINKED CORE ABILITIES

- Do your share as a good citizen in your school, community, country, and the world

- Treat self and others with respect

SKILLS AND KNOWLEDGE YOU WILL GAIN ALONG THE WAY

- Describe principal physical features of the continent of North America

- Summarize the physical and human characteristics of countries and regions in North America

- Explain how the interactions between groups of people in North America affect the area's cultural, economic, and political characteristics

- Define key words contained in this lesson

Introduction

North America spans a vast area and covers all different weather situations from arctic cold to tropical heat. The geography of North America is diverse, and includes the following:

- **Parts of both the United States and Canada lie within the Arctic Circle.**
- **Seattle, Washington, and Vancouver, Canada, are both important port cities.**
- **The Great Lakes are an important resource to both Canada and the United States.**
- **The Appalachian Mountains were formed by tectonic forces about 250 million years ago. Their once-sharp peaks have been worn down by rain, ice, and wind. Only a few reach elevations higher than 6,000 feet (1,829 m).**
- **The beaches of North America range from fine, white sand to sharp and rocky coastlines.**

This lesson looks at every part of the North American continent, from the lay of the land to the people who inhabit it. You learn that the geography of North America has much to do with how its inhabitants make their living and live their daily lives.

The Lands of North America

North America (see Figure 2.2.1) is the third largest continent comprising all the land and adjacent islands north of and including the **Isthmus** of Panama. A principal physical feature of North America is the North American **Cordillera**, a mountain region in the west that extends from Alaska to Mexico and includes the Rocky Mountains. Other important physical features are the Appalachian Mountains, the Great Lakes, the Great Plains, and the Mississippi River which, along with the Missouri and Ohio Rivers, makes up one of the world's longest river systems.

Key Note Terms

isthmus – a narrow strip of land connecting two larger land areas

cordillera – a system of mountain ranges often consisting of a number of parallel chains

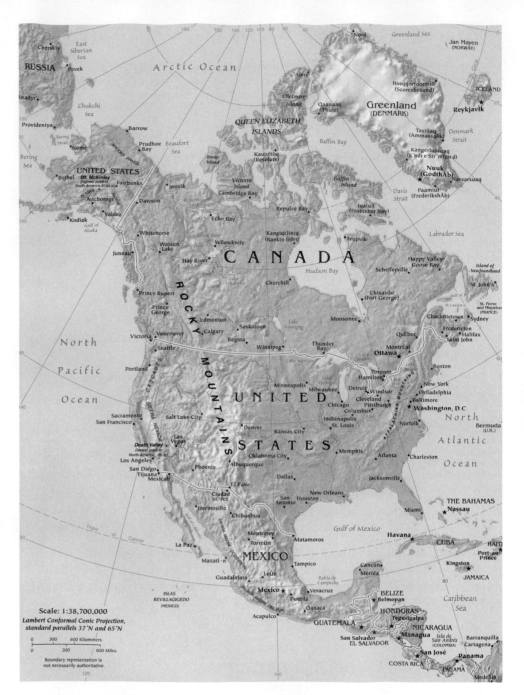

Figure 2.2.1: North America.

Reproduced from *The 2004 World Factbook*, courtesy of the CIA, modified by Pearson Custom Publishing.

The Bering Strait separates Asia in the Eastern Hemisphere from North America in the Western Hemisphere. Many scholars believe that between 7,000 and 20,000 years ago the Bering Strait was a land bridge that allowed people from Asia to migrate to and populate North and South America. These people are the ancestors of today's Native Americans—North American Indians and Eskimos of Greenland, Canada, and the U.S., and Central American Indians of Central America. In addition to Native American culture, European and African influences shaped North America as Europeans colonized the continent and brought slave labor from Africa. Over centuries, these cultures combined in a variety of ways to create the human landscape of today's North America.

History: Settlement of the Americas

More than any other part of the world, the countries of the Americas are nations of immigrants. Geography helps explain how and why people first migrated to these countries.

The Bering Land Bridge

For most of the past several million years, two great oceans have separated the American continents from the rest of the world. But during the Ice Ages—between about 20,000 and 12,000 years ago—geographers believe that much of the earth's water was frozen into glaciers and ice sheets. As a result, ocean levels dropped, exposing a flat bridge of land between Alaska and eastern Asia, where the Bering Strait is today.

Eastern Asia was home to groups of wandering hunters. When animals wandered onto the land bridge to graze, most scientists believe that the hunters followed. Both animals and hunters gradually moved onto the new land. Over thousands of years, different hunting groups gradually spread out over North and South America. These Paleo-Indians were the first humans in the Americas, ancestors of all the Native American peoples.

Worlds Apart

For thousands of years more, the Americas remained worlds apart. People traveled only on land or in small ships that did not venture far from sight of land. Isolated by rugged mountain ranges and great distances, people in different regions of the Americas developed their own distinctive language, families, and cultures.

Compared with Europe and Asia, the population of the Americas was small. A few settlements grew into populous towns and cities, but most Native Americans remained hunters and farmers. Thick forests and broad, tall grass prairies covered most of the land.

The Age of Exploration Brings Newcomers

In Europe and Asia, however, populations were growing and cities were becoming crowded. Good land—the main measure of wealth—was scarce. By the 1500s, better ships and navigation methods allowed European explorers to find their way to the two huge continents to the west.

The first European newcomers, mainly from Spain, settled in areas what are now Florida, the Southwest, and Mexico. Their first goals were gold and conquest (Figure 2.2.2 shows a gold

Figure 2.2.2: Gold figurines attracted European explorers.

Courtesy of the Lee Botlin Library/Bridgeman Art Library.

figurine, one of many that attracted European explorers), but in time people settled there permanently. Later, Spanish settlers went south into Central and South America. About a century later, settlers from France and Great Britain set up colonies on the eastern coast of North America. North America had rich resources: forests, farmlands, and wild animals that supplied valuable furs. Europeans also settled on many Caribbean islands, and established profitable plantations in the warm climate.

For several hundred years, nearly all those who chose to move to North America were Europeans. They came because of wars, religious unrest, and lack of land or opportunity at home. In addition, millions of Africans were brought unwillingly as slaves. Railroad building and gold-mining attracted the first immigrants from Asia in the mid-1800s, but for a long time, discriminatory laws kept the number of Asian immigrants low.

Dramatic changes in patterns of immigration to the United States began in the 1960s. Today the greatest number of immigrants come from Asia and from other parts of the Americas.

Reading a Population Density Map

Before you begin studying North America or any area that is populated, it's important to know how to read a population density map. This type of map shows the most densely or sparsely populated areas, and can help answer crucial questions such as: Where are new roads needed? Where will a business find the most customers? Government officials, business leaders, and social scientists study population density maps to find answers to questions like these. Figure 2.2.3 shows the population density of North America. Use the following steps to help you analyze it.

Figure 2.2.3: North America: Population density.

Courtesy of GeoSystems Global Corporation.

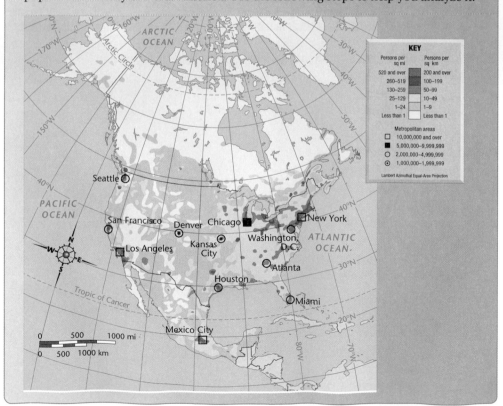

1. Know what information is covered on the map. Maps can show population density for small areas, such as a neighborhood or city, or for very large areas, such as a continent or the entire world.

   Study the map key to find out the colors and codes that are used. Maps usually show density with shading. Other symbols may indicate the sizes of cities. (a) How many categories of population density does this map include? (b) What areas average fewer than one person per square mile?

2. Study the data to draw conclusions. A population density map can make a very dramatic first impression. It is immediately obvious that population is very unevenly distributed. In this case you can also see at a glance the overall patterns of human settlement in North America. (a) What areas of North America appear to be quite uninhabited? (b) What different physical factors do you think might keep people from settling there? (c) Name four large cities in North America that have populations greater than one million people.

3. Analyze population density patterns. Move from your general impressions to think about the data available on the map. For instance, think geographically as you consider the areas of highest population density on this map. (a) What region of the United States has the greatest concentration of people? (b) What factors contribute to the population density of this region? (c) Where are population densities lighter? Why?

Greenland: The Frozen Island

Key Note Term

semiautonomous – largely self-governing within a greater political organization

Greenland (see Figure 2.2.1) is the world's second largest island—the largest being Australia. Lying mostly within the Arctic Circle, an ice sheet, which is more than two miles thick in some places, covers over four-fifths of Greenland. Most of the population, however, lives on the island's warmer southwest coast, which is not within the Arctic Circle. A former Danish colony, Greenland is now a **semiautonomous** state of Denmark. About 90 percent of its people are of mixed Eskimo and Danish ancestry.

Canada: A Plural State

Key Note Terms

dominion – a self-governing nation of the British Commonwealth, other than the United Kingdom, that acknowledges the British monarch as the head of state

commonwealth – a group of self-governing countries loosely associated in common allegiance

Canada (Figure 2.2.4), a self-governing **dominion** within the British **Commonwealth** of Nations, is the second largest country in the world (only Russia is larger). It consists of ten provinces and three territories. Starting in the east are the Atlantic Provinces (Newfoundland, Nova Scotia, Prince Edward Island, and New Brunswick). Moving west, the provinces of Quebec and then Ontario are next. Moving farther west are the Prairie Provinces of Manitoba, Saskatchewan, and Alberta. The westernmost province is British Columbia. In the north are the territories known as the Yukon, Northwest Territories, and Nunavut (created from the eastern half of the Northwest Territories in April 1999).

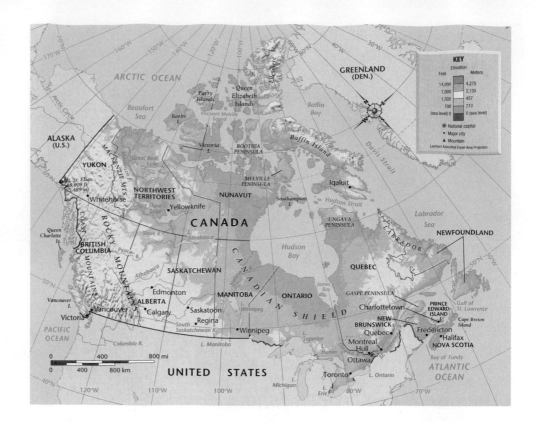

The capital of Canada is Ottawa, located in southeast Ontario. The largest and most populous cities are Montreal, located in Quebec on the Saint Lawrence River, and Toronto, located in Ontario on Lake Ontario. The Great Lakes along with the Saint Lawrence River form a major shipping artery navigable by ocean-going vessels.

> ### Note
>
> The greatest drop between Great Lakes occurs between Lakes Erie and Ontario, falling 167 feet at Niagara Falls.

The Canadian Shield (see Figure 2.2.5) stretches from the Saint Lawrence River and the Great Lakes northwest to the Arctic Ocean. Formerly referred to as a plateau, it is a region of ancient rock and many lakes formed by the advance and retreat of ice sheets. Centered on the Hudson Bay, the shield covers over half of Canada. The area is rich in minerals and water power.

Figure 2.2.5: The Canadian Shield.

Courtesy of Photographers Aspen.

Southeast of the Canadian Shield in the Atlantic Provinces is the northern section of the Appalachian Mountains which extend down into the southeastern U.S. West of the shield in southwest Manitoba as well as most of Saskatchewan and Alberta are wheat-growing, oil-rich plains or prairies. This area includes the northern reaches of the Great Plains, a semi-arid grassland that extends south into Texas. Along the western border of Alberta and in British Colombia and the Yukon is the North American Cordillera. The cordillera in Canada includes the Rocky Mountains, known as the Canadian Rockies, and the Coast Mountains.

> **Note**
>
> The Rocky Mountains are a cordillera that stretches for more than 3,000 miles (4,827 km) from northern Alaska to Mexico, making it the longest mountain chain in North America.

The Canadian People

Most Canadians possess high living standards and live in an urbanized, **postindustrial** society. The majority of the population is of European descent (approximately 48 percent of British origin and 31 percent of French origin) and of Christian faith (approximately 46 percent are Roman **Catholic** and 45 percent are **Protestant**). In Ontario and the territories are large Indian minorities, and there is a rapidly growing Asian population in the west. Although Canada is a huge country, its population is small—only one-tenth that of the U.S. Moreover, most Canadians live within 100 miles of the U.S. border.

Key Note Terms

postindustrial – dominated by production and manipulation of information, skilled services and high-technology manufacturing

Catholic – a follower of the Roman Catholic Church, a Christian church which accepts the absolute authority of the Pope on decisions of faith and morals

Protestant – broadly defined, a Christian not of a Catholic or Orthodox Church, including the Amish, Anglican, Assemblies of God, Baptists, Congregationalists, Episcopalians, Evangelicals, Lutherans, Mennonites, Methodists, and Presbyterians, among others

Unlike the U.S., Canada has two official languages. English is the home language to about 62 percent of the population, and French is the home language to 26 percent. Most French-speaking Canadians live in Quebec, where 80 percent of the people are of French origin. Montreal, Quebec, is second only to Paris, France, as the largest French-speaking city in the world.

French-Canadians hold strongly to French history, tradition, and culture, while most other Canadians prefer British customs. This separation of French and British language and culture has inhibited the formation of a single combined culture in Canada and makes Canada a **plural state**.

Canada's Economy

Canada's wealth of natural resources makes it a prosperous nation. Forests covering 46 percent of the country support wood-processing industries. Minerals found in the Canadian Shield make Canada one of the world's leading mineral exporters. Coal, oil, and natural gas are abundant in the Prairie Provinces, and agriculture in these provinces produces major exports of grains and meat. The Atlantic Provinces and British Columbia provide most of Canada's fishing catch, and the area's natural beauty attracts many tourists.

Manufacturing is a chief economic activity in Quebec and Ontario. The Great Lakes and Saint Lawrence River form a chief trading artery, with Montreal and Toronto as principal ports. Toronto is also English-speaking Canada's leading financial and communications center. The U.S. is Canada's leading trade partner and an important financial investor.

> ### North America's Inhabitants
>
> Compared with many nations of the world, the populations of Canada and the United States have long life expectancies, high per capita incomes, and high **literacy** rates. These and other statistics show that people in Canada and the United States have a high **standard of living**.

The United States of America: From Sea to Shining Sea

The United States of America (Figure 2.2.6), the fourth largest country in the world, includes 50 states and one federal district, the District of Columbia. Canada and the Pacific Ocean separate Alaska and Hawaii, respectively, from the other 48 states, making the U.S. a **fragmented state**. The U.S. also holds territories in the Caribbean Sea and Pacific Ocean.

Key Note Term

plural state – a country in which there has been extensive contact between two or more national groups without any real cultural mixing

Key Note Terms

literacy – the condition or quality of being literate, especially the ability to read and write

standard of living – a level of material comfort as measured by the goods, services, and luxuries available to an individual, group or nation

fragmented state – a discontinuous country whose national territory consists of two or more individual parts separated by foreign territory and/or international waters

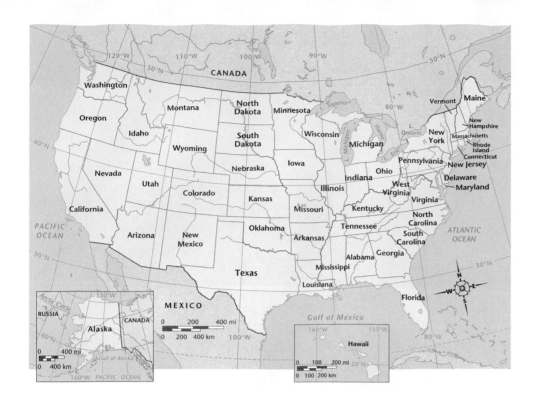

Figure 2.2.6: The United States.

Courtesy of maps.com.

Similar to Canada, significant terrain features of the U.S. include the Great Lakes, Great Plains, Appalachians, and the North American Cordillera. The Appalachians run 1,600 miles from eastern Canada to Alabama. East and south of the Appalachians is the Gulf-Atlantic Coastal Plain, characterized by flat, low-lying coastlines in contrast to the mountainous coastlines along the Pacific. Stretching west of the Appalachians are the Interior Plains, fertile lowlands that were once covered by an inland sea. Even farther west is the Great Plains, a tree-less plateau area that gradually rises to the foothills of the Rockies.

As mentioned previously, the Rocky Mountains, or Rockies, are part of the North American Cordillera and extend from New Mexico north through the U.S. (Southern, Central, and Northern Rockies) into Canada (Canadian Rockies) and Alaska (Brooks Range). The Cordillera also includes the Alaska Range along the south coast of Alaska, home to Mount McKinley, the highest point in North America (see Figure 2.2.7). Farther west of the Rockies in the continental U.S., the Cordillera includes the Cascade Range with volcanic peaks like Mount Rainier; the Sierra Nevada; and the Coast Ranges.

North America's Landforms

Because rivers wend their way downhill, the pattern of landforms determines the direction in which they flow. A continental divide is the boundary that separates rivers flowing toward opposite sides of a continent. In North America, the Rockies separate the rivers that flow west from the rivers that flow east. A divide also separates one **drainage basin** from another. The Mississippi River and its tributaries drain the largest area in the United States.

Key Note Term

drainage basin – an area drained by a river system

Key Note Term

continental divide – an extensive stretch of high ground from each side of which the river systems of a continent flow in opposite directions

Between the Rockies and these western ranges is the Intermontane Region. This region consists of plateaus, basins, and lower ranges. There are also several deserts in this area, one of which is Death Valley in Southern California and Southern Nevada.

Rivers such as the Columbia and Colorado have cut deep gorges through the Intermontane Region. One such gorge cut by the Colorado River in Arizona is the Grand Canyon, which is up to 1 mile deep, 4 to 18 miles wide, and more than 200 miles long.

The **Continental Divide**, which follows the crest of the Rocky Mountains, separates the rivers that drain into the Pacific Ocean from those that drain into the Atlantic. The Columbia and Colorado Rivers flow west from the Rockies supplying power, irrigation, and water to western states. On the other side of the Rockies, the Missouri River flows east then south to meet the Mississippi River near St. Louis, Missouri. Farther south at Cairo, Illinois, the Ohio River meets the Mississippi. These three rivers make up the Mississippi River System, which drains the mid-western U.S. and is the chief river system of North America.

The People of the United States

People of the U.S. have been shaped by the wide variety of immigrant groups who have made the U.S. their home over the past two centuries. Many of the original European settlers came to the "New World" to build better lives based on freedom and equality. Their beliefs became the basis of American social and political life.

Unlike Canadians, people of European descent in the U.S. mixed to form a **collective** group, and immigrants to the U.S. continue to become a part of mainstream American society—thus, the U.S. nickname "the melting pot." In some cases, however, this mixing does not occur. Consequently, immigrants and their descendants find themselves, willingly or not, in ethnic communities.

Similar to their Canadian neighbors, Americans enjoy a high standard of living. Both countries are rich in natural resources that contribute to a productive economy. Many Americans relocate as economic opportunities shift from place to place. In fact, Americans are the most mobile people in the world, with 19 percent of the population changing residence each year.

North America: Largest Metropolitan Areas

North America boasts the largest metropolitan areas in the world. These areas include:

New York City, United States	19,342,000
Mexico City, Mexico	15,525,000
Los Angeles, United States	14,532,000
Chicago, United States	8,240,000
Washington, D.C., U.S.A.	6,727,000
San Francisco, United States	6,253,000
Philadelphia, United States	5,893,000
Boston, United States	5,455,000
Detroit, United States	5,187,000
Dallas, United States	4,037,000
Toronto, Canada	3,893,000

Regions of the United States

The continental U.S. is often divided into the following regions (Figure 2.2.8) based on physical landscapes, dominant cultures, and/or major economic activities.

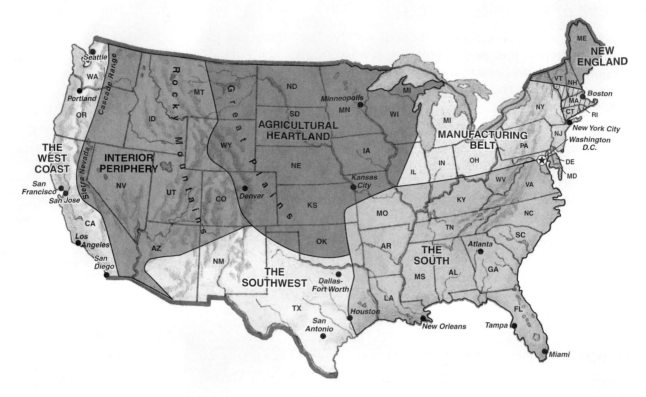

Figure 2.2.8: Regions of the United States.

Map courtesy of Dorling Kindersley, modified by Pearson Custom Publishing.

New England is famous for its natural harbors, colorful autumns, picturesque villages, and historic sites dating from colonial times. Tourism, recreation, fishing, forestry, and farming in the region's fertile valleys are important economic activities. Manufacturing is a leading source of income in southern New England states, making them part of the Manufacturing Belt as well.

The Manufacturing Belt was the country's economic leader between the Civil War (1861–1865) and the decline of the industrial age in the 1970s. Since then, America's economy has turned from traditional manufacturing to high-tech industries. Although manufacturing remains important, fast-growing areas in the west and south provide competition for the Manufacturing Belt. Nevertheless, some cities such as Boston, New York City, and Washington, D.C. are booming in this high-tech age.

Key Note Term

hydroelectric power – a form of energy generated by the conversion of free-falling water to electricity; the generation of electricity by using the motive power of water; also called hydroelectricity

Note

Detroit is a major United States industrial city near Lake Erie. Canada's industry and its population are also concentrated in the Great Lakes region and along the St. Lawrence River. **Hydroelectric power** is used to supply power to many of these industries.

The Agricultural Heartland has vast areas of fertile land for crop growth and dairy and livestock production. Iowa and Illinois are the center of the Corn Belt. West of the Corn Belt in the Great Plains is the Wheat Belt. Even the economies of large cities in the region, such as Kansas City, Minneapolis, and Denver, are based on agriculture operating major processing centers for grains and livestock.

The South remained isolated economically and culturally from the rest of the country following the Civil War. Then, in the 1960s, interest in the South resurfaced, and it became the United States' most rapidly changing region. With its warm climate and fertile soils, agricultural areas began to produce high-value products like beef, poultry, and soybeans. At the same time, tourists began flocking to the region's coastal beaches. Atlanta, Houston, Miami, Tampa, and New Orleans grew into booming cities practically overnight, and high-tech industries continue to move into the region today.

The Southwest is an area of vast, open space, characterized by long, hot summers. The eastern portion of the region contains abundant supplies of oil and natural gas that provide much of its economic wealth. This region also successfully represents the postindustrial revolution with electronic and space-technology facilities located between Houston (on the dividing line between the South and Southwest regions), San Antonio, and Dallas-Fort Worth.

The Interior Periphery includes Alaska and the area stretching from the Sierra Nevada-Cascade Range to the Rocky Mountains. The region is isolated, rugged, and sparsely populated. Despite its disadvantages, the Interior Periphery is one of the Earth's major storehouses of mineral and energy resources. During the oil shortage of the 1970s, oil companies explored Alaska, Wyoming, and Colorado in search of petroleum and natural gas. Minerals mined in the region include coal, uranium, copper, lead, zinc, platinum, gold, silver, and nickel.

The West Coast covers the area on the Pacific coast between the Sierra Nevada-Cascade Range and the Pacific Ocean. This region, despite being earthquake prone, has a hospitable environment with year-round agreeable weather south of San Francisco.

Major development of the region took place after World War II (1939–1945), much of it in California, an innovator of national culture and industry and the most populated state. In Oregon and Washington, long-standing economic activities like logging and fishing still thrive. Industrialization also exists in the form of aluminum and aircraft manufacturing.

A great advantage to this region in the current global economy is its proximity to Asia.

North America's Climate Regions

Grasses grow well in the dry, interior plains of Canada and the United States. Blocked by the Rockies, rainfall on the plains averages 10 to 20 inches (25 to 51 cm) a year. This is just enough moisture for healthy grasses to grow. This temperate grassland is also called **prairie** and is characterized by a great variety of grasses.

Key Note Term

prairie – an extensive area of flat or rolling, predominantly treeless, grassland; especially the large tract of plain in central North America

Central America: Separating Atlantic and Pacific

Central America (see Figure 2.2.1) constitutes all the land and islands south of the U.S. and north of the South American continent. It is a crucial barrier between the Atlantic and Pacific Oceans and a bridge from North America to South America. Central America consists of:

- **Mexico, a large country that dominates Central America in size, population, and economic wealth**

- **Central America, consisting of seven countries: Belize, Guatemala, Honduras, El Salvador, Nicaragua, Costa Rica, and Panama**

- **The West Indies, which separate into the Bahamas, the Greater Antilles that include the larger islands (Cuba, Hispaniola, Jamaica, and Puerto Rico), and the Lesser Antilles that include all other islands**

A major geographic feature of Central America is the Sierra Madre Mountain System, which is the southernmost part of the North American Cordillera. This area forms the junction of the North American Cordillera and the outlying reaches of the Andes, a similar cordillera in South America. The area also marks the collision of several tectonic plates. Because of this, Central America is mostly mountainous, with active volcanoes and earthquakes.

Unfortunately, Central America is the least developed region in the Americas, and many Central American people live in poverty. Much of the area is also politically unstable. These two factors drive many Central Americans to cross the border into the U.S. looking for a better existence.

Mexico: Merging Cultures

Mexico (see Figure 2.2.9) consists of 31 states and the Federal District of Mexico City, its capital. Mexico's significant geographic features include the Baja California Peninsula in the northwest, an extension of California's Coast Ranges; the Gulf of California that separates the Baja California Peninsula from the rest of Mexico. Also noteworthy is the Rio Grande River which separates Texas from Mexico. The Yucatán Peninsula in the southeast and the Sierra Madre Mountain System comprise two other major features of Mexico.

Figure 2.2.9: Mexico.

Courtesy of MapQuest.com.

Mexico's Mountain Ranges

Mountain ranges dominate the landscape of Mexico, defining the country's regions. The central plateau, a huge, bumpy highland region that ranges in altitude from 6,000 to 8,000 feet (1,800 to 2,400 m), lies between two great mountain ranges. Continuing south, mountains, including active volcanoes, form the highlands of Central America.

Sierra Madre Del Sur in the south splits as it nears Mexico City, dividing into Sierra Madre Occidental in the west and Sierra Madre Oriental in the east. These mountains frame Mexico's central plateau, which is 8,000 feet in elevation in the south near Mexico City and declines to 3,600 feet at the Rio Grande. The plateau is desert in the north, contains shallow lakes and swamps in the center, and has tropical forests in the south. Generally, Mexico has a dry climate with only 12 percent of the country receiving adequate rainfall.

Important Historical/Political Considerations of Mexico

Mexico was the birthplace of several great Indian civilizations, including the Maya and Aztec. In the 1500s, Spanish conquistadors conquered the Indians and made Mexico a Spanish colony. Indians became laborers for the Spanish, and a mestizo class (of mixed Spanish and Indian blood) developed. Colonists gained independence from Spanish rule in 1821, and Mexico became a federal republic in 1823.

North America's History

The Americas were home to several great Indian civilizations. Long before A.D. 1000 the Maya had built cities in the Yucatán Peninsula and nearby areas. Tenochtitlán, capital of the even larger Aztec empire, stood on the site of modern Mexico City.

The Mexican People

Mexico's population has grown rapidly in the twentieth century more than tripling from 1940 to 1980. In 1991, it was 19 million, more than the combined populations of all the other Middle American countries and islands. Only one-third of the population lives in rural areas; 68 percent reside in towns and cities. Over one-half of the people in Mexico live in a zone that centers on Mexico City (see Figure 2.2.10) and extends from Veracruz in the east to Guadalajara in the west.

Figure 2.2.10: The Independence Monument in Mexico City.

Courtesy of Prentice Hall.

Sixty percent of Mexicans are mestizo, 29 percent are Indian, and 9 percent are European. Ninety-five percent are Roman Catholic. Spanish is the official language of Mexico. Five million Mexicans also speak an Indian language, and 1 million speak an Indian language only. In addition to language, Mexican culture has been influenced by Indian dress, food, art, and architecture. In fact, Mexican culture is truly a mixture of both European and Indian cultural traits.

Mexico's Economy

For almost 100 years after Mexican independence, most of the farmable land belonged to wealthy Spanish landowners who left much of the land uncultivated. Consequently, the country did not produce enough to feed its citizens. In 1910, a revolution to redistribute land began. The Constitution of 1917 made redistribution the law. Today, the government has redistributed over half of the cultivable land to mostly peasant communities. Although these communities tend to use outdated farming methods to grow Mexican staples (corn, beans, and squash) for their own consumption, commercial agriculture uses modern irrigation and farming techniques to produce high-value crops and livestock, like cotton, wheat, and cattle.

Since World War II, Mexico has enjoyed considerable economic growth. The country's mineral resources include silver, copper, zinc, and lead. Mexico is a leading producer of oil and natural gas. Manufacturing is also a source of economic wealth, especially in Mexico City and the border cities of Cuidad Juárez/El Paso and Tijuana/ San Diego.

Although the discovery of oil and natural gas brought Mexico great prosperity, the country borrowed heavily in the 1970s as oil prices soared. When oil prices fell it was saddled with a huge foreign debt it could not pay off. Today, Mexico continues to strive for improvements in industry and agriculture as it struggles with its huge national debt and a skyrocketing population growth rate.

Central America: A Land of Unrest

Central America (see Figure 2.2.11) occupies the narrow strip of land in the southernmost part of North America between Mexico and South America. The narrowest point in Central America spans 40 miles from the Pacific to the Caribbean and lies in Panama. The Panama Canal, constructed by the U.S. from 1904 to 1914, is a 51-mile-long waterway cut across central Panama connecting the Atlantic Ocean, by way of the Caribbean Sea, to the Pacific Ocean. Instead of sailing around South America to get from the Atlantic to the Pacific (which can take about two weeks), ships can make the trip in seven to eight hours by way of the canal.

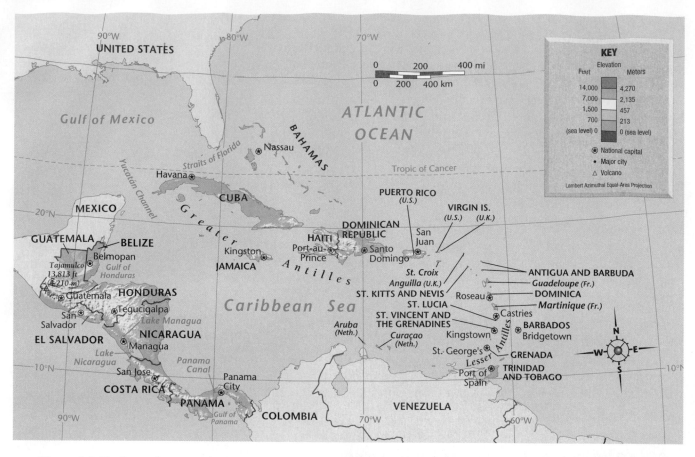

Figure 2.2.11: Central America.

Courtesy of maps.com.

The interior of Central America is mostly mountainous, with low-lying coastal plains on both the Pacific and Caribbean sides. The area has an active zone of volcanoes and earthquakes. The highlands and the Pacific side of Central America are more hospitable to human habitation than the Caribbean side which tends to have hotter, wetter weather. Much of the area receives adequate rainfall, with heavy rainfall in the east. Where rainfall exceeds 100 inches and humankind has left nature untouched, tropical rain forests thrive in Central America.

Important Historical/Political Considerations of Central America

Much of Central America's history parallels Mexico's history. Spanish explorers conquered the area along with Mexico. With the exception of Belize (formerly under British rule), Spain ruled Central America until the colonies declared independence—most in the early 1800s.

Since their independence, Guatemala, El Salvador, and Nicaragua have had a history of repressive governments, military rule, armed rebellions, terrorism, and civil war. Their proximity to Honduras, a democratic republic, has also caused that more stable country to suffer. As in Mexico, problems have occurred over the huge gap between wealthy landowners and the poor, and conflicts also exist between various Indian and mestizo groups.

In contrast to this political instability, Costa Rica, which has an old democratic tradition, has remained politically stable for most of the past 175 years. Panama, also a democracy, is buffered from the rest of Central America's strife by Costa Rica. Belize, Central America's only monarchy, is fairly stable as well.

The People of Central America

In general, the majority of Central Americans are mestizo with Indian and white minorities (see Figure 2.2.12). Exceptions include Guatemala where almost half of the population is pure Indian; Belize where half of the population is black or mulatto (of mixed black and white ancestry); and Costa Rica where there is a large majority of Spanish and relatively recent European immigrants.

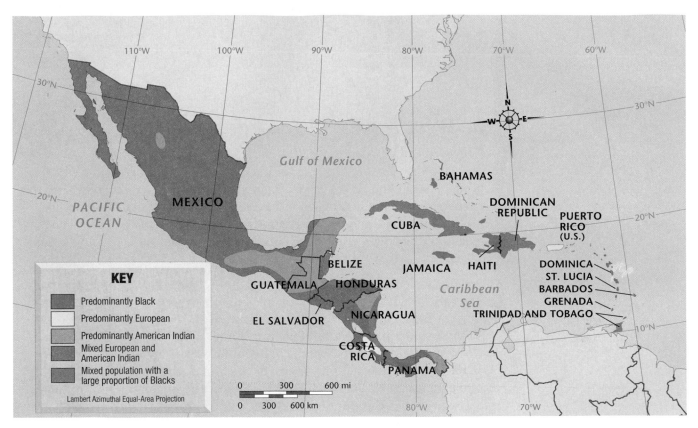

Figure 2.2.12: Central America: Major ethnic groups.

Courtesy of maps.com.

Similar to Mexicans, the majority of Central Americans are Spanish-speaking Catholics; some speak Indian languages as well. Because of its British heritage, Belize is an exception: English is the official language and 35 percent of its population is Protestant. Many Panamanians also speak English because Panama has had significant contact with the U.S. due to U.S. interest in the Panama Canal.

Many people in Central America become refugees, leaving their countries because of political and economic instability. Honduras is the poorest, least developed country in Central America, while Costa Ricans have the highest standard of living and a literacy rate and life expectancy more like that in the U.S.

Central America's Economy

Agricultural exports such as bananas, coffee, and sugarcane, are the mainstay of Central America's economy. Unfortunately, political instability and feuds over the redistribution of farmland have hurt agriculture in many countries and discouraged foreign investment and tourism. The Caribbean-like Belize and stable Costa Rica, however, attract many tourists. Costa Rica also produces beef for export, and Panama earns much of its income from shipping through the use of the Panama Canal.

North America's Tourism

Most of the Caribbean islands have a warm tropical climate all year, making tourism an important economic activity. Summer temperatures average 80°F (27°C), but the northeast trade winds blowing over the ocean keep the days comfortable. Rainfall on the islands varies dramatically. Sudden rains may fall daily on the northeast, or windward side of an island, while mountains protect the leeward side.

The West Indies: Island Paradise

The West Indies (see Figure 2.2.11) is an archipelago that extends in an arc from Florida in North America to Venezuela in South America. This arc separates the Caribbean Sea from the Gulf of Mexico and the Atlantic Ocean. Many of the islands are the tops of mountains rising from the floor of the sea. The islands divide into three main groups: the Bahamas, the Greater Antilles, and the Lesser Antilles.

The Bahamas consist of about 700 islands and 2,400 reefs. Because most of the islands are low, flat, and riverless, people inhabit only about 20 of them. They begin 50 miles off the southeast coast of Florida and extend for 600 miles southeast into the Atlantic Ocean, ending near the island of Hispaniola. Hispaniola, divided into Haiti and the Dominican Republic, is part of the Greater Antilles along with Cuba, Jamaica, and Puerto Rico. These four islands located in the Caribbean Sea are the largest in the West Indies. The remaining smaller islands are known as the Lesser Antilles.

Key Note Terms

cay – low-lying island

coral – rocklike skeletons of tiny sea animals

North America's Island Nations

Some of the islands in the Caribbean Sea are the jagged tops of a vast underwater mountain chain. Flatter islands of the Caribbean are **cays** formed over thousands of years from the accumulation of **coral**. The islands are divided into three main groups: the Bahamas, the Greater Antilles, and the Lesser Antilles.

Important Historical/Political Considerations of the West Indies

In 1492, Columbus discovered the Bahamas, and European colonization of the entire Caribbean area quickly followed. Sugar plantations prospered at the expense of the Caribbean Indians, the original inhabitants, who perished in slavery. African slaves replaced them. Countries disputed over rights to many of the islands, and some islands passed from colonial power to colonial power. Today, most of the islands have gained independence.

Christopher Columbus and the Foods We Eat Today

What's so unusual about tomatoes on Italian pasta or hamburger in a Mexican taco? Today, nothing. But tomatoes are not native to Italy. Neither are cattle native to Mexico. How did they get there?

For most of human history, the Americas have been cut off from the rest of the world by great expanses of ocean. That isolation ended abruptly in 1492, when Christopher Columbus reached what Europeans called the "New World." Soon other Europeans arrived, bringing their customs—and foods—with them. They took back to Europe some foods from the Americas. This two-way trade is known as the **Columbian Exchange**. As the chart on the facing page shows, the exchange included food plants, animals—and, unfortunately, diseases. These diseases killed millions of Native Americans. Weakened as a result, Native American societies found it hard to resist European invaders.

Corn, or maize, was one of the first plants domesticated in the Western Hemisphere. Native Americans began growing it about 5,000 years ago. Along with squash and tomatoes, corn was a staple food. It was so important that it was included in Indian creation stories as one of the most treasured gifts from the gods to humans. In one such story, the creator of the earth gave people corn before giving them water, sun, or wind.

With the growth of transatlantic travel, corn soon became an important food crop in western Africa. It also thrived in parts of southern and central Europe.

Not only corn, but also potatoes soon fed a rapidly growing world population. People of the Andes not only domesticated the potato but also found ways to preserve it. At night, they froze potatoes in the cold mountain air. The next day, after the potatoes had thawed, people squeezed out the water and set the potatoes out to freeze again. After a few days of this, the potatoes were "freeze dried" and could last for years without spoiling.

Potatoes were well suited to the cool, rainy parts of northern Europe, such as Ireland and Germany. They soon became a staple food, especially for poorer people. When disease ruined the Irish potato crop in the mid-1840s, famine resulted, causing many Irish to emigrate to the United States.

Tomatoes were another American food. While it is hard to imagine Italian pasta without them, tomatoes were one of the most exotic imports from the Americas. For many years, they were thought to be dangerous and even poisonous. After the tomato became popular, it was widely grown and eaten throughout Europe.

Sugar cane, a tall tropical grass from the islands of Southeast Asia, thrived in the Caribbean islands, but with terrible consequences. Harvesting sugar cane was hard and painful work, needing the labor of many people. At first, European plantation owners forced the native islanders to do this work. But as the islanders died off, plantation owners turned to African slaves to do the work.

Animals were one import that improved life for people in the Americas. Spanish soldiers brought horses, which soon became important in many Native American cultures for hunting and war. Sheep and goats from Spain flourished in mountainous regions like Chile and northern Mexico. Cattle did well in both North and South America. Pigs also adapted to the Western Hemisphere. Two dozen pigs brought to Cuba in 1498 were estimated to have increased in number to 30,000 only sixteen years later.

Key Note Term

Columbian Exchange – upon the arrival and interchange of native lifeforms of the Europeans to North America in 1497, there began a massive transformation in the global ecosystem resulting from the exchange of flora, fauna and disease between the Old World and New

The U.S. acquired Puerto Rico from Spain after the Spanish-American War (1898). In 1917, Puerto Ricans attained U.S. citizenship, and in 1952, the country became a self-governing territory of the United States. The U.S. purchased the 52 western Virgin Islands from Denmark in 1917, and the people of these islands became U.S. citizens in 1927. The 36 eastern Virgin Islands belong to England.

The People of the West Indies

The West Indies is one of the most densely populated parts of North America. There are currently 34 million people living in the West Indies, almost 11 million of them in Cuba. Unlike the rest of Middle America, the original Indians of the Caribbean did not survive European colonization. Forced into plantation labor, they died by the thousands. The few hundred remaining Indians mixed with African slaves brought to replace them, and the pure Caribbean Indian disappeared.

With the exceptions of Cuba and Puerto Rico where the majority of people are of Spanish descent, people of African descent make up the majority in the West Indies (see Figure 2.2.10). African heritage is visible in village construction, local markets, food, and art.

Because of the islands' history of European colonization, European influences also exist. For example, British influence survives in the Bahamas, Jamaica, and Grenada; Spanish influence can be seen in Cuba, the Dominican Republic, and Puerto Rico. French influence is evident in Haiti, Guadeloupe, and Martinique. Dutch customs are readily observed in the Netherlands Antilles. Likewise, languages spoken in the islands include English, Spanish, French, and Dutch. Because of this diversity, the people of the West Indies practice many religions, with Roman Catholicism the most predominant. In Cuba, which is a communist country, religious practice is discouraged.

Economy of the West Indies

The warm climate of the West Indies, the clear Caribbean waters, and the beautiful beaches support a large tourist industry, particularly cruise ships. Yet, with the exceptions of Puerto Rico and Cuba, poverty is the rule in this area. Haiti is the poorest nation in the Western Hemisphere, and the slums in its capital, Port-au-Prince, are among the worst in the world. Agriculture (sugar, coffee, bananas, among other crops) is the main economic activity in the West Indies (see Figure 2.2.13). Because the best land grows crops for export, rather than for local consumption, many local people are undernourished.

North America's Weather Patterns

Most Atlantic storms begin to form off the coast of Africa during the summer and early fall, when ocean temperatures are warmest. A few gain strength to become tropical storms. In an average year, only six Atlantic Ocean tropical storms grow to become powerful **hurricanes**. These destructive storms can devastate island homes and businesses, such as what occurred in Florida in 2004.

Key Note Term

hurricane – a tropical storm with winds of at least 74 miles (119 km) per hour

Conclusion

North America is an exciting and diverse continent, spanning from the Arctic Circle almost to the equator. It includes Greenland, Canada, the United States, Mexico, all the countries of Central America and all the island nations of the Caribbean. North America has an extremely diversified terrain as well as diversified inhabitants. Once known as the "New World," North America is now a place where people want to study, visit, and live. From the **tundra** of Greenland and Northern Canada to the tropical climates of Central America and the West Indies, North America is a place where cultures come together and exciting things happen.

In the following lesson, you will learn about South America. This part of the world runs from the tropics nearly all the way to Antarctica, and holds a population just as diverse and colorful as that of North America.

Key Note Term

tundra – a treeless area between the icecaps and the tree line of Arctic regions, having a permanently frozen subsoil and supporting low-growing vegetation such as lichens, mosses, and stunted shrubs

Lesson Review

1. **Name the landform that dominates the central United States and Canada.**

2. **How has human activity affected the landscape of Canada and the United States?**

3. **What role have abundant natural resources played in the economies of the United States and Canada?**

4. **What are the three groups of islands in the Caribbean region?**

Lesson 3
South America–Through the Tropics Toward Antarctica

Key Terms

basin
canopy
El Nino
mestizo
savanna

WHAT YOU WILL LEARN TO DO

- Explore the unique geographic characteristics of South America

LINKED CORE ABILITIES

- Do your share as a good citizen in your school, community, country, and the world

- Treat self and others with respect

SKILLS AND KNOWLEDGE YOU WILL GAIN ALONG THE WAY

- Describe principal physical features of the continent of South America

- Summarize the physical and human characteristics of South American countries and regions

- Explain how the interactions between groups of people in South America can affect the area's cultural, economic, and political characteristics

- Characterize places in South America based on common characteristics and recognize the distribution of those characteristics across the earth's surface

- Define key words contained in this lesson

Chapter 2

Introduction

The continent of South America is as diverse and colorful as North America. Much of the population of South America can trace its roots back to the native Indians that inhabited this land prior to the Spanish explorers. This lesson explores the geographic characteristics of South America, from the tropics to near Antarctica. You learn what affects the region's cultural, political, and economic structures, and also learn about the history of the people of this lush continent.

South America

South America (Figure 2.3.1) is the fourth largest continent, extending about 5,000 miles from north to south. It reaches farther south than any other continent except Antarctica, with its southern tip at Cape Horn only 620 miles from that frozen continent.

A principal physical feature of South America is the Andes Mountain System, which extends almost 5,000 miles from Venezuela in the north to Tierra Del Fuego (an archipelago divided between Chile and Argentina) in the south. The system widens in Bolivia and Peru, forming an altiplano. Similar to the North American Cordillera, the Andes follow the Pacific coast. They are rich in minerals, contain active volcanoes, and experience earthquakes.

Another principal physical feature of South America is the Amazon River, the second longest river in the world after the Nile. It flows almost 4,000 miles across the country from Peru through Brazil to the Atlantic Ocean. The Amazon drains almost half of the continent, carries more water than any other river in the world, and travels through the world's largest rain forest. There are no obstructions along the course of the river, and ocean-going vessels travel almost its full length. Other important rivers include the Orinoco River in the north and the Paraná River in the south.

South America's largest lowland is the **basin** of the Amazon River, the area drained by this huge river and its tributaries. The Amazon Basin covers 2.7 million square miles (7 million sq km), a region two thirds the size of the United States. It carries a larger volume of water than any other river on earth.

Important grasslands in South America include the Pampas in Argentina and Uruguay, a 300,000 square-mile plain that supports livestock and agriculture; the Gran Chaco in Argentina and Paraguay, a lowland that supports livestock; and the Llanos, a savanna-like area in the Orinoco River basin in Colombia and Venezuela that has oil reserves and great agricultural potential yet to be tapped.

Key Note Term

basin – a large or small depression in the surface of the land or in the ocean floor

Figure 2.3.1: The regions of South America.

Map reproduced from *The 2004 World Factbook*, courtesy of the CIA, modified by Pearson Custom Publishing.

Between the Andes and the highlands of the east, wide plains fill the center of the continent of South America. In the north is a lowland region of tropical grasslands, or **savanna**, called the Llanos (YAH nohs). Savannas have long dry seasons and short, warm rainy seasons. In the south are the pampas, a large region of temperate grasslands in Argentina and Uruguay.

Also of note are the Atacama Desert in northern Chile, a coastal, desert plateau with great mineral wealth that is considered one of the driest places on Earth; Patagonia in the south, a semi-arid plateau rising from the Atlantic coast to the base of the Andes, also with great mineral wealth; the Galapagos Islands belonging to Ecuador that are famous for their unique geology, plants, and animals, including the giant tortoise; and the British-owned Falkland Islands, which Argentina claims is theirs and tried unsuccessfully to take over in 1982.

Important Historical/Political Considerations of South America

Similar to North America before the arrival of the Europeans, Indians were the original inhabitants of South America, with the Incas creating the greatest South American Indian empire along the west coast. After conquering Central America, the Spanish turned to conquering and colonizing South America, taking control of western and southern South America and forcing the Indian population into labor. In the meantime, the Portuguese claimed the east coast of South America and much of the South American interior. This area became Brazil. Because there were few native Indians living east of the Andes to use as labor, the Portuguese brought Africans to the continent to work on plantations.

A Bit of South American History

Colonization by Spain and Portugal made a lasting imprint on South American culture. Spanish and Portuguese, both derived from Latin, became and remain the region's major languages. Many towns built in the colonial period were built around a central plaza, following a Spanish model. Roman Catholicism, taught and spread by priests who arrived with the soldiers in the 1500s, became the major religion. Today, about 90 percent of South America's people are Roman Catholic.

The remaining South American territories along the northeast coast (now Guyana, Suriname, and French Guiana) became British, Dutch, and French colonies, respectively. Africans, East Indians, and Indonesians (an island in Southeast Asia) were brought or immigrated to this area to work on sugar plantations.

With the exception of French Guiana, which is an overseas department of France, the other South American countries gained their independence in the early 1800s. Since then, they have fought each other over territory and experienced political instability marked by military rule, oppressive dictatorships, and civil war—making it difficult for many of these countries to maintain democratic governments.

The People of South America

Unlike North American, South America never drew a large European immigrant population, and its current population of about 302 million people is small for a continent of its size. More people live along the northwest, west, and east coasts of the continent, with few people living in the south, northeast, or interior. About half of the population lives in Brazil. Most of South America is still considered underdeveloped and standards of living are low. Many people move to the cities in hopes of finding work and a better life, so three out of four South Americans currently live in urban areas (see Figure 2.3.2). Similar to other underdeveloped countries, however, many unskilled workers end up living in poverty in the crowded, rundown areas surrounding these cities.

Figure 2.3.2: Sao Paulo, Brazil, one of the largest cities in Brazil.

Courtesy of Getty Images, Inc.

South America: Largest Metropolitan Areas

Although not as populated as North America, South America has its share of densely populated areas.

Buenos Aires, Argentina	10,686,000
Rio de Janeiro, Brazil	9,817,000
São Paulo, Brazil	9,480,000
Lima, Peru	6,415,000
Santiago, Chile	4,386,000
Bogota, Colombia	3,975,000
Salvador, Brazil	2,056,000
Belo Horizonte, Brazil	2,049,000

A majority of South Americans are of European and/or Indian ancestry. The main European influences are Spanish and Portuguese, with most people speaking one of those two languages. In certain countries, however, many people also speak Native Indian languages. The majority of South Americans are Catholic.

> **Note**
>
> In a number of places, South Americans of Indian ancestry follow older, traditional lifestyles. Many Indians continue to dress, speak, farm, and trade much as their ancestors did.

Regions of South America

The continent of South America can be divided into four regions based on cultural as well as geographical characteristics. These regions are the Caribbean region, the Indian region, the South, and Brazil.

The Caribbean Region: Colombia, the Guianas, and Venezuela

Colombia, the Guianas, and Venezuela have a common northern, Caribbean coastal location. All of them at one time had plantation economies, and today each country still has a tropical plantation area. Because of their plantation history, the countries' population mix, in addition to Spanish and South American Indian, includes people of African, East Indian, and Indonesian descent.

Colombia is the only South American country with both Pacific and Caribbean coastlines. The Pacific coast is swampy and humid, while the Caribbean side is dry and hot. Colombians grow sugar, tobacco, and coffee (see Figure 2.3.3). Oil and coal are its other leading exports.

Figure 2.3.3: Growing coffee in Colombia.

Courtesy of National Geographic Society.

Unlike the majority of South America, the Guianas have British, French, and Dutch heritage. Because of this, English, French, and Dutch are official languages. Exports from this area include sugar, fish, lumber, rum, coffee, and bauxite, a principal source of aluminum.

Venezuela also exports coffee, and it is a leading oil producer. One of the world's greatest oilfields is in Lake Maracaibo, which is really a gulf open to the Caribbean Sea. Unfortunately, the lake now has major pollution problems due to oil spills. Venezuela is one of South America's wealthier countries because of its oil production. Similar to Mexico, however, it borrowed against its future oil profits and faces problems paying off its large foreign debt.

The Indian Region: Bolivia, Ecuador, Paraguay, and Peru

In west and central South America, the countries of Bolivia, Ecuador, Paraguay, and Peru have large Indian populations, almost 90 percent being Indian or **mestizo**. These Indian populations have very low incomes, and the region is the least urbanized in South America.

In the altiplano in Bolivia, freshwater Lake Titicaca, the highest large lake in the world, creates milder weather at its elevation of 12,500 feet and makes agriculture possible. Bolivians have grown grains in the area for centuries. They also export mineral oil, gas, zinc, silver, copper, and tin (see Figure 2.3.4). Bolivia, however, is at a disadvantage economically because it is landlocked with no seaports of its own.

Key Note Term

mestizos – a person of mixed European and American Indian ancestry

Figure 2.3.4: Tin mining in Bolivia.

Courtesy of Woodfin Camp and Associates.

Ecuador is one of the leading exporters of bananas and is South America's second largest exporter of crude oil. Although it is not a poor country, the Indian population in the interior lives in poverty.

Paraguay is the only non-Andean country in this region. It is also the poorest. Its most important commercial activity is cattle grazing in the Gran Chaco. Like Bolivia, Paraguay is landlocked and must transport its exports of meat, timber, cotton, and tobacco on the Paraná River to Argentina's Buenos Aires. Possible oil reserves in the Gran Chaco could provide future income for both Paraguay and Argentina.

Peru's economic activities include a large fishing industry on the coast, and agriculture where mountain streams irrigate valleys in the coastal desert. These areas produce cotton and sugar for export, and rice, wheat, fruit, and vegetables for the country's consumption. Northeastern Peru has oil, and its rain forests supply nuts, rubber, herbs, and wood. The country also exports copper, zinc, silver, and lead.

Key Note Term

El Nino – a disruption of the ocean-atmosphere system in the tropical Pacific having important consequences for weather around the globe

South America's Economy

One of South America's richest fishing regions is where two cold-water currents, the Peru (Humboldt) and California currents, meet off the coast of Peru and Ecuador. Winds blowing across this cold surface water lose their moisture at sea and are dry when they reach the land. About every three years, around December, a current known as **El Niño** warms these cold surface waters. The change in water temperature disrupts fishing. Birds and animals that usually feed on the fish die. El Niño also alters world weather patterns, causing both droughts and floods.

The Andes are home to half of Peru's population, but the many Indians living there have little political or economic influence. Most work on family-owned small farms, or are laborers on larger farms.

The South: Argentina, Chile, and Uruguay

In southern South America, Argentina, Chile, and Uruguay have large European populations. Spanish is the official language, and the area is better developed economically than others on the continent.

Argentina's wealth comes from the Pampas (see Figure 2.3.5) that produce abundant livestock and grains. Transportation of the Pampas' products to Argentina's cities is on the densest railroad system in South America, which radiates from Argentina's capital, Buenos Aires. In the cities, manufacturing to process the Pampas' products is a major economic activity. In addition, Argentina has an oilfield in Patagonia, where sheep are also raised. In the future, there is also the possibility of oil drilling in the Gran Chaco.

Uruguay is also a prosperous, agricultural country because of the Pampas. Surrounding Montevideo, its capital, is the major agricultural area, producing vegetables, fruit, and wheat for the country's internal consumption. Raising sheep and cattle is the main economic activity in the rest of the country, and Uruguay's chief exports are wool, hides, and meat. Like Buenos Aires, railroads radiate from Montevideo into Uruguay's interior aiding in the transport of agricultural products.

Chile has the world's largest reserves of copper. Found mainly in the Atacama Desert, it has become Chile's major export. Most of Chile's population lives in middle Chile, where agriculture is the chief economic activity. The area also supports cattle. In southern Chile, the coast breaks up into many islands, and few people live there.

Brazil: On the Rise

As the largest country on the continent, Brazil makes up its own region within South America. It is almost the size of all other South American nations combined. It is the fifth largest country in the world and the sixth largest in population. Interestingly, it is the only country in the world that intersects both the Equator and a tropic. The Amazon River basin takes up almost 60 percent of the country, gets heavy rainfall, and is covered in tropical forest. The Brazilian Highlands cover much of the rest of Brazil, with steep cliffs and slopes dropping to sea level along the coastline and leaving little coastal living space.

South America's Vegetation

The Amazon rain forest is the single largest mass of vegetation anywhere on earth, home to millions of species. Tangles of vines line the banks of the rain forest's rivers. The forest is dimly lit, for little sunlight can filter through the **canopy**. Only small, low-growing plants grow on the brown forest floor.

Key Note Term

canopy – the topmost forest layer where branches of tall trees meet

Brazil's heritage gives it a strong national culture, with one dominating language, Portuguese, and one main religion, Catholicism. Because of the millions of African slaves brought to work on Brazil's sugar plantations, Brazil has South America's largest black population. About 12 percent of Brazilians are black, 30 percent are of mixed African, white, and Indian ancestry, and more than half are of European descent. Indians make up a very small minority.

Brazil's economy is on the rise in the world because of its abundant natural resources, rapid urbanization, growing industry, enormous mineral deposits, and major oil and gas fields. In agriculture, Brazil is a leading producer and exporter of coffee, soybeans, and oranges. It has built huge hydroelectric plants, including the world's largest dam, the Itaipu, which is 600 feet high and five miles long (see Figure 2.3.6).

Figure 2.3.6: The Itaipu dam in Brazil.

Courtesy of Odyssey Productions, Inc.

Conclusion

South America is a fascinating continent with rich history and perhaps the most strikingly beautiful scenery on Earth. It also contains perhaps the most important ecosystem on Earth in the Amazon rain forest. It has strong Spanish and Portuguese influences, which can be seen in its religion, languages and architecture. The continent has many poor areas, and its residents are constantly moving to the cities for a better life. The South American continent is dominated by the large nation of Brazil, which has been working hard to modernize its economy in recent decades.

In the next lesson, you will learn about Europe, home to some of the world's most beautiful, famous, and historic cities. The lesson will cover the basic geography of the region as well as give you information about the economic and cultural climate.

Lesson Review

1. What are the important physical features of the South American continent?
2. What are the four regions of South America?
3. What types of economic activities take place in the Andes?
4. List three ways that Brazil different from the rest of South America.

Chapter 2

Lesson Review

Lesson 4
Europe—The Peninsular Continent

Key Terms

Celtic
clans
fjords
geysers
Gulf Stream
Orthodox Church
Slavs

WHAT YOU WILL LEARN TO DO

- Explore the unique geographic characteristics of Europe

LINKED CORE ABILITIES

- Do your share as a good citizen in your school, community, country, and the world

- Treat self and others with respect

SKILLS AND KNOWLEDGE YOU WILL GAIN ALONG THE WAY

- Describe principal physical features of the continent of Europe

- Summarize the physical and human characteristics of the countries and people of Europe

- Characterize places in Europe based on common characteristics of the earth's surface

- Define key words contained in this lesson

Introduction

Europe is rich in historical, cultural, and geographical diversity. Spanning from near the Arctic to the Mediterranean, the climate differences are as vast as the people who inhabit the land. This lesson looks at Europe, from its mountains to its rivers.

Europe

Some geographers consider Europe and Asia as one continent, Eurasia. It is generally accepted, however, that Europe and Asia are two separate continents, with Europe taking up the vast western peninsula of the European/Asian landmass. The Ural Mountains, Caspian Sea, Caucasus Mountain System, Black Sea, and Bosporus and Dardanelles Straits (Figure 2.4.1) separate Europe from Asia.

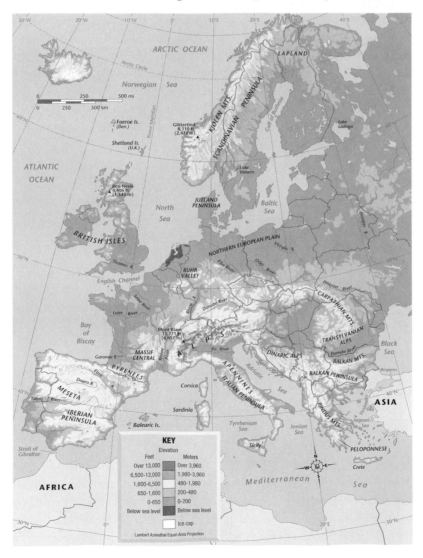

Figure 2.4.1: The European continent.

Courtesy of GeoSystems Global Corporation.

Although Europe, the second smallest continent, is itself a peninsula, it also consists of many peninsulas surrounded by many seas including:

- **The Scandinavian Peninsula, home to Norway and Sweden, between the Norwegian and Baltic Seas**

- **The Kola Peninsula in Russia on the Barents Sea**

- **The Jutland Peninsula, home to Denmark and part of Germany, between the North and Baltic Seas**

- **The Iberian Peninsula, home to Portugal and Spain, west of the Mediterranean Sea and separated from the African continent by the Strait of Gibraltar**

- **The Italian Peninsula, home to Italy, Vatican City, and San Marino, on the Mediterranean and Adriatic Seas**

- **The Balkan Peninsula, home to Greece, Bulgaria, European Turkey, Albania, Macedonia, Yugoslavia, Bosnia-Herzegovina, Croatia, Slovenia, and part of Romania, on the Mediterranean, Adriatic, Aegean, and Black Seas**

- **The Crimean Peninsula, which is part of the Ukraine, on the Black Sea**

Entering the many seas of Europe are major rivers, including the Volga, Danube, Dnieper, and Rhine. The Volga is the longest river in Europe, flowing south through Russia to enter the Caspian Sea. The Danube starts in Germany, flows through or creates borders with eight countries (Austria, Slovak Republic, Hungary, Croatia, Yugoslavia, Bulgaria, Romania, and Ukraine), and enters the Black Sea. Also flowing into the Black Sea is the Dnieper, passing through Russia, Belarus, and the Ukraine. The Rhine River is the main waterway of Western Europe. It begins in Switzerland, forms part of the Germany-France border, then flows through the Netherlands to the North Sea.

The source of the Rhine River is in the Alps, the principal mountain range of Europe, which passes through Switzerland, France, Germany, Austria, Liechtenstein, Italy, Slovenia, Croatia, and Yugoslavia. The Alps are part of the Alpine Mountain System that crosses Europe from west to east. Other important mountain ranges in the Alpine Mountain System are the Pyrenees which separate France from Spain and are home to the country of Andorra; the earthquake prone Apennines that extend down the Italian Peninsula; the Carpathians extending from the Czech Republic along the Poland-Slovak Republic border into the Ukraine and Romania; and as previously mentioned, the Caucasus Mountains.

> **Note**
>
> The Caspian Sea is not really a sea. It is the largest lake in the world, spanning over 140,000 square miles.

Another important physical feature of Europe is the North European Plain that stretches from the Atlantic coast of France to the Ural Mountains in Russia. The area is a low land, much of it below 500 feet in elevation. It contains Europe's best farmland, where the practices of agricultural diversity and high productivity help feed Europe's large population—about 25 percent of the Earth's total population in an area about half the size of the U.S.

People of very different backgrounds and cultures exist together on this small continent, which is home to over 40 different countries (see Figure 2.4.2). Historically, European countries have been economically and politically fragmented, their borders shaped by conflict and the rise and fall of political powers. Yet, Europe also has a history rich in science, art, literature, music, religion, commerce, world exploration, and industry. Today, Europe continues to possess thriving cities, excellent transportation networks, high productivity, and innovative technology.

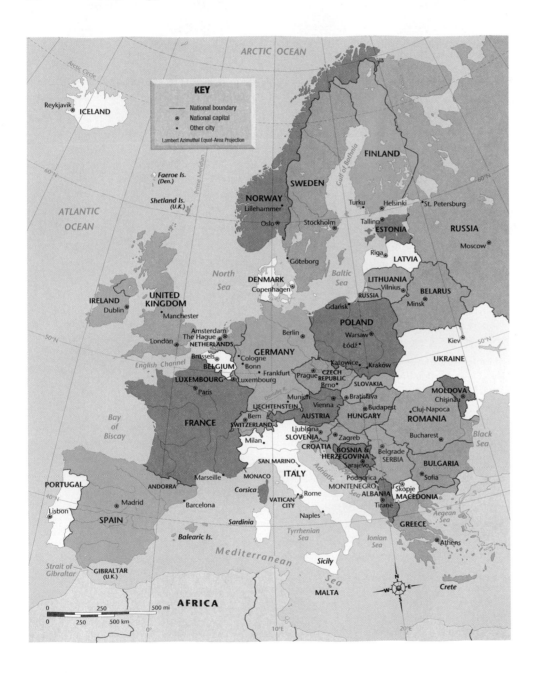

Figure 2.4.2: The European Continent: Political.

Courtesy of GeoSystems Global Corporation.

In Western Europe, 11 countries formed the Economic and Monetary Union, and in the pursuit of economic unity, created one currency, the euro, issued in

2002. In contrast, many countries in Eastern Europe are struggling with internal conflicts and economic problems following the dissolution in the early 1990s of the U.S.S.R., of which many were a part.

The European Union

The European Union (EU) is the world's largest trading block—and it is still growing. Here are some of the challenges success has created for this economic giant.

Fifteen Western European countries currently belong to the EU. Member countries pay no tariffs when trading with one another. As a result, trade among member countries has increased and the standard of living of citizens living in EU countries has risen. Several Eastern European countries, including Poland, Hungary, and Romania, are eager to join their European cousins and enjoy the economic benefits of EU membership. Some EU members, particularly Great Britain, are opposed to expanding the EU.

In 1992 representatives of the EU countries agreed to create a common currency called the euro. They planned to begin using the euro by 1999, but now there are some concerns that the launch of the euro will be delayed. Before adopting the euro, each country must meet strict criteria to ensure that its economy is strong. Few countries seem able to meet these requirements.

The European Union acts to regulate trade relations with countries outside the union. Members of the European Parliament voted in favor of a customs union between Turkey and the EU on December 13, 1995.

In addition to working together for economic growth, EU members also cooperate politically. Citizens of EU countries enjoy a single European citizenship that allows them to live and work anywhere in the Union. They can also vote in local elections in the country where they live, even if they are not citizens of that country. Despite this level of unity, disagreements among leaders of member countries sometimes weaken the EU's ability to act quickly and forcibly on important issues.

The EU is a leading economic power. It produces more goods than the United States and is the largest importer and exporter in the world. As a result, it plays a crucial role in negotiating and managing world-trade rules. In addition, its economic power has given it responsibilities for providing financial help to poor, nonmember countries and negotiating peace treaties between warring nations.

Leaders of EU member states are meeting the challenges the EU faces so that their union can remain strong. Here are some of the solutions they are working on.

Formal talks concerning the admission of new members are planned to begin before the end of 1997. Germany is particularly eager that modern Eastern European countries, such as Poland, be admitted into the Union. It is concerned that denying nations entry into the EU could condemn them to poverty and create two classes of European nations—the haves and the have-nots.

EU representatives are meeting to talk about ways to bring monetary union to Europe. Some leaders suggest relaxing the strict criteria that countries must meet in order to adopt the euro. Others have suggested extending the 1999 deadline so that countries that are temporarily experiencing slow growth can recover. These countries are now using the euro.

The British Isles: Great Britain and Ireland

The British Isles (Figure 2.4.3) are home to the United Kingdom (England, Scotland, Northern Ireland, and Wales) and the Republic of Ireland. They consist of two large islands—Great Britain and Ireland—and smaller islands off their coasts. The North Sea and the English Channel, which is one of the world's busiest shipping lanes, separate the British Isles from mainland Europe. London, located on the Thames River, is the capital of England and the United Kingdom. The Pennines Mountain Range is "the backbone of England," and the Highlands in Scotland is a mountainous region known for its rugged beauty and distinctive culture based on **clans**. The British Isles tend to have wet weather, with Ireland receiving the heaviest rainfall.

Key Note Term

clans – groups united by common interests or characteristics, particularly Celtic groups in the Scottish highlands claiming descent from common ancestors

Figure 2.4.3: The British Isles: Political and physical.

Courtesy of maps.com.

Important United Kingdom Historical/Political Considerations

From 1801 until 1922, all of Ireland was part of the United Kingdom; however, the Irish, especially the large Catholic population, fought British rule. In the 1920s, Britain divided Ireland—Northern Ireland was mostly Protestant and stayed in union with the United Kingdom, while the rest of Ireland eventually became the Republic of Ireland.

The People of the British Isles

The United Kingdom is one of the most densely populated nations in Europe. Of the United Kingdom's 57 million people, England has the largest population, with 20 million people living in and around London. In contrast, Ireland has a shrinking population. Each year, 30,000 Irish leave their country, usually because of Ireland's economic problems. Since 1999, however, these problems seem to be on the decline due to Ireland's promotion of new industries, trade, and foreign investments.

The population of the United Kingdom is 81 percent English, 10 percent Scottish, 2 percent Irish, 2 percent Welsh, and 2 percent Asian and African from former British colonies. English is the universal language of the British Isles, with **Celtic** languages (Welsh, Irish Gaelic, and Scots Gaelic) spoken as well.

Similar to North and South Americans, people from the British Isles are overwhelmingly Christian. In the United Kingdom, a majority of people are Protestant, in contrast to the Republic of Ireland where the majority is Catholic. Since the 1960s, Northern Ireland has experienced violence between Catholics and Protestants based on Catholic claims of discrimination and Protestant fears of reunification with the Republic of Ireland.

The European Economy

The United Kingdom is a leading industrial nation (see Figure 2.4.4). Yet, because of its small size, it lacks the raw materials needed for industry; therefore, it exports manufactured goods in exchange for the raw materials and food needed for its large population. This makes the United Kingdom one of the most active trading nations in the world. Industries include food processing, publishing, shipbuilding, and production of oil and gas from the North Sea. Other economic activities include agriculture, livestock, fishing, and tourism.

Key Note Term

Celtic – pertaining to the Celts, an ancient people who dominated Europe in the 4th century B.C. and eventually withdrew to the British Isles

In the Republic of Ireland, agriculture is the primary economic activity, with much of the land used for grazing sheep and cattle. Tourism is also a large source of income. Other economic activities include fishing, forestry, and a recent growth in engineering, electronics, and software development.

Western Europe: The Continental Core

Western Europe (Figure 2.4.5) consists of Andorra, Austria, Benelux (created when Belgium, the Netherlands, and Luxembourg formed a trade union in 1948), France, Germany, Liechtenstein, and Switzerland. Territorially, France is the largest country; Liechtenstein is the smallest composed of just 62 square miles.

Physically, the region possesses a variety of landscapes. The Alps in France, Switzerland, and Austria contrast with the extremely flat land of Benelux, also referred to as the Low Countries because they lie near sea level. In the Netherlands, more than 25 percent of the land is actually below sea level; the Dutch have claimed land from the sea by connecting coastal islands in the North Sea with dikes, then pumping out the trapped water.

Continental Europe's Terrain

The mountains in northern Scandinavia formed more than 400 million years ago. The mountains in the southern part of Europe, the Alps, are higher and younger. They formed about 25 million years ago. Mont Blanc is the tallest mountain in the Alps mountain range. Its summit, or highest point, is 15,771 feet (4,807 m) above sea level. Name at least three other mountain ranges in Europe besides the Alps.

The North European Plain is an important source of agricultural products. Its flat, fertile land is irrigated by some of Europe's great rivers. The plain stretches more than 1,200 miles (1,931 km) from France through Germany and into Eastern Europe and Northern Eurasia.

Throughout history, these rivers have carried much of the region's commerce. Two major rivers flow east or south. The Rhône in France empties into the Mediterranean. The Po in Italy empties into the Adriatic.

Many Western European cities are located on the banks of rivers. Paris, the capital of France, was founded more than 2,000 years ago on an island in the Seine (SEHN) River. Describe the advantages of such a location.

Similar to the Netherlands and Belgium of Benelux, Germany and France also have coastlines. The rest of the countries in Western Europe are landlocked, and rely on rivers connected by canals and artificial waterways.

The North Atlantic Drift, a powerful ocean current, carries tropical waters toward the coast of Europe. The winds that blow across this warm current are the prevailing westerlies. The ocean currents and winds produce a warm, moist climate in most of Western Europe. Because southern mountains block the moist Atlantic winds, the climate along the Mediterranean Sea is hot and dry in summer. In winter, winds blow off the Mediterranean, bringing regular rainfall. On the Scandinavian Peninsula, northern mountains block warm Atlantic winds creating a very dry, cold, subarctic climate.

The People of Western Europe

Similar to the United Kingdom, the countries of Western Europe are densely populated. Comparing size and population, the countries of Benelux are some of the most densely populated on earth (see figure 2.4.6). Twenty-five million people inhabit an area about the size of the state of Maine. Maine, by comparison, contains only 1.2 million people.

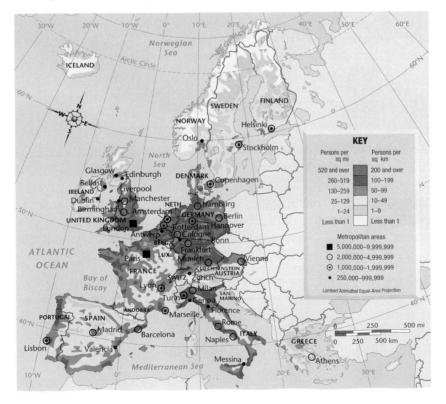

Figure 2.4.6:
Western Europe:
Population density.

Courtesy of GeoSystems Global Corporation.

Western Europe: Largest Cities

Although London, England, is the most densely populated city in Europe, other large cities are located on the continent.

London, England	6,803,000
Berlin, Germany	3,438,000
Madrid, Spain	2,991,000
Rome, Italy	2,828,500
Paris, France	2,151,500
Barcelona, Spain	1,667,500
Hamburg, Germany	1,660,500
Vienna, Austria	1,560,500
Milan, Italy	1,548,500
Munich, Germany	1,236,500

Similar to the British Isles, a majority of people are Christian. Unlike the British Isles, the countries of Western Europe do not share a common language. In the Netherlands, Dutch is the official language. In Germany, Austria, and Liechtenstein, a majority of the people speak German. In Luxembourg, both German and French are official languages, although the common language is Luxembourgish, a form of German. In Switzerland, German, French, and Italian are spoken. French is the official language of France.

In Belgium, more than half of its people are Flemings, natives of Flanders who speak Flemish, a Dutch language; while a third are Walloons, inhabitants of southern Belgium who speak French. Political tensions between the Flemings and Walloons caused the collapse of several governments; and in 1989, a new constitution split Belgium into three regions: Flanders, Wallonia, and the bilingual city of Brussels.

The Economy of Western Europe

Industry and commerce make Western Europe the continental core. Many internationally important cities in the region include Brussels, Belgium, which is headquarters of the European Union and NATO; Geneva, Switzerland, which is headquarters to over 200 international organizations, including the International Red Cross and the World Health Organization; Paris, France, one of the world's main tourist destinations and a world center of art, high fashion, and luxury goods; and Rotterdam in the Netherlands, which is one of the largest ports in the world.

Switzerland, with a history of political stability and neutrality, strong commerce, and technological advancement, is one of the richest countries in the world. It is famous for cheese, chocolate, watches, and banking. Luxembourg is another important banking center. Belgium is one of Europe's most heavily industrialized nations. In addition to industry, the Netherlands boasts a large agricultural base.

France, however, is Europe's leading agricultural producer. Although wheat is its major crop, the country has enormous agricultural diversity, and French wine and cheese are world-famous (see Figure 2.4.7). France also specializes in high-quality textiles and precision equipment. It is active in the telecommunications, biotechnology, and aerospace industries.

In Germany, a division exists between the economies of old East and West Germany (separated by a Soviet blockade in 1949 and reunited following the fall of the Berlin Wall in 1989). Because of the east's previous socialist economy, it has limited industrial development compared to the west. Despite these problems, Germany has a strong economy. It exports high-technology goods and among its most famous exports are its automobiles, which include BMW, Mercedes, Porsche, and Volkswagen.

Figure 2.4.7: The Vineyards of the Rhone Valley in France.

Courtesy of Getty Images, Inc.

Scandinavia: The Northernmost Countries

For historical, ethnic, and geographical reasons, Scandinavia (Figure 2.4.8) consists of Norway and Sweden on the Scandinavian Peninsula, as well as Denmark, Finland, and Iceland. These are the world's northernmost countries. The U.S., Canada, and Russia all have territory at similar latitudes, but they also possess more southerly land.

Figure 2.4.8: The Scandinavian Peninsula.

Courtesy of maps.com.

fjords – narrow inlets of the sea between cliffs or steep slopes

geysers – natural springs that periodically eject fountains of heated water and steam from a crack in the earth's surface

Gulf Stream – a warm ocean current that originates in the Gulf of Mexico, flows along the east coast of the U.S., then across the Atlantic Ocean as the North Atlantic Drift; its warm water helps moderate the climate of northwest Europe

Norway's coastline is irregular with many islands and **fjords**. Its interior is mountainous, with much of it over 5,000 feet in elevation. The Kjölen Mountains in the north form a border with Sweden. Forest covers over half of Sweden and Finland, and both countries have much inland water in the forms of rivers and lakes. Unlike Norway and Sweden, Finland and Denmark are low-lying countries. Iceland has snowfields and glaciers as well as active volcanoes, hot springs, and **geysers**. Underground hot water heats many towns in Iceland, and warm water from the **Gulf Stream** flows around the country keeping its ports ice-free.

The People of Scandinavia

For its size, Scandinavia has a small population with most people living in the southern portion of the region. People from Scandinavian countries have much in common. Most have a high standard of living; and not only are a majority Protestant, but also over 90 percent of all Scandinavians are specifically Lutheran. Each country has its own language, yet Danish, Swedish, and Norwegian are mutually understandable. These three languages and Icelandic are of German origin. Only Finnish is totally different, but many Finns also speak Swedish.

In the Arctic region of Scandinavia, known as Lapland, there is a Lapp minority believed to have originated in central Asia. The Lapps use the reindeer as a pack animal as well as, for milk, meat, leather.

The Economy of Scandinavia

Denmark's level land and good soil support intensive agriculture. Estimates indicate its farm production could feed 20 million people a year. Since Denmark has few natural resources, it trades exports for raw materials to support processing industries. One famous Denmark product is Lego toy building blocks. Unlike Denmark, only three percent of Norway's land is under cultivation, and one of its important economic activities is the extraction and processing of raw materials including North Sea oil. Both its fishing industry and its merchant marine are among the world's largest. Similarly, three-fourths of Iceland's income comes from fishing.

Chief exports of both Finland and Sweden are wood products. Both have shifted from traditional economic activities of farming and forestry to industries like electronics, food processing, and chemical manufacturing. Bordering Russia, Finland has experienced economic problems due to changes in the former Soviet Union and Eastern Europe in the 1990s.

Mediterranean Europe: Peninsulas and Islands

Greece, Italy, Malta, Monaco, Portugal, San Marino, Spain, and Vatican City make up Mediterranean Europe (Figure 2.4.9). Similar to Scandinavia, this region consists of many peninsulas and islands. In addition to the Iberian and Italian Peninsulas (refer back to Figure 2.4.1), the southern part of the Balkan Peninsula is a peninsular region of Greece known as the Peloponnese. Over 1,400 islands make up 20 percent of Greece, with Crete being the largest.

Figure 2.4.9: Mediterranean Europe.

Reproduced from *The 2004 World Factbook,*
courtesy of the CIA.

Most of Mediterranean Europe is mountainous or hilly. As in Western Europe, the Alps and Pyrenees Mountains are important physical features of this region. Other features include the Apennine Mountains that run through Italy and are home to San Marino, a 23 square mile republic land-locked in Italy; the 2.5 square mile city of Gibraltar on the Strait of Gibraltar, which the United Kingdom owns and Spain wants; the Italian city of Venice, built on 118 islets in a lagoon, allowing transportation by boat only through a system of canals; and the rivers Tagus, Ebro, Po, and Tiber.

The Tiber River flows through Rome, Italy, an important historical and cultural city for more than 2,000 years. Located in Rome on the Tiber is Vatican City, the smallest independent nation in the world at less than one-fifth of a square mile. Often called simply the Vatican, it is the world center of the Catholic Church and home of the Pope, who is its spiritual leader. Although the Vatican is small, decisions made there by the Pope often affect politics in other predominantly Catholic countries. His influence is particularly great with laws on moral issues.

The People of the Mediterranean

In general, the people of Mediterranean Europe have a lower standard of living than their neighbors in Western Europe, Scandinavia, and the British Isles. Monaco, a luxury resort area that is home to many wealthy people, is an exception. Of the larger Mediterranean countries, Portugal and Greece have the lowest standards of living. Although its island of Sicily still has much poverty, Italy, in general, has the highest standard of living in the region.

Whereas Spain has the largest territory, Italy has the largest population at 57 million—almost equal to Portugal, Spain, and Greece combined. Yet, the smaller countries are the most crowded, especially Malta. Except for the Greeks, most of whom belong to the **Orthodox Church**, the majority of people in Mediterranean Europe are Roman Catholic.

Like Western Europe, languages in Mediterranean Europe differ from country to country: Greek in Greece; Portuguese in Portugal; Italian in Italy and San Marino; English and Maltese (a mixture of Arabic and Italian) in Malta; and French in Monaco. Latin, an ancient language from which the Romance languages evolved, is the official language in Vatican City. In Spain, Spanish is the official language, but other dialects and languages spoken are Catalan and Basque.

Key Note Term

Orthodox Church – a community of Christian churches that originated in Eastern Europe and southwest Asia after separating from the Catholic Church in 1054 over differences in doctrine, including acceptance of the Pope's supremacy

How Languages Spread

Why do millions of people around the world speak languages that come from Western Europe? Over centuries of history, European colonial powers took their cultures and languages to other parts of the world.

Europe is a small continent, but its nations have built great empires that influenced people in all parts of the world. The first was the Roman Empire, which reached its height about A.D. 120. Along with Roman laws, its soldiers took Latin, the language of Rome, to western and central Europe.

The Roman Empire itself fell apart in the fifth century A.D., but Latin continued to have an important influence in Western Europe because of the Roman Catholic Church. Church officials and all educated people spoke and wrote Latin.

Centuries of Roman rule also influenced people's everyday language. At one time, various groups in Europe had their own languages—Celtic, Iberian, Germanic. By the Middle Ages, most people in Western Europe were speaking rough versions of Latin called the vernacular. These developed into modern languages such as Italian, French, Spanish, and Romanian.

A later conquest led to modern English. Even in Roman times, most people in northern Europe spoke Germanic languages. When the Angles and Saxons migrated to the British Isles, they took their Germanic language with them.

Then, in 1066, William of Normandy led his soldiers across the English Channel to conquer England. The Normans brought their Latin-based French language. For a time, nobles, law court officials, and scholars spoke Norman French. Most ordinary English people went on speaking Anglo-Saxon. Gradually the two languages mixed. They created the English language we speak today.

Beginning in the 1500s, western European nations competed to build colonial empires around the world. Spain and England in particular took their national cultures and languages to their colonies.

Spain's colonies included Mexico and most of Central and South America. Spanish was the official language; Roman Catholicism the only religion. Spanish conquistadors, friars, and officials did all they could to eliminate native languages and religions. Today, while Spain's population is about 40 million, the Spanish language is spoken by about 300 million people worldwide.

Portugal's empire lay mainly in Asia. The Portuguese language and its Catholic religion took hold in its one American colony, Brazil.

England and France were rivals in several places. In North America, they fought over territory and colonies. The English language, along with English law, became dominant in the original American colonies and in most of Canada. French language and customs, however, persisted in Quebec and in some Caribbean islands.

France and England also competed in India and Africa. India was Britain's most prized colony until it gained independence in 1947. English is still an official language in both India and Pakistan. English is also spoken in many former British colonies in Africa and the Caribbean, while people in France's former colonies in northern and western Africa speak French.

The Basques, located in north Spain and southwest France, are probably Europe's oldest ethnic group. The majority live in Spain and preserve their unique traditions and ancient language, unrelated to any present-day European language. Many Basques desire political independence, and some engage in terrorism to force the establishment of a Basque state.

The Economy of Mediterranean Europe

The warm climate in Mediterranean Europe makes tourism an important economic activity, while dry summers and rocky soil make agriculture difficult in many areas. The region lags behind much of Western Europe in industrial development.

Greek islands and ancient structures still standing in Athens make Greece a major tourist attraction, with the service sector accounting for almost 60 percent of Greek income. Other industries include shipping (Greece's maritime fleet is one of the largest in Europe), textiles, food processing, and chemicals. Agricultural exports include grapes, olives, and olive oil. Olives and grapes are also the main crops in Spain where industry supplements a traditionally agricultural economy. Since the late 1980s, Spain's economy has grown at a fast rate. High-technology industries, resorts, and retirement communities have multiplied, especially along the Mediterranean coast.

Eastern Europe: In Transition

Political instability, changing boundaries, and internal ethnic and religious problems mark the countries of Eastern Europe. Although not all of these countries were part of the U.S.S.R., communist parties and communist economics controlled this region for much of the twentieth century. With the collapse of the Soviet-dominated communist system in the late 1980s and early 1990s, many problems surfaced as countries declared their independence and struggles for political control and economic reform began. At the turn of the century, Eastern Europe remains an area in transition.

Eastern Europe's Nations

In 1989, Eastern Europe included eight nations: Albania, Bulgaria, Czechoslovakia, East Germany, Hungary, Poland, Romania, and Yugoslavia. List the nations of the region today.

Political changes have dramatically altered boundaries in Eastern Europe. For example, what was once East Germany has merged with West Germany to form Germany.

Many of the nations of Eastern Europe have no seacoast. It is no surprise, then, that none of the capital cities of Eastern Europe are located on seacoasts.

Eastern Europe has four broad bands of distinct landforms (see Figure 2.4.10). The North European Plain forms the northernmost landform region. It stretches from the Atlantic Ocean in the west to the Ural Mountains in the east.

Figure 2.4.10:
Eastern Europe.

Courtesy of United Nations
Publications.

The Dinaric Alps run along much of the Adriatic Seacoast. The Danube River dominates the region below the Carpathians (see Figure 2.4.11). It has been called "a lifeline" in the region. The southernmost landform region in Eastern Europe is the Balkan Peninsula. It is the tangled web of mountain ranges and valleys south of the Danube River.

Figure 2.4.11:
The Danube River.

Courtesy of Robert Harding World Imagery.

European Russia

In its entirety, Russia is the largest country in the world (see Figure 2.4.12), stretching more than six million square miles from Eastern Europe across northern Asia to the Pacific. European Russia is Russia's core area with major industry and transportation networks, well-cultivated land, and a large portion of Russia's population. This area also has many large cities including Moscow, Russia's capital and largest city, and St. Petersburg (formerly Leningrad), a Baltic port and Russia's second largest city.

Figure 2.4.12: Russia.

Courtesy of maps.com.

Except for the Caucasus and Ural Mountains, most of European Russia is flatland consisting of the fertile Russian Plain (part of the North European Plain) and drained by the Volga and Don Rivers.

The People of European Russia

After years of living under restrictive and repressive government regulations, the Russian people witnessed a move in the late 1980s toward greater cultural freedom, freedom of the press, and open public debate. This move was part of the policy of glasnost that affected not only Russia but also the rest of Eastern Europe as well.

Russians make up part of Europe's largest ethnic group, the **Slavs**. Over 80 percent of Russia's total population is Russian with over 100 other ethnic groups making up the rest. Russian, a Slavic language, is official, with over 100 other languages spoken as well. Many people are non-religious, but 25 percent consider themselves Orthodox. There is also a Muslim minority.

Key Note Term

Slavs – the largest group of Europeans sharing common ethnic and linguistic origins, including Russians, Belorussians, Ukrainians, Serbs, Montenegrins, Poles, Macedonians, Czechoslovakians, Slovaks, Croats and Bulgarians

Eastern Europe's Inhabitants

Roughly two thirds of the people of Eastern Europe are descended from the Slavs. The Slavs arrived in the Carpathian Mountains about 2,000 years ago. They then moved north to the Baltic Sea, south toward Greece, west toward Germany, and east into Russia.

Dozens of other ethnic groups live in the region. They include the Bulgars, the Romanians (linked to the ancient Romans), Albanians (linked to a very ancient people on the Adriatic Sea), Germans, Turks, Roma (once called Gypsies), and Jews. Why would the Romans have been involved in Eastern Europe, hundreds of miles from Rome?

The Economy of European Russia

Since the late 1980s, Russia has restructured its communist economy in a move toward capitalism. Currently it is struggling with legal problems related to private property, food and fuel shortages, unemployment, and cutback or suspension of social services. European Russia has a wealth of mineral resources in the Ural Mountains as well as oil and natural gas along the Volga River. The greatest industrial regions are around Moscow and along the Volga. Fruit and tobacco are major export crops.

The Northern Countries

The remaining northern countries in Eastern Europe include Belarus, the Czech Republic, Estonia, Hungary, Latvia, Lithuania, Moldova, Poland, the Slovak Republic, and the Ukraine (Figure 2.4.13). The lands of Belarus, Estonia, Latvia, Lithuania, and Poland are covered in part by the North European Plain, while the Carpathian Mountains begin in the Czech Republic and extend through southern Poland and the Slovak Republic.

The People of the Northern Countries

The majority of the populations of the Czech Republic, Hungary, and Poland are Czechoslovakian, Hungarian, and Polish, respectively. The populations of the remaining countries are a diverse mix of ethnic groups. (*Note:* Through the rest of this chapter, names of ethnic groups and languages discussed are numerous and may be more unfamiliar to you than those covered previously. The point is not that you must specifically know the names of each region's ethnic groups and languages, but that you gain an appreciation for the diversity of people living in the different regions discussed.)

Eastern Europe: Largest Cities

Some of the most beautiful cities in the world are situated in Eastern Europe. Although not as populated as other areas of Europe, these cities are just as bustling and viable.

Budapest, Hungary	2,017,000
Bucharest, Romania	1,807,000
Warsaw, Poland	1,654,500
Prague, Czech Republic	1,212,000
Sofia, Bulgaria	1,141,000
Belgrade, Serbia	1,137,000
Lódź, Poland	846,500
Kraków, Poland	750, 500

The Belorussians, Czechoslovakians, Poles, Slovaks, and Ukrainians are of Slavic origin, like the Russians. Likewise, the official languages of these countries (Belorussian, Czechoslovakian, Polish, Slovak, and Ukrainian, respectively) are Slavic languages like Russian. The Hungarians (or Magyars) and the Hungarian language (or Magyar) are of Asian origin. The Moldovans and the Moldovan language are essentially Romanian, since the Soviets took Moldova from Romania in the 1940s. Latvian and Lithuanian are related languages, while the Estonians and their language bear similarities to their neighbors, the Finns. Most people in this region are Christian (a mix of Protestant, Roman Catholic, and Orthodox).

The Economy of the Northern Countries

Under communist rule, much of the agriculture and industry in this region came under government control. However, in Hungary in the 1960s, individual farms and factories gained greater independence. This mix of capitalism and communism allowed the Hungarian economy to progress. Much of Hungary is flat farmland, and its industries include engineering, chemicals, textiles, food processing, and mining. Its industrial and commercial center is Budapest, also Hungary's capital (see Figure 2.4.14).

Figure 2.4.14:
Budapest, Hungary.

Courtesy of Getty Images, Inc.

Much of Poland is also flat farmland, and over 50 percent of it is under cultivation. Poland is a major producer of coal and has huge shipbuilding factories. The Ukraine contains the 10,000 square mile Donets coalfield and has been in heavy industry since the late 1800s. It has a wide variety of natural resources, but limited water resources. With its fertile soils, the Ukraine is a major exporter of grain.

Forty-six percent of Belarus is farmland, and Moldova has fertile soils that produce grapes for wine. The Czech Republic has coal and iron, while the Slovak Republic is more of an agricultural region. Both produce steel; however, since the division of Czechoslovakia into two republics, heavy industry in the Slovak Republic has suffered due to loss of state subsidies. The economy of the Baltic Republics (Estonia, Latvia, and Lithuania) relies on manufacturing, agriculture, livestock, and fishing.

The Southern Countries

The remaining countries in Eastern Europe lie entirely or partially on the Balkan Peninsula. Often referred to as the Balkan States, they include Albania, Bulgaria, Bosnia-Herzegovina, Croatia, Macedonia, Romania, Slovenia, European Turkey, and Yugoslavia (Figure 2.4.15).

Note

Turkey will be discussed in its entirety in the following lesson on Asia.

Except for land near the Danube River, most of this region is mountainous. It contains the Dinaric Alps which are part of the Alpine Mountain System; Balkan Mountains; and Carpathian Mountains which include the Transylvanian Alps in Romania. All but Macedonia, which is landlocked, have coastlines on the Adriatic or Black Seas.

Important Historical/Political Considerations of the Southern Countries

This region is the most troubled in Europe. In fact, because of the Balkan States' reputation for division and fragmentation, the term "balkanize" means "to break into small and often hostile units." As late as the 1990s, civil war occurred when the former Yugoslav Republics of Bosnia-Herzegovina, Croatia, Macedonia, and Slovenia declared their independence leaving Yugoslavia with only Serbia and Montenegro. Fighting occurred between ethnic and religious groups in Croatia and Bosnia-Herzegovina. NATO conducted bombing raids against Serbian forces in Serbia to halt hostilities against ethnic Albanians in the Serbian province of Kosovo. Warfare in these nations destroyed vast quantities of property and cost hundreds of thousands of lives (see Figure 2.4.16).

Figure 2.4.16: A city in war-torn Croatia.

Courtesy of TRIP/H. Sayer.

History: The Balkan "Powder Keg"

Why have conflicts so often erupted in the small nations of southeastern Europe? The answers lie in the region's central location, which has given it a long and troubled history.

For thousands of years southeastern Europe, between the Black Sea and the Adriatic, has been the scene of conflicts. Forces from east and west have pulled at the people of the northern Balkan peninsula. Invaders and groups on the move have added to the ethnic mix. The region has been split by religion, by ethnic differences, by politics, and by language. Although great empires have ruled the Balkans, its people never really became part of a larger national identity. Each group's ethnic and religious loyalties remained strong, ready to resurface.

The ancient Roman Empire unified much of Europe. But as the Empire weakened, its eastern provinces in the Balkans were the first to fall. Goths and other Germanic invaders moved across the countryside. Huns from Asia settled on the broad Danube Plain.

Before the Roman Empire finally fell, it split into eastern and western halves. The split cut across the Balkans. Part of the region was in the Eastern Empire, later the Byzantine Empire. The Adriatic coast was in what remained of the Western Empire. Attila and the Huns ruled the north.

Other influences had an impact on the region. The Roman Empire became officially Christian in the 4th century, but Christianity itself was divided into the Greek-speaking Orthodox Church in the east and the Latin-speaking Roman Catholic Church in the west.

For the next several centuries, an assortment of ethnic groups, mostly from central Asia, moved through Eastern Europe.

By the late 1400s, the Muslim Turkish sultans of the Ottoman Empire ruled the entire Balkan Peninsula. To the north was the Austrian Empire. For hundreds of years the border between those two empires shifted back and forth in the Balkans.

Divisions between ethnic groups increased. The South Slavs, for instance, had converted to Christianity but split over religion. Croats became Roman Catholic; Serbs were Orthodox. Their spoken languages were almost alike, but Croats wrote in the Roman alphabet, Serbs in the Cyrillic. Croatia was part of Hungary for centuries; for most of that time, Serbs lived within the Ottoman Empire.

Early in the 1800s the Ottoman Empire was weakening. Serbs, Greeks, Romanians, and Bulgars all saw a chance to gain independence. By the 1870s, other European rulers wanted to help Balkan peoples escape from Muslim rule. The actual task was left up to the Czar of Russia. When Russian troops finished their mission, the northern Balkans were a patchwork of small nations, some in the Austro-Hungarian Empire, some with their own rulers. The map below is a snapshot of the region at that time, 1885.

World War I brought the end of both the Austro-Hungarian and Ottoman empires. Nationalist groups demanded and got their own countries. Yugoslavia, for example, was supposed to bring together all the South Slavs. Many people, however, simply found themselves minorities in the new nations. Along with centuries of history, this set the stage for still more conflicts to erupt in the Balkans in the 1990s.

The People of the Southern Countries

Like the northern countries of Eastern Europe, the southern countries have a mix of ethnic groups (Albanian, Bulgarian, Romanian, Slovene, Slavic, Serbian, Croatian, and Turkish) and languages (Albanian, Serbo-Croatian, Bulgarian, Macedonian, Romanian, and Slovene). Unlike their northern counterparts that have mainly Christian populations, many of the southern countries have a mix of Christians (Orthodox and Roman Catholic) and Muslims.

Economy of the Southern Countries

This region is one of the poorest areas of Europe, with Albania being the poorest country in Europe despite its rich mineral resources. Albania is attempting industrial expansion especially in oil, mining, chemicals, and natural gas. Bulgaria is less industrial than other countries in this region. Much of its land, collectivized in the 1950s, is being returned to former owners or privatized. The state owns a third of the farm land in Romania, which moved from agriculture to industry after World War II.

Yugoslavia's industry has also grown since World War II. The country has natural resources like copper, coal, and timber, as well as fertile valleys for agriculture; however, its economy and the economies of its former republics have been badly affected by civil war.

Conclusion

Europe is a small continent, but there are numerous nations, religions, languages, ethnic groups and types of terrain. Often divided into Western Europe and Eastern Europe, the continent is dominated by peninsulas. Western Europe, stretching from the Scandinavian Peninsula in the north to the Iberian Peninsula in the South, is one of the most heavily industrialized areas and one of the most densely populated areas on earth. Much of Eastern Europe is still struggling economically due to its former communist legacy.

Next, you will learn about Asia. Asia is the largest continent in the world, totaling more than one third of the earth's landmass. It is also the most populated continent with more than 3 billion people or 60 percent of the Earth's population.

Lesson Review

1. Why does Western Europe have so many different languages?

2. How have Western European nations cooperated in recent years?

3. Why are some Eastern European nations torn by ethnic conflict?

4. Why do you think Europe is so densely populated? What types of economic activity support this sizeable population?

Lesson 5
Asia—The Largest, Most Populous Continent

Key Terms

atheist
Buddhist
Confucianism
homogenous
monsoon
sultanate

WHAT YOU WILL LEARN TO DO

- Explore the unique geographic characteristics of Asia

LINKED CORE ABILITIES

- Communicate using verbal, non-verbal, visual, and written techniques

SKILLS AND KNOWLEDGE YOU WILL GAIN ALONG THE WAY

- Describe principal physical features of the continent of Asia

- Summarize the physical and human characteristics of Asian countries and regions

- Explain how the interactions between groups of people in Asia affect the area's cultural, economic, and political characteristics

- Define key words contained in this lesson

Introduction

At over 17 million square miles, Asia is the largest continent possessing more than a third of the world's total land. A sprawling realm of diverse terrain and climate, it is also the most populated continent with more than 3 billion people or 60 percent of the Earth's population. Asia is as rich in history as it is in natural resources, and has a great influence on the political and economic climate of the world.

Asia

Site of some the earliest civilizations, today Asia is a complex mosaic of languages, races, religions, and politics. Although over half of Asia's land is claimed by only 2 countries, China and the Asian portion of Russia, 46 countries make up the remaining half (Figure 2.5.1).

Figure 2.5.1:
Asian countries.

Courtesy of GeoSystems
Global Corporation.

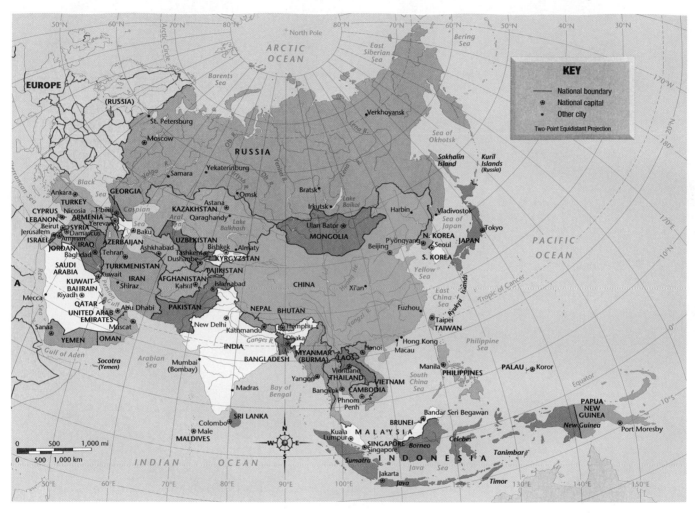

The Asian landscape (Figure 2.5.2) is full of extremes and record-breaking measurements.

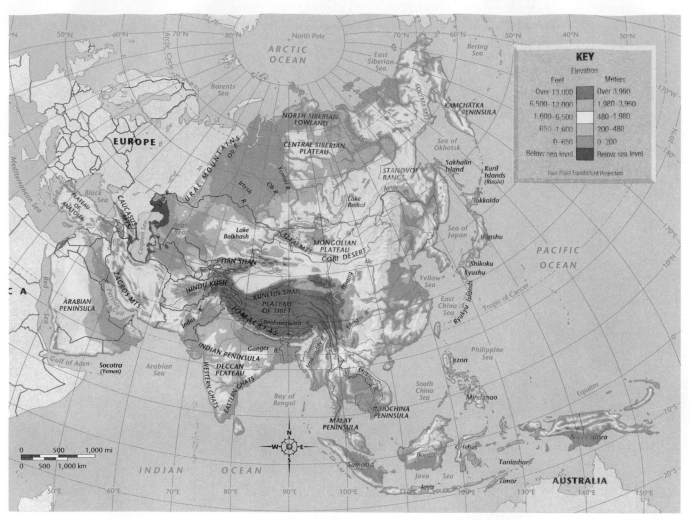

Stretching 1,500 miles across the continent is the highest mountain system in the world, the Himalayas (see Figure 2.5.3). They rise over 29,000 feet at Mount Everest, the highest mountain in the world, and include the Karakoram Range among others. The Hindu Kush, the world's second highest mountain range, is an extension of the Himalaya Mountain System. Other important mountain ranges in Asia include the Tien Shan and Altai.

Figure 2.5.3:
The Himalayas.

Courtesy of Tropix
Photographic Library.

> **Note**
>
> The 28 highest mountains in the world are in Asia, with the 10 highest located in the Himalayas.

Other highlands in Asia include the Plateaus of Mongolia and Tibet. At an average altitude of 13,000 feet, the Plateau of Tibet is the world's highest plateau, covering almost one million square miles. On another plateau ranging from 3,000 to 5,000 feet in altitude is the Gobi Desert, which covers almost 500,000 square miles.

In contrast, the Dead Sea is the lowest point on Earth at 1,312 feet below sea level. The Dead Sea is one of the most saline lakes in the world, and contains no life.

Two other important Asian lakes are Lake Baykal, the deepest lake in the world with a maximum depth of 5,315 feet, and the Aral Sea. Once the world's fourth largest lake, it is now less than half its original size because of water diversion for cotton irrigation.

The rivers in Asia play an important role in ancient history as well as in the lives of Asians today. Many of the world's first great civilizations developed in the river valleys of the Tigris and Euphrates, Indus, and Huang He (Yellow) Rivers. Three of the greatest population densities in the world are along the Ganges, Yangtze, and Huang He Rivers. Other rivers of note include the Mekong, Amur, Lena, Yenisey, and Ob. The latter three rivers are in Siberia, a vast region of Asian Russia known for its harsh climate which is being used as a prison colony.

Other important geographic regions of Asia include the Arabian, Kamchatka, and Malay Peninsulas, and Asia Minor, a peninsula that forms Asian Turkey.

Important Historical/Political Considerations of Asia

Asia was the birthplace of great civilizations, religions, and philosophy. The Chinese, Indians, and Muslims made major contributions to medicine, mathematics, astronomy, and literature. The Japanese developed a strict military code of behavior. At its peak (750 to 1200 A.D.) the Muslim Empire under the control of the Turks and the Arabs, stretched across northern Africa, Mediterranean, and southeastern Europe, southwestern Asia and parts of India acted as a buffer between Christian Europe and eastern Asia until the 1400s when Europeans found a sea route around Africa.

After the 1500s, European colonialism, as well as Russian and Japanese expansion greatly affected the borders within Asia. The opening of the Suez Canal in 1869, which connected the Mediterranean Sea to the Red Sea, aided this expansion by providing easier access to eastern Asia. Following World War II, foreign influence in Asia gave way to Asian nationalism with many countries gaining their independence. However, a return to self-rule in Asia was not without problems, and political, ethnic, and religious conflicts erupted—among them the Korean, Vietnam, Arab-Israeli, and Iran-Iraq Wars. Conflicts still affect many Asian countries today.

Russia, Central Asia, and Transcaucasia

This region (Figure 2.5.4) includes all the former Soviet Socialist Republics in Asia: Russia, the central Asian republics, and the three republics of Transcaucasia (the area south of the Caucasus Mountains and north of Turkey and Iran.) In Asian Russia, the West Siberian Lowlands extend from the Ural Mountains to the Yenisey River. The Central Siberian Plateau then extends to the Lena River.

Russia, Central Asia, and Transcaucasia's Climate and Vegetation

Russia, Central Asia, and Transcaucasia has four broad east-west bands of vegetation: tundra, forest, steppe, and desert. Only tundra vegetation can grow in the polar conditions near the Arctic Ocean. Vegetation grows rapidly during the short summer, when the surface of the permafrost thaws and becomes marshy.

The largest forest region in the world covers nearly half of Northern Eurasia, south of the tundra. The northern part of this region is scattered with coniferous trees. This type of forest is called the taiga (TY guh), the Russian word for "little sticks." Farther south, with decreasing rainfall, come the vast, grassy steppes. East of the Caspian Sea lay dry lands, where the natural vegetation is desert scrub.

Outside the interior, Northern Eurasia has a variety of climates. In the north, chilling winds from the Arctic Ocean create a tundra climate, while a subarctic climate extends from northeastern Russia across most of Siberia. The southern part of the European Plain has a humid continental climate with warm summers. South of that, from Ukraine to Kazakhstan, is a semiarid climate zone, with warm winters and hot summers.

Winds from the Atlantic Ocean and the Baltic Sea bring moisture to coastal European parts of Northern Eurasia. Autumn in the European Plain is often cool, gray, and rainy. In northwestern Russia, heavy precipitation means frequent, heavy snowfalls. Snow often stays on the ground in Moscow for six months of the year.

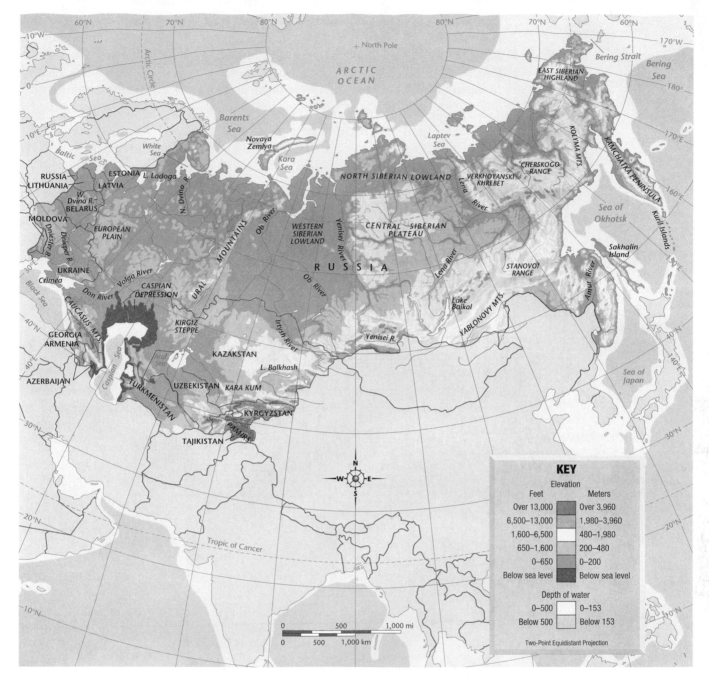

The five central Asian republics are located east of the Caspian Sea. Both Kyrgyzstan and Tajikistan are mountainous. Kazakhstan, the second largest republic of the former U.S.S.R. at over one million square miles, is steppe land (prairie) and desert. Most of Uzbekistan is a sandy plain, and desert covers 80 percent of Turkmenistan. Much of the area experiences very hot summers and freezing winters.

Much milder weather exists in the small, mountainous republics of Transcaucasia (Armenia, Azerbaijan, and Georgia). Note that Armenia splits Azerbaijan into two parts.

Figure 2.5.4: Russia, Central Asia, and Transcaucasia.

Courtesy of GeoSystems Global Corporation.

Even though the area of Russia, Central Asia, and Transcaucasia is huge, its basic landform follows one overall pattern. The land is flat in the west and becomes increasingly mountainous toward the east and south. In the Russian far east, the East Siberian Highlands are a jumble of ridges, steep valleys, and volcanic peaks. Along the southern border of the region lie great lakes and high mountains.

The steppes sweep across central Russia, divided by a low-lying mountain range, the Ural Mountains. The Urals are usually considered the boundary between Europe and Asia. They average only 3,000 to 4,000 feet (900 to 1,200 meters) in elevation. The fertile, rolling western plain is the continuation of the European Plain, a huge lowland that stretches from the Atlantic Ocean across Europe.

Siberia is the Asian part of Russia, the land from the Ural Mountains eastward to the Pacific Ocean. The Western Siberian Lowland covers more than 1 million square miles (2.6 million square kilometers) and is the largest area of unbroken lowland in the world. Much of this land is swampy or remains partly frozen all year. Although Siberia is famous for its harsh subarctic climate, its short summers can be hot.

Highlands, lakes, and seas line the southern edge of Northern Eurasia. Between the Black Sea and the Caspian Sea stand the rugged, forested peaks of the Caucasus Mountains (see Figure 2.5.5). They form Russia's border with Georgia and Azerbaijan. Farther east are other steep, forbidding mountain ranges. The highest peaks in the region reach 25,000 feet (7,600 meters) above sea level and are found in the Pamirs, where the borders of Tajikistan, China, and Afghanistan meet.

Figure 2.5.5: Caucasus Mountains.

Courtesy of Woodfin Camp and Associates.

The People of Asian Russia

Russia, Central Asia, and Transcaucasia: Largest Cities

Some of the larger cities in Russia, Central Asia, and Transcaucasia include:

City	Population
Moscow, Russia	8,746,500
St. Petersburg, Russia	4,436,500
Kiev, Ukraine	2,643,000
Tashkent, Uzbekistan	2,094,000
Kharkov, Ukraine	1,622,000
Minsk, Belarus	1,613,000
Novosibirsk, Russia	1,442,000

Although Russia, Central Asia, and Transcaucasia have a population of nearly 300 million, the average population density is low. The most densely settled area is in the west, which has fertile soil and industry. The intensely cold climate of Siberia discourages settlement, except along rivers or in planned industrial cities. People have settled the deserts only in places where a canal, a river, or a moisture-catching mountain range makes farming possible.

Almost 75 percent of the people of Russia, Central Asia, and Transcaucasia live in the European Plain. Three large historic cities are population centers: Moscow and St. Petersburg in Russia, and Kiev in Ukraine. Other areas of high population are near rivers, canals, railways, and mines.

Similar to the countries of Eastern Europe, the countries of this region possess a mix of ethnic groups. The people of Russia, Central Asia, and Transcaucasia belong to more than 100 ethnic groups and speak more than 200 different languages. The Slavs are the largest ethnic group in Russia and the European republics. Most people in central Asia are of Turkic background. The population of the central Asian republics is a mix of Kazahks, Russians, Germans, Ukrainians, Kyrgyz, Tajiks, Uzbeks, and Turkmen. In Transcaucasia, Armenia's population is mostly Armenian with Azeri, Kurd, and Russian minorities, while Azerbaijan is mostly Azeri with Russian and Armenian minorities. In Georgia, the population is mostly Georgian with other minorities.

Russia, Central Asia and Transcaucasia's History: Russian Expansion

The huge country of Russia dominates the northern parts of two continents—Europe and Asia. How did one nation acquire so much territory?

The Russian state began in the 800s in a city that is no longer in Russia: Kiev (a city in Ukraine). There, on a forested bluff above the wide Dnieper River, Viking traders built a fort. Another fort, Novgorod, was farther north. The traders came from Scandinavia, bringing furs, honey, and beeswax for candles, along with amber from the Baltic Sea area. They followed a river route from the Baltic Sea to the Black Sea and Constantinople, center of the Byzantine Empire.

Viking leaders organized the local Slavic peoples under their rule and became Grand Princes of Kiev. The two ways of life blended. Traders also brought Byzantine culture to Russia. Kiev's rulers adopted Orthodox Christianity in about A.D. 988.

Around 1240, nomadic Mongols from central Asia invaded and conquered Kievan Russia. During more than 200 years of Mongol rule, Russia was an isolated agricultural country, cut off from trade and contact with Europe.

Power shifted from Kiev to Moscow. In 1480 Ivan III, prince of Moscow, stopped paying tribute to the Mongol rulers and unified the other Russian towns. Since the Byzantine Empire had collapsed, Ivan declared himself the successor to the emperors of both Rome and Constantinople. He took the title czar—the Russian equivalent of "Caesar."

Czar Ivan "the Great" quickly moved to expand Russia in all directions. His armies retook land from the Mongols and gained new territory across the Ural Mountains, the traditional dividing line between Europe and Asia.

Later rulers were equally ambitious. They fought neighboring rulers in Poland and Sweden for land. Cossacks, peasant groups organized in military units, led the conquest of the vast eastern lands of Siberia.

Under Peter the Great, who ruled from 1682 to 1725, and Catherine the Great, who ruled from 1762 to 1796, the Russian Empire expanded greatly. Peter went to war for land on the Baltic Sea. He brought in technology from Western Europe and built a new capital city, St. Petersburg, as Russia's "window to the West." Catherine also took many ideas from Western Europe. She acquired territory on the Black Sea and annexed rich farmlands in Ukraine and Poland. The map on the previous page shows how much the country grew between the reigns of Ivan the Great and Catherine the Great.

Czars during the 1800s made Russia still larger, adding territory around the Caspian Sea. In 1891 construction began on the great Trans-Siberian Railroad, which runs some 5,700 miles (9,300 km) from Moscow to Vladivostok on the Sea of Japan. By 1914, on the eve of World War I, the huge Russian Empire included Poland, Finland, and much of central Asia.

The Bolshevik Revolution in 1917 destroyed the empire and created the Soviet Union. Many ethnic groups had separate republics within the Soviet Union. When the Soviet Union broke apart in 1991, the republics became independent nations. Even without the rest of its empire, Russia is still the largest country in the world in land area.

Most Georgians and Armenians are Christian; Kazakhstan is a mix of Christians and Muslims; and the people of the remaining republics are mostly Muslim. Ethnic and religious conflicts, as well as conflicts over territory, have occurred in this region as late as the 1990s.

In the Soviet era, Russian was the official language and is still widely spoken. Today each republic has its own official language. Azerbaijan, Kazakhstan, Kyrgyzstan, Turkmenistan, and Uzbekistan all have languages of Turkic origin. The official languages of Armenia and Georgia are Armenian and Georgian, and the official language of Tajikistan is Tajik, a Persian (Iranian) language.

Russia, Central Asia and Transcaucasia's Inhabitants

Urbanization varies greatly from country to country in Russia, Central Asia, and Transcaucasia. In the European-influenced countries, such as Estonia, Belarus, and Ukraine, 65 percent or more of the population live in cities. In Russia, nearly 75 percent live in cities of over a million in population, from Moscow and St. Petersburg in the west to Omsk and Novosibirsk in the east.

The Economy of Asian Russia

Siberia in Asian Russia has a wealth of natural resources, including oil, natural gas, forest, and precious metals. In the past, forced labor and population resettlement to Siberia increased mining and industrial development where Siberians still remove gold, diamonds, gas, and oil from the frozen land today. In the warm climate of Transcaucasia, there are tropical fruits, cotton, tobacco, grain, and olives, as well as mineral resources.

In the central Asian republics, there are coal deposits, oil, natural gas, and mineral resources. In the past, Soviet planners dictated industrial development of the area and invested in irrigation for the growth of cotton crops (see Figure 2.5.6). Although the area still has oil refining, gas extraction, mining, and cotton as major industries, the Soviet's development plans have left many environmental problems, including the shrinking of the Aral Sea.

Figure 2.5.6: An irrigated field in Turkmenistan.

Courtesy of TRIPP Photographic Library.

> **Note**
>
> Russians built the Trans-Siberian Railway from 1891 to 1905 to encourage development in Siberia. The trip from Moscow to Vladivostok is 5,786 miles, takes seven days, and crosses seven time zones.

Southwest Asia: The Middle East

Loosely defined, the term Middle East refers to the Arab countries east of the Mediterranean Sea and on the Arabian Peninsula, and includes Turkey, Cyprus, and the countries of North Africa (discussed in the following lesson about Africa). Characteristics of the Middle East include vast oil reserves, a desert environment, and the Islamic religion, which heavily influences life in much of the region. Bahrain, made up of 35 islands in the Persian Gulf, is the smallest country in the Asian part of the Middle East, and Saudi Arabia is the largest, covering four-fifths of the Arabian Peninsula.

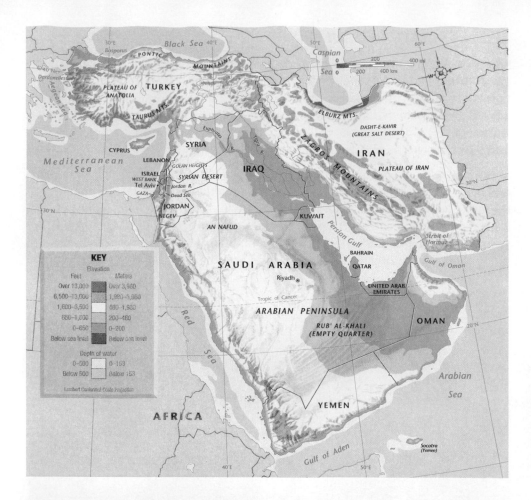

With the exception of coastal areas, most of the peninsula is flat desert. Iran and
Turkey, however, are more mountainous. The Tigris-Euphrates River valley is
fertile area in the Middle East's arid landscape. Most of the region receives less
than 10 inches of rain a year, and there are frequent sandstorms.

The Middle East's Terrain

Much of the land of Southwest Asia is desert. Wind shapes the landscape into great
expanses of sand dunes. The Tigris, Euphrates, and Jordan rivers are important
sources of water for many countries in the region. Rising populations, agriculture,
and industry have increased demands on limited water supplies. Countries that
share these rivers compete for their water. Dams built by one country can create
political conflict. Mountains in the region have an effect on climate. The highest elevations in the region are found in the Zagros Mountains of Iran.

An important waterway in this region is the Strait of Hormuz through which
ships must pass to reach the oil terminals in the Persian Gulf. The strait was the
location of international tension during the Iran-Iraq and Gulf Wars. Jutting into
the strait is a peninsula belonging to Oman but separated from it by the United
Arab Emirates. Another location of conflict in this region is Israel, a Jewish state
in an Islamic world.

Important Middle Eastern cities include:

- **Jerusalem on the border of Israel and the Israeli-occupied West Bank of Jordan, a holy city for Jews, Muslims, and Christians**

- **Jericho in the Israeli-occupied West Bank of Jordan, site of the world's oldest known settlement dating from 9000 B.C.**

- **Mecca, Saudi Arabia, the birthplace of Mohammed and Islam's holiest city, which is closed to non-Muslims**

- **Istanbul, Turkey, formerly Constantinople, the only city in the world on two continents (see Figure 2.5.8)**

Figure 2.5.8: Mosque in Istanbul, Turkey.

Courtesy of eStock Photo.

The Middle East: Largest Metropolitan Areas

Some of the most populated metropolitan areas of the Middle East include:

Istanbul, Turkey	7,309,000
Tehran, Iran	6,042,500
Baghdad, Iraq	3,841,000
Ankara, Turkey	3,236,500
Damascus, Syria	1,444,500
Jidda, Saudi Arabia	1,300,000

The People of the Middle East

A majority of Middle Easterners are Arabic-speaking Muslim Arabs. Exceptions include:

- **Sizable Christian populations in Cyprus and Lebanon, and a Jewish majority in Israel**

- **Turkish and Greek spoken in Cyprus, Turkish spoken in Turkey, Farsi (Persian) spoken in Iran, Hebrew spoken in Israel**

- **A Persian (Iranian) majority in Iran, a Turkish majority in Turkey, and large Kurdish minorities in Iraq and Turkey. The Kurds are the largest ethnic group in the world without their own state. Often politically oppressed and persecuted, they fight and negotiate for an independent Kurdish state.**

The Birthplace of Three Major Religions

The Middle East is the birthplace of three of the world's major religions. These include Judaism, Christianity, and Islam.

Judaism: Judaism first developed around 1000 B.C. along the eastern shore of the Mediterranean Sea. It was the religion of the Hebrews. Five holy books, together known as the Torah, record the early history of the Hebrews and their religion. A large temple located in the city of Jerusalem served as a religious center. The site of this temple is sacred to Jews.

Christianity: Christianity first developed around A.D. 30 along the eastern shore of the Mediterranean. It is based on the teachings of Jesus, who Christians believe to be the son of God. Jesus was tried and crucified—put to death on a cross—in Jerusalem. The Christian Bible consists of the Old Testament (the Torah of Judaism) and the New Testament, which includes four gospels, or accounts, of Jesus' life.

Islam: Islam first developed around A.D. 600 in Arabia. It is based on the teachings of the prophet Muhammad. A prophet is a person whose teachings are believed to be revealed by God. The Five Pillars of Islam are described in the Koran, the Muslim holy book. The Five Pillars include stating a belief in one God, performing daily prayers, giving to charity, daytime fasting during the holy month of Ramadan, and at least one pilgrimage to Mecca, known as the Hajj, during one's lifetime.

Many problems in the Middle East have occurred because of these ethnic and religious differences. In Cyprus, the Turkish part of the island declared independence in 1983. In Lebanon, a civil war between Christians and Muslims started in 1975 and lasted almost 15 years. After World War I, Palestine (a holy land for Jews, Muslims, and Christians) came under British supervision. After World War II, most of Palestine became the Jewish homeland of Israel, and Arabs living in Palestine, or Palestinians, became refugees in neighboring countries. In the Arab-Israeli War of 1967, Israel occupied and held the remaining Palestinian territory belonging to Egypt (Gaza Strip), Syria (Golan Heights), and Jordan (West Bank). As of 1999, although negotiations for a peaceful solution are ongoing, animosity between Israelis and Palestinians continues in the form of terrorist and retaliatory activities.

Global Issues: The Palestinians

Lasting peace in Southwest Asia depends on Israel and the Palestinians reaching a permanent settlement regarding the future.

In 1993 there was a dramatic breakthrough in the Middle East peace talks. On September 13, Yasir Arafat, longtime leader of the PLO and Nobel Prize winner, and Yitzhak Rabin, the Israeli prime minister, signed an agreement in Washington, D.C. They agreed to establish limited Palestinian self-rule in the Gaza Strip and the ancient West Bank town of Jericho. The agreement also set the stage for negotiations on the status of the rest of the West Bank, as well as for peace talks with other Arab countries.

Most of the over 2 million Palestinians living in the occupied territories strongly supported the new peace plan. One Palestinian said: "We have started on the road to establishing our state, independent and free. People can't quite grasp it yet, because the tragedy has been going on for decades. It's about time that both governments, Israeli and Palestinian, have stood up and thought about what's good for both people."

In 1995, the agreement made in 1993 was expanded to include more than 450 other Palestinian cities, towns, and villages in the West Bank. Large parts of the West Bank remained under Israeli control. These included areas where there were Israeli towns and cities with sacred Jewish religious sites. In addition, although Palestinians elected their own government, Israel kept control of foreign policy.

Some Palestinians called Arafat's agreement with Israel a sell-out. They demanded that the West Bank and Gaza Strip be completely independent. Radical Palestinian groups carried out suicide bombings and launched missile attacks against Israel. For these reasons, many Israelis remained deeply suspicious about the idea of Palestinian self-rule.

The world is dependent on oil from the Middle East. In the past, fighting between Israel and its Arab neighbors erupted into major conflicts in the region, severely disrupting the world's oil supply. In addition, more and more governments around the world believed that the Palestinian people were entitled to an independent homeland.

By the late 1990s, many encouraging steps had been taken, although several difficult issues remained unresolved, even after talks in 2000. In the mid-1990s, some Israeli leaders considered the idea of an independent Palestinian state. These leaders realized, however, that many Israelis would feel that their security might be jeopardized.

When Israel took control of the West Bank, it allowed Israeli citizens to settle there. Some of these settlers claimed they had a historic right to the land. In addition, they opposed living under the authority of a Palestinian state.

Yassar Arafat died on November 11, 2004. His death has the potential to drastically change the face of politics in the Middle East. Arafat's successor, Mahmoud Abbas, could very well do much to further the peace efforts in this part of the world.

Religious sites that are important to both Jews and Muslims are located in Hebron and East Jerusalem. Many Jews and Muslims alike want to control those sites. A particularly difficult issue concerns East Jerusalem. Both sides are steadfast about it being included in their territory. One suggestion is that control of East Jerusalem might be shared between the two groups.

The Economy of the Middle East

Many countries in the Middle East have economies based on oil production, making them some of the world's richest countries. Bahrain is a major center for oil trading, banking, and commerce. Iraq and Iran are two of the world's largest producers of oil, but recent wars have disrupted production. Oil provides

95 percent of Kuwait's government revenue and 90 percent of Oman's. Qatar's off-shore oil makes up an eighth of the world's known reserves; reserves in Saudi Arabia, the world's leading oil exporter, account for a fourth of the world's known oil supply. Syria and the United Arab Emirates also have economies based on oil. To avoid relying too heavily on oil income, Kuwait, Oman, and Saudi Arabia, are attempting to diversify their economies.

In the remaining countries, light manufacturing and agriculture are major economic activities. Tourism is important in Cyprus, Israel, and Turkey. Lebanon, once a commercial and financial center, is attempting to revive its economy devastated by civil war.

South Asia: The Triangular Subcontinent

The countries of south Asia are on or near the triangular peninsula known as the Indian subcontinent (Figure 2.5.9). Characteristics of this region include thousands of small villages, as well as large, overpopulated cities, much poverty and underdevelopment, and intense faith in various religions. Mountains outline the region. The Hindu Kush, Karakoram, and Himalayas in the north spread across Afghanistan, Bhutan, Nepal, and part of Pakistan and India. The much smaller mountains of the Western and Eastern Ghats ranges dot the southwest and southeast coasts of India, with the Deccan Plateau, noted for its cotton, lying between them.

Figure 2.5.9: South Asia.

Courtesy of GeoSystems Global Corporation.

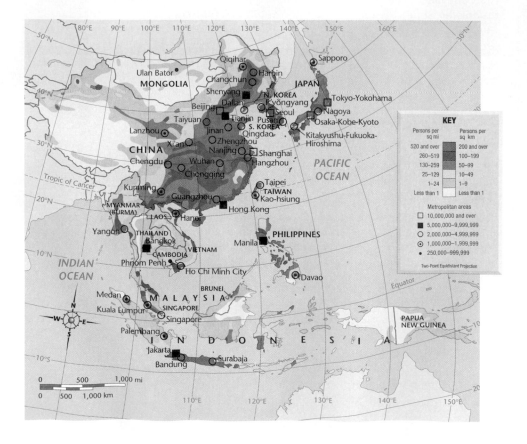

The Thar Desert covers 125,000 square miles in northwest India and East Pakistan. In the mostly desert country of Pakistan, the Indus River (see Figure 2.5.10) helps irrigate crops. Crossed by the Brahmaputra and Ganges Rivers, Bangladesh, which is flat and low-lying, is subject to frequent flooding. The Maldives are also low-lying, and only 202 of its 1,190 islands have inhabitants.

Figure 2.5.10:
Indus River.

Courtesy of Corbis Images.

South Asia's Terrain

Three great rivers flow through the northern region of the Indian subcontinent: the Indus, the Ganges, and the Brahmaputra. These rivers begin their journey to the sea as trickles moving down the icy crags of the Himalayan slopes.

As the Indus, Ganges, and Brahmaputra rivers travel through the low, flat land, they slow down and deposit rich silt that they picked up during their journey. When the rivers flood, they leave broad expanses of fertile land along their banks forming alluvial plains.

The Himalayan range includes more than thirty of the world's highest mountains and is often called the "rooftop of the world." Scientists believe that the Himalayas started pushing upward millions of years ago when the tectonic plate carrying what is now India collided with the Eurasian plate. These plates are still moving, and the Himalayas are getting taller all the time. The highest elevations in the region are found in the Himalayas in Nepal.

The southern tip of India is shaped by two sets of mountain ranges that give the subcontinent its distinctive wedge shape. Name these mountain ranges.

The geographic landscape of South Asia varies greatly. Deserts stretch throughout Pakistan. Lush rain forests spread across the slopes of India's west coast. Glacier-covered mountains overlook the villages of Nepal.

The People of South Asia

More than one billion people live in South Asia, which has the world's second largest population cluster. India's population of 890 million is greater than that of Europe, the Middle East, and northern Africa combined. In Bangladesh, more than 120 million people live in an area the size of Iowa, which, by comparison, has less than 3 million inhabitants.

South Asia: Largest Cities

Some of the most populated cities in South Asia include:

City	Population
Mumbai, India	12,572,000
Calcutta, India	10,916,000
Delhi, India	8,375,000
Chennai, India	5,361,500
Karachi, Pakistan	5,180,500
Lahore, Pakistan	2,952,500

Many of the people on the Indian subcontinent are of Dravidian and/or Aryan descent. The Dravidians were original inhabitants of the region, and the Aryans were invaders. Most people of Dravidian origin live in south India and Sri Lanka. People of Aryan descent live in northern India, Pakistan, the Maldives, and Sri Lanka. The Nepalese of Nepal are a mix of Aryan and Mongolian blood.

Many of the languages spoken are Indo-Aryan. They include, among others, Hindi, Bengali, Nepali, and Sinhalese. Afghanistan's official languages are Iranian-related, and Bhutan's is a variant of Tibetan. Since much of this region was once a British colony, English is also widely spoken here.

Islam is the major religion in Afghanistan, Bangladesh, the Maldives, and Pakistan. There are **Buddhist** majorities in Bhutan and Sri Lanka, and Hindu majorities in India and Nepal. Racial and religious hostilities exist between Hindu and Muslim animosity in Kashmir (officially Jammu and Kashmir), an Indian-administered state claimed by both Pakistan and India.

Key Note Term

Buddhist – a follower of Buddhism, a religious and philosophical system based on the teachings of Guatama Buddha, who rejected certain Hindu beliefs, particularly the caste system

Religions of South Asia

For thousands of years geography has made South Asia a crossroads. The towering Himalayas protect the subcontinent on the north and east, but invaders have poured in through the mountain passes on the northwest frontier. Trade routes across the region brought merchants and missionaries.

Two major world religions began in South Asia and spread to other places. Another religion, brought by conquerors, had a great impact on society and politics.

Much of the mainstream culture of modern India derives from long-ago invaders. About 1500 B.C., people known as Aryans crossed the mountains from the high plains of central Asia. The Aryans' language and culture soon drove the earlier inhabitants, the Dravidians, southward. The Dravidian traditions continued to survive in southern India.

The Aryans believed in many gods, who were related to natural forces such as fire, water, and thunder. These beliefs became the basis of Hinduism, which has many gods who can take different forms. Aryan society was strictly divided along class lines. These divisions, in which class determined each person's life and work, eventually developed into the Hindu caste system. Brahmins, the priest class, had the most power and privilege.

In the 6th century B.C., a very different religious leader was born in northern India (Nepal). Siddhartha Gautama, an Indian prince, underwent a number of experiences that sent him into a lifetime of teaching. Followers of the Buddha, as Siddhartha later was known, practiced his guidelines for living, the Eightfold Path, in order to reach enlightenment, or nirvana.

Buddhism appealed to people of all classes and spread throughout India. Missionaries and traders carried Buddhism eastward, and the religion took firm root across Asia. But since Hinduism was flexible enough to absorb most of its beliefs, Buddhism slowly disappeared as a separate religion in India. The map above shows the spread of Hinduism and Buddhism across East Asia.

Soon after the religion of Islam emerged in Arabia in A.D. 622, some Muslims moved into northwest India. Over the next centuries four different groups of Muslims reached the peninsula. In the early 1500s, Muslims from Persia led by Babur conquered and united most of South Asia under the Mogul Empire. Mogul rule had a lasting influence on India's culture and society, especially in the arts, architecture, and literature.

Differences between Islam and Hinduism were so deep that the two religions could not mix, as Hinduism and Buddhism had done. Devout Muslims, who believe in one God, could not tolerate the many Hindu deities. Attitudes toward class differences were also very different. Neither group could easily accept the other's ways. Deep and sometimes violent conflicts eventually led to the partition of South Asia into two modern nations: India, with a Hindu majority, and Pakistan, an Islamic state.

The Economy of South Asia

As previously indicated, South Asia is a very crowded part of the world, and innovations in health and medicine continue to increase population growth. The amount of cultivated land per person continues to decline. Farming methods are inefficient, and there are food shortages. Many people in this underdeveloped region live in hunger and poverty.

Agriculture is the main economic activity in south Asia, in some countries employing as much as 90 percent of the population. Rice is an important food crop, growing well in south Asia's famous **monsoon** climate. Other crops include wheat, sugarcane, coffee, tea, spices, corn, and jute, a native south Asian plant with fibers used in burlap, sacking, twine, rope, and insulation.

South Asia's Monsoon Climate

Monsoons are seasonal shifts in the winds. In winter the winds blow from the northeast and bring dry air from Asia's mainland to much of South Asia. In summer the winds reverse direction, pick up moisture from the warm Indian Ocean, and drop heavy rains as they move over the land.

When summer monsoon winds meet mountain ranges, they release their moisture as they are pushed upward. Because the Western Ghats block the rain, the land to the east is hot and dry.

Key Note Term

monsoon – a wind system that changes with the seasons, especially in the Indian Ocean and southern Asia; heavy rainfall that is associated with this type of wind system

Much of South Asia is hot and dry for half the year (left). Farmers wait anxiously for the life-giving monsoons to arrive (right). However, if the rain hits too hard, lowland areas face the danger of floods. Other areas can be threatened by landslides.

Areas out of the path of the monsoon wind in South Asia receive little rain. In its wettest month Karachi, Pakistan, receives an average of only 2.5 inches of rain. But Chennai, India, receives 14 inches in its rainiest month.

Manufacturing of textiles, especially cotton products, is important in this region. In India, industrial production has increased considerably since independence, and tourism is expanding in the Himalayan countries.

Southeast Asia: Peninsulas and Islands

Key Note Term

sultanate – a country governed by a sultan, the title given to the supreme authority usually of a Muslim state

Southeast Asia (Figure 2.5.11) is a region fragmented into peninsulas and islands. Indonesia is the region's largest country and the world's greatest archipelago, made up of more than 13,000 islands and stretching for almost 3,500 miles. Over 6,000 of these islands have inhabitants. The main islands are Sumatra, Java, Sulawesi, the western part of New Guinea called Irian Jaya (the eastern part, Papua New Guinea, is considered part of Oceania), and the southern part of Borneo (Kalimantan). The northern part of Borneo mostly belongs to Malaysia except for the small country of Brunei, an Islamic **sultanate** far from the Middle East. The Philippines is also a country of islands—more than 7,100. The Malay Peninsula forms part of Thailand and Malaysia, with the island country of Singapore at its southern tip. Important rivers cross the region's mainland countries: the Ayeyarwady (formerly Irrawaddy), the Mekong, and the Red. Many people in this region live in the valleys surrounding these rivers. Mountains and thick tropical forests cover much of the rest of Southeast Asia making human settlement difficult. Many of Indonesia's peaks are actually volcanoes. Indonesia has 77 active volcanoes, more than any country in the world.

Figure 2.5.11: Southeast Asia.

Courtesy of maps.com.

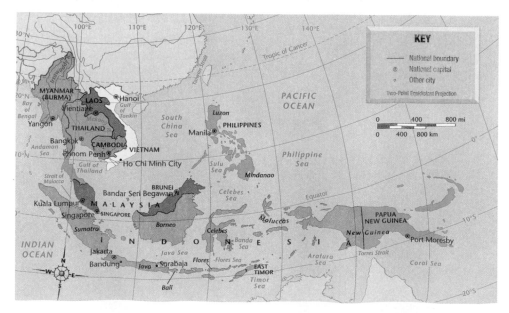

The People of Southeast Asia

In Southeast Asia, the Burmans make up the majority of the population in Myanmar (formerly Burma), the Malays make up the majority in Brunei and Malaysia. Other people groups in the region include the following: the Khmer or Cambodians in Cambodia; the Laotians (related to the Thai) in Laos; the Filipino in the Philippines; the Thai or Siamese in Thailand (formerly Siam); the Vietnamese in Vietnam; and the Chinese in Singapore. The Chinese also make up large minorities throughout the area. Indonesia is a mix of many ethnic groups.

Languages in the region include Burmese, Malay, Khmer, Bahasa Indonesian, Lao, Pilipino, Thai, and Vietnamese. In Singapore, the chief languages are English, Malay, Chinese, and Tamil. English and French are also widely spoken in many of these countries because of their colonial heritage, and Indonesia has more than 250 different languages spoken.

Indonesia and Brunei are predominantly Muslim; Myanmar, Laos, and Thailand are predominantly Buddhist; and the Philippines is 83 percent Roman Catholic. The populations of Malaysia, Singapore, and Vietnam practice several different religions. Buddhism was the chief religion in Cambodia until the Khmer Rouge (communist revolutionaries) outlawed religion in 1975.

The Economy of Southeast Asia

Southeast Asia is an underdeveloped region of the world. The economies in most of these countries depend largely on agriculture (see Figure 2.5.12) with rice, sugarcane, tobacco, and rubber as important crops. Java's rich volcanic soil makes it one of the most agriculturally productive places on Earth.

Figure 2.5.12: Terraced land in Southeast Asia.

Courtesy of Woodfin Camp and Associates.

Brunei is a large oil producer, and oil and natural gas from Borneo and Sumatra account for 60 percent of Indonesia's income. Singapore, a major shipping center, is Southeast Asia's most developed country. It has a diversified industrial economy with a well-educated workforce. In contrast, Laos has little industry, no railroads, few paved roads, and is this region's poorest country, and in many parts of the Philippines, major overpopulation contributes to poverty and malnutrition.

Considering Southeast Asia's geography, fishing is also a profitable economic activity. Tourism is important in the more politically stable countries.

Eastern Asia: China, Japan, and Neighbors

Territorially, China dominates eastern Asia (Figure 2.5.13). Twenty-two provinces and five autonomous regions cover the country's 3,700,000 square miles. Tibet is home to the Plateau of Tibet and is known as the "roof of the world." It is an autonomous region, as is Inner Mongolia, an area of desert and semi-desert, are two of the autonomous regions. They are part of the western two-thirds of China, which is mountainous, sparsely populated, and arid. The remaining third of the country along the east coast is heavily populated, fertile, and flat.

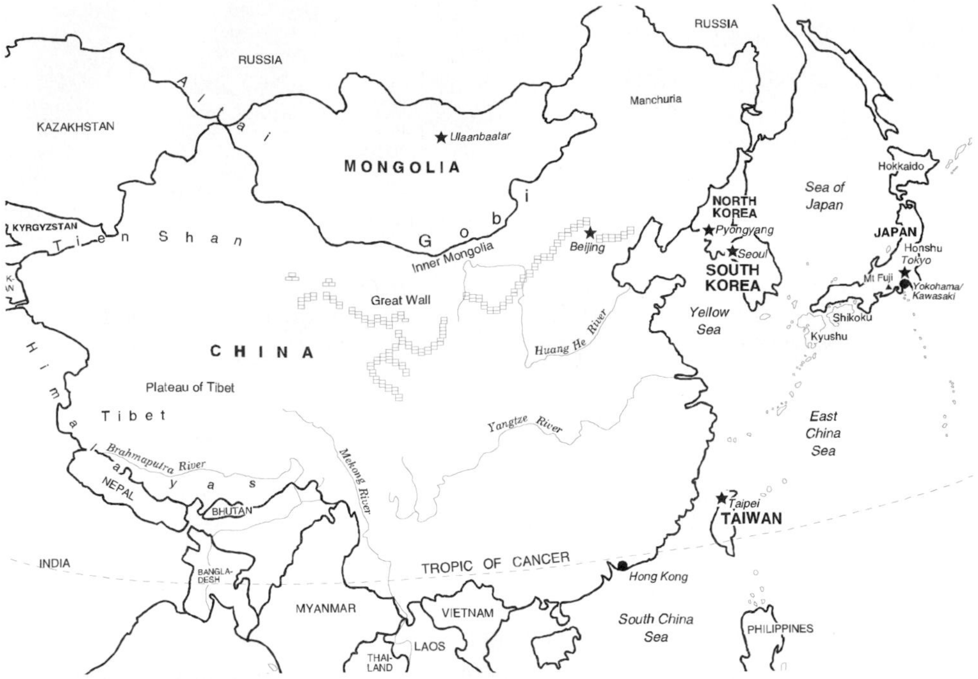

Figure 2.5.13: East Asia.

Courtesy of US Army JROTC.

East and Southeast Asia: Largest Cities

Some of the most populated cities in East and Southeast Asia include:

Seoul, South Korea	10,628,000
Tokyo, Japan	8,278,000
Jakarta, Indonesia	7,885,500
Shanghai, China	6,293,000
Bangkok, Thailand	5,876,000
Beijing, China	5,531,500
Tianjin, China	5,152,000
Shenyang, China	3,994,000
Wuhan, China	3,287,500
Yokohama, Japan	3,220,500

Mongolia, a large desert country, lies to China's north. Taiwan, an island of less than 14,000 square miles, lies 80 miles off the southeast coast of China. Taiwan is two-thirds mountains and crossed by the Tropic of Cancer. Japan is also an island country. Despite having a total area less than the size of California, Japan is politically and economically powerful. Its four largest islands are Hokkaido, Honshu, Kyushu, and Shikoku. The islands are mountainous with 54 active volcanoes.

East and Southeast Asia's Terrain

Almost 20 percent of the world's earthquakes occur in East and Southeast Asia. In 1995, an earthquake in Kobe, Japan (left), took some 5,000 lives and caused $60 billion in damage.

The collision of the Eurasian and Indo-Australian tectonic plates created much of East and Southeast Asia's physical landscape, raising the Himalayas, the Kunlun Shan, the Altun Shan, and the Tian Shan.

The Malay and Japan archipelagoes form part of the Ring of Fire—a circle of volcanic and seismic, or earthquake-related, activity that surrounds the Pacific Ocean. The island of Java, for example, has thirty-five active volcanoes.

Note

To combat overpopulation, China has a population policy that limits most families to only one child. Many Chinese understand their country's population problem and willingly comply with the policy.

To Japan's west on a peninsula bordering northeastern China are North (communist) and South (democratic) Korea. A 487 square mile demilitarized zone separates them from each other. South Korea has hot summers and cold winters, while the more mountainous North Korea experiences warm summers and severely cold winters. Typhoons, or hurricanes that form over the Pacific Ocean, bring heavy rains to Japan, Taiwan, South Korea, and southeast China in late summer and early fall.

Note

The Great Wall of China, built between 221 B.C. and the 1600s to repel invaders, is over 1,500 miles long and an average of 25 feet high and 12 feet wide.

Important Historical/Political Considerations of East Asia

The two political giants in East Asia are China and Japan. In fact, the remaining countries in the region have been under either Japanese or Chinese control, or both, at one time or another in their past. When the communist government took over China in 1949, the nationalist government moved to Taiwan and founded the Republic of China. Today, Taiwan continues to proclaim its independence from China, and China continues to claim Taiwan.

The People of East Asia

With almost 1.2 billion people, China has the largest population of any country in the world. By contrast, the United States, which is only slightly smaller in size than China, has only 252 million people. One out of every five people on Earth lives in China, most of them in the east.

For their size, Japan, South Korea, and Taiwan have some of the greatest population densities in the world. In contrast, Mongolia is the world's emptiest country with little over 2 million people spread out over 1.5 million square miles. Mongolia's population is 90 percent Mongol, descended from nomadic tribes in Mongolia and southern Siberia with a reputation for skilled warfare and horsemanship. Many Mongols also live in China's Inner Mongolia. Mongolia's official language is Khalkha Mongol, and its chief religion is Buddhism.

The Chinese make up the majority of the populations in Taiwan and China, but China also has over 50 different minorities. Mandarin Chinese is the chief language in both countries, but China has many other dialects. Minority languages are spoken here as well. China is officially an **atheist** country, but many Chinese follow **Confucianism**, Buddhism, and Taoism (a philosophy and religion that teaches harmony between the individual and the natural world).

Despite the border that divides them, the people of North and South Korea have the same ancestry, language, religion, and until recently, history. Both countries have Korean majorities, and Korean is their official language. Buddhism and Confucianism, as well as Christianity, are some of the religions practiced in South Korea. Although Buddhism and Confucianism are also practiced in North Korea, religious activities there are minimal.

Japan's society is very different from the other countries in this region. It is both modern and traditional. With a population over 99 percent Japanese, it has few minorities and is one of the most ethnically **homogeneous** populations of its size in the world. Japanese is Japan's official language, and its chief religions are Buddhism and Shintoism, an ancient native religion that incorporates features of Buddhism and also involves reverence to Japanese ancestors.

The Economy of East Asia

Japan is one of the world's industrial and technological giants. Since it has limited natural resources, it buys raw materials and sells finished products worldwide. These products include, among many others, electrical goods, electronics, automobiles (see Figure 2.5.14), cameras, and film. The country also supplies engineering and financial services, as well as information technology. Agriculture in Japan is very efficient and productive, even though less than 20 percent of Japanese land is under cultivation. There is intensive crop production of rice, and other economic activities include timber and fishing.

Key Note Terms

atheist – one who denies the existence of God or any supernatural being

Confucianism – a moral and religious system of China that does not teach the worship of a god or the existence of life after death, but is a guide to ethics and government based on sympathy or "human-heartedness" with others through ritual and etiquette

homogeneous – of the same or similar nature; uniformity of structure or composition

Figure 2.5.14: Robotics in a Japanese car factory.

Courtesy of Woodfin Camp and Associates.

Taiwan is another country that has few raw materials but is still very successful in manufacturing. Following Japan's lead, the country is now switching to high technology.

Unlike Japan and Taiwan, China is rich in natural resources. China's heavy industry produces iron, steel, coal, machinery, and armaments. More recently, the country is turning to light industry, like household goods, and is attempting to disperse factories and manufacturing into its interior. To feed its large population, China uses agricultural technology and diversifies crops to increase food production.

Urbanization in China—Filled to Capacity

Migration to urban areas in China has caused extreme overcrowding. The crowded neighborhood in the Chongwenmen district of Beijing is overflowing its boundaries. New cities, like the one being built on Hainan Island, are also quickly filling up to capacity.

Millions of people are migrating from the countryside to cities in China. Here are a few of the reasons why this is causing concern.

- **A Population Boom in the Cities.** The population of China's cities is exploding. In recent years, as China's economy has improved, millions of people have left the countryside and moved to cities in search of jobs and a better life. Fifteen years ago, approximately 80 percent of China's population was rural. Today that figure is roughly 70 percent.

- **A River of Migrants.** In Beijing an estimated 3.2 million migrants have streamed into the city. This is about one fourth of the city's population. The migrants cluster together on the outskirts of the city. They live in rundown buildings where some operate small businesses such as restaurants or workshops that make clothes and shoes. Most of them have no official residency papers, giving them permission to live in the city.

- **Global Impact.** Social problems are widespread in overcrowded cities like Beijing and Shanghai. Many people are jobless. Crime is on the rise. In addition, city services, such as transportation systems, housing, schools, and sewerage are stretched to the limit. As a result, the air and water are polluted. Beijing's air pollution level, for example, is 16 times that of Tokyo's. In Shanghai, tons of waste are dumped daily into the Huangpu River. These conditions pose threats to public health and encourage epidemic diseases that thrive in crowded conditions.

Government officials and urban planners have made some progress in developing policies and plans to handle the urban influx.

- **Controlling Migration.** Officials in cities have taken steps to control migration. They are enforcing residency requirements and checking job permits. In Beijing, migrants must pay a steep registration fee if they want to become residents.

- **Building New Cities.** Urban planners are designing new cities. If all goes as hoped, as many as 200 new cities will be built in China. Local governments will provide the basic infrastructure. The rest is up to private developers. One city on Hainan Island, one of China's special economic zones, is not even finished; yet it already contains some 800,000 people—200,000 more than its planned population of 600,000.

Regarding North and South Korea, most of the mineral wealth is in the north. South Korea, however, has one of the world's largest deposits of tungsten, a metal used in light bulb filaments and steel. North Korea is especially rich in iron and coal and has more heavy industry than South Korea. South Korea, which has a more rapidly growing economy, produces light consumer products but is shifting to heavy industry. Only about 20 percent of the total land in both countries is good for agriculture, and fishing is an important economic activity.

Mongolia is the least industrialized country in this region and relies on raising livestock and processing animal products for its income. Some cultivation of its arid land is possible with irrigation.

Conclusion

With more than three billion inhabitants, the continent of Asia contains the largest country, the highest mountain, the deepest lake, and some of the earliest world civilizations. Southwest Asia, often referred to as the Middle East, is the birthplace of three major world religions. South Asia, which includes the Indian subcontinent, has one of the most densely settled populations on Earth. South-east Asia, with all its island and peninsular nations, is a focus of world trade. East Asia, dominated by China and Japan, is an important market in the global economy.

In the following lesson, you will learn about Africa, sometimes referred to as "The Dark Continent." Africa's inhabitants are as diverse as the natural resources this land offers. Africa is the second largest continent on Earth.

Lesson Review

1. How do the areas of Central Asia and Transcaucasia still reflect their Soviet influences?

2. Why is the Middle East such an important region in global affairs?

3. What are the two largest religions of South Asia?

4. How did Japan, a country with limited natural resources, become an industrial giant?

Lesson 6
Africa—The Plateau Continent

Key Terms

deforestation
desertification
famine
nomadic
oases

WHAT YOU WILL LEARN TO DO

• Explore the unique geographic characteristics of Africa

LINKED CORE ABILITIES

• Communicate using verbal, non-verbal, visual, and written techniques

• Apply critical thinking techniques

SKILLS AND KNOWLEDGE YOU WILL GAIN ALONG THE WAY

• Describe principal physical features of the continent of Africa

• Summarize the physical and human characteristics of countries and regions of Africa

• Characterize places in Africa based on characteristics across the earth's surface

• Examine current events in Africa

• Define key words contained in this lesson

Introduction

Africa is a land of mystery and cultural diversity. Although the African continent is rich in natural resources, Africa is one of the most economically poor areas of the world. In this lesson, you learn about the people, cultures, and land of the African continent. You also learn some of the history that has brought Africa to where it is today.

Africa

Africa (Figure 2.6.1) is the second largest continent. It is connected to the largest continent, Asia, by the Sinai Peninsula. With much of its land over 1000 feet in elevation, and few lowlands or mountainous areas, it is often called a plateau continent. In contrast to the Americas, Europe, and Asia, Africa is without a mountain range of continental proportions such as the North American Cordillera, Andes, Alpine, and Himalaya Mountain Systems.

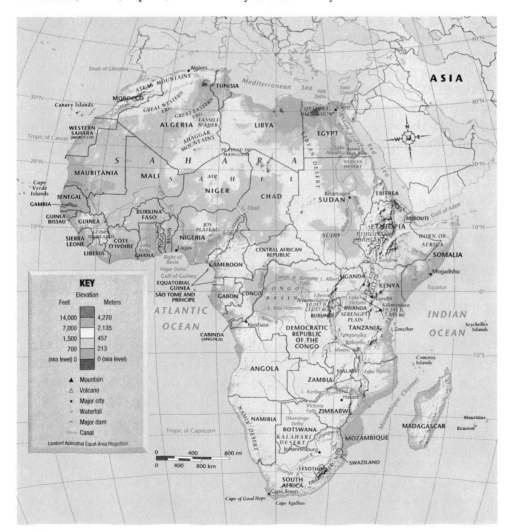

Figure 2.6.1:
Africa: Physical.

Courtesy of maps.com.

Similar to South America, Africa extends about 5,000 miles from north to south, but it is located farther north than South America. It is the only continent crossed by both tropics and the Equator. Because the Equator bisects it, Africa has similar climate and vegetation in its northern and southern halves. It is an excellent example of basic climate as discussed in the first lesson of this chapter. Africa is hot and rainy at the Equator with jungle vegetation. Moving away from the Equator, the land becomes a savanna with wet and dry seasons. At the tropics, there are deserts and semi-deserts.

Africa's Climate Regions

Much of Africa is tropical rain forest. The rain forest is always hot and rainy, with an average of 100 inches (254 cm) of rainfall each year. North and south of the rain forest, much of the land is savanna, an area of tall grasses with scattered trees. South of the desert that covers much of North Africa, the Sahara, lies a broad band of semi-arid land known as the Sahel. The Sahel nations must constantly struggle with the approaching desert. Parts of extreme southern Africa have milder climates. This region, which is good for farming, is heavily populated.

Key Note Term

famine – an extreme scarcity of food resulting in the starvation of many people

In the south where the Tropic of Capricorn crosses Africa are the Namib and Kalahari Deserts. To the north where the Tropic of Cancer crosses Africa are the Libyan and Sahara Deserts. The Sahara, which is mostly a plateau between 500 and 2000 feet high, is the largest desert in the world extending 3000 miles east to west and 1200 miles north to south. Covered by areas of sand, rock, and gravel, the Sahara includes the Ahaggar and Tibesti Mountains and part of the Atlas Mountains. The Sahel south of the Sahara marks a zone between desert and savanna where rainfall is irregular and drought and **famine** often occur.

The three greatest rivers in Africa are the Nile, Zaire (formerly the Congo), and the Niger. The Nile is the longest river in the world flowing over 4,000 miles from the Equator north to the Mediterranean Sea. Its main trunk is formed by the joining of the Blue Nile and the White Nile. These flow from Lake Victoria, the largest lake in Africa at almost 27,000 square miles. Other large lakes include the following: Lake Chad at the meeting point of four countries—Chad, Niger, Nigeria, and Cameroon (Figure 2.6.1); Lake Tanganyika, the second largest lake in Africa; and Lake Malawi, often called the Calendar Lake because it is 365 miles long and 52 miles across at its widest point.

Africa's Terrain

Africa has wide deserts, high mountains, and vast forests that divide one region from another.

South of the Sahara, Africa is a vast plateau interrupted by basins. Along the coast, the plateau drops sharply down an escarpment, or steep cliff, to a narrow coastal plain. Cataracts, areas of the rivers that are broken by waterfalls and rapids, often prevent navigation up the rivers.

Great rivers like the Nile, the Niger, and the Congo flow thousands of miles through Africa, supplying water, electric power, and transportation. Humans change the ecology of African rivers as they dam them to provide irrigation or hydroelectric power.

Lakes Tanganyika and Malawi make up part of the Great Rift Valley in eastern Africa (see Figure 2.6.2). A rift valley forms when parallel cracks occur in the Earth's crust and the land between them sinks. The deepest parts of the valley contain long, narrow lakes.

The eastern rift of Africa's Great Rift Valley includes Lake Turkana and the Red Sea, a trench cut through the Ethiopian Highlands into Kenya and Tanzania (Figure 2.6.2). The western rift runs down western Uganda, Rwanda, Burundi, and Tanzania, then through Malawi to southern Mozambique, and includes Lakes Tanganyika and Malawi. Lake Victoria lies between the eastern and western rifts but is not part of the Great Rift Valley.

Figure 2.6.2: Great Rift Valley.

Courtesy of MapQuest.com, Inc.

Important Historical/Political Considerations of Africa

As in Asia where great civilizations flourished along rivers, the ancient Egyptians created a kingdom along the Nile about 5000 years ago. They developed a form of writing, built huge pyramids that still stand today, and made important contributions to art, astronomy, medicine, architecture, and geometry. After being conquered by the Greeks and Romans, among others, Egypt was conquered by the Arabs in 640 A.D. Eventually the Arabs extended their influence and Islam over the entire north coast of the continent, south into Sudan, and along the east coast. Meanwhile, several great African states developed, including Ghana, Mali, and Ethiopia.

In 1467, the Portuguese sailed around the Cape of Good Hope in search of eastern Asia. Soon, Europeans had set up stations and forts along Africa's west coast. By the 1800s, explorers had crossed the continent and the Suez Canal had been dug, dramatically shortening the shipping route from Europe to Africa's east coast. Competition among European powers for African territory grew fierce.

In 1884, a conference of 14 countries, including the U.S., met in Berlin to attempt to settle colonial rivalries. Even though 80 percent of Africa was still under African rule at the time, the entire continent was divided up among European colonial powers without regard to the physical or human landscape that already existed on the continent. The only two African countries that remained independent were Ethiopia, which fought successfully against the Italians, and Liberia, established in 1822 as a home for freed African-American slaves.

History: Legacies of Colonialism

A century or more of European colonial rule has left modern African nations with many problems that work against their political stability.

In 1884, delegates from twelve European countries, the Ottoman Empire, and the United States met in Berlin, Germany. All of them already had interests or claimed colonies in Africa. They wanted to set ground rules for taking over the continent without clashes among themselves. No representatives from Africa were invited, however.

The Berlin Conference was called because of a sudden expansion in European imperialism, or empire building, in the 1870s. National pride was strong in Europe, and ambitious nations wanted empires. Colonies and trading rights were also important because of the rapid growth of industries. Africa offered both rich resources and new markets for European goods.

European nations carved up Africa to suit themselves. The slave trade in preceding centuries had weakened societies and economies in many parts of Africa. Still, some African rulers resisted strongly. The Ashanti kingdom battled British rule in a series of wars between 1824 and 1900. Mandinka warriors led by Samori Toure battled the French along the Niger River. Nonetheless, by 1914, only Liberia and Ethiopia remained free of European rule.

In most African colonies, European officials set up governments and laws like those in their home countries. They replaced local rulers with officials sent out from Belgium or Germany or Portugal. Africans were kept out of government and had few chances for education or professional training.

French colonial officials also took direct control, but they tried to make the local Africans into French citizens. They brought in French schools and political ways to replace African institutions.

In British colonies, African officials and local leaders were allowed to run local governments and community affairs. Final authority, however, rested with the local British residents.

In the 1950s and 1960s, most African colonies gained independence. But the years of colonial rule left many problems for the new nations. New national boundaries usually followed colonial borders, which had been drawn by Europeans who knew little about Africa. They often put together within one nation people from rival ethnic groups with different languages, religious beliefs, and traditions. These differences led to bloody violence and political unrest in a number of nations, such as Nigeria and present-day Rwanda.

Few Europeans were interested in Africa's long-term development. As a result, Africans gained no training as government workers or administrators. Education was not encouraged. The economy, moreover, was run only to profit the colonizing country. Colonial industries stripped away valuable minerals and timber, while ignoring economic development in Africa itself.

Today African governments work to reverse these patterns. In many African nations, the struggle for true economic independence continues.

Since World War II, African countries have struggled for independence, most gaining it in the 1960s and 70s. Yet, as in other world regions with a history of colonial rule, the transition to independence has not been easy. Many ethnic and political conflicts have continued, and as a result, the political boundaries of Africa are still in transition today. In addition, much of Africa is plagued by poverty, disease, inadequate healthcare, malnutrition, agricultural problems, and a high illiteracy rate. Despite an abundance of natural resources, Africa's economic growth has been slow and its rapidly growing population is not adequately supported. Parts of Africa are some of the most underdeveloped areas on Earth.

Regions of Africa

Africa is generally divided into two main regions: North Africa and sub-Saharan Africa. The two regions are vastly different in terms of economy, ethnic groups, and history.

Africa: Largest Cities

Cairo, Egypt	6,800,000
Alexandria, Egypt	3,380,000
Kinshasa, D.R. Congo	2,664,500
Casablanca, Morocco	2,263,500
Giza, Egypt	2,144,000
Abidjan, Côte d'Ivoire	1,929,000
Addis Ababa, Ethiopia	1,912,500
Cape Town, South Africa	1,911,500
Algiers, Algeria	1,740,500

North Africa: The Most Prosperous Region

North Africa's location historically and geographically has put it in contact with people from Europe and Asia. In North Africa, most people are descendants of Arab, Berber (believed to be the oldest inhabitants of North Africa having settled along the Mediterranean by 3000 B.C.), and Black African ancestors. Due to this Arab ancestry and to Arab rule for over a thousand years, North Africa is more closely associated with the Middle Eastern region of Asia than with the rest of Africa. There are also huge oil and natural gas reserves in North Africa, just as there are in the Middle East. These reserves, along with industrial development and stable economies in most North African countries, make the region the most prosperous in Africa.

The People of North Africa

The Sahara Desert covers most of North Africa and is sparsely populated. Small groups of people live around its **oases**, and **nomadic** people travel across it in search of vegetation and water for their livestock. More and more, however, nomadic people are encouraged to settle in one place so that governments have better control of them. Unfortunately, fragile lands which could recuperate when used in rotation, are often overused once they become a permanent settlement. In the semi-deserts along the Sahara's edges, the overuse of land and frequent droughts have resulted in **desertification**. See Figure 2.6.3 for a map of North Africa.

Key Note Terms

oases – fertile or green area in an arid region (as a desert)

nomadic – living without a fixed location; moving from place to place for trading purposes or in search of pasture and water for livestock

desertification – a process in which fertile land is turned into desert over time, usually due to overuse of the land and/or inadequate rainfall

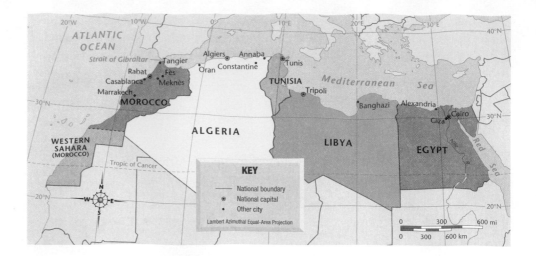

Most people in North Africa, however, live either in the Atlantic and Mediterranean coastal lowlands, in the Atlas Mountains (all of which receive adequate rainfall), or along the Nile River (the only large river providing water to the region). The Nile River basin is one of the most densely populated places on Earth and contains some of the most fertile land in the world. Lake Nasser, created on the Nile by the Aswan Dam (see Figure 2.6.4), allows irrigation of many more millions of acres of farmland.

Figure 2.6.4: The Aswan Dam.

Courtesy of Ed Kashi.

In Morocco, Algeria, and Tunisia, Arabs make up 70 percent or more of the population, with many Berbers living in the Atlas Moutains. Most Egyptians are a mixture of Arabs and descendants of ancient Egyptians, while most Libyans are a mixture of Berbers and Arabs. In Sudan, half the population is Arabic (mostly in the north) and the remaining half is Black African—mostly Nilotic, including the Dinka, Nuer, and Shilluk. There are also European minorities in the region traced to colonial times.

Regardless of background, most people in North Africa, like their Asian neighbors in the Middle East, speak Arabic and follow the Islamic religion, which is a major force in North African society and government. In addition to Arabic, many people also speak a European or African language.

Non-Muslim minorities include a 10 percent Christian population in Egypt. In Sudan's southern sections, 8 percent follow the Christian faith and 17 percent follow various African religions. Attempts by Sudan's government in the late 1980s to impose Islamic holy law on the non-Muslim south resulted in rebellion and a continuing civil war.

The Economy of North Africa

Economically, as already mentioned, North Africa is a prosperous region. Egypt, Libya, and Algeria are all major oil exporters (see Figure 2.6.5), and Morocco, Tunisia, and Western Sahara (under Moroccan occupation) all have large supplies of phosphates, which are used in fertilizers. Other industry in the region produces iron, steel, chemicals, textiles, cement, and food products.

Figure 2.6.5:
Oil field in Libya.

Courtesy of
Jim Holland/Black Star.

Morocco has strong fishing and tourism industries. Tourism is also important in Tunisia and Egypt. A great cultural, financial, and commercial center, Egypt is also politically the strongest country in the region and one of the strongest in the Middle East. Its capital, Cairo, is the largest African city, as well as one of the largest cities in the world.

Climate in the Atlas Mountains supports farming and livestock, and the Mediterranean climate along the Tunisian and Algerian coasts supports crops like grapes and olives. Egypt grows cotton, among other crops, and is famous for its cotton products.

Sudan is the poorest country in this region with most of the population employed in agriculture. Its economic development has been hindered by chronic civil war and major famines in the 1980s and 1990s.

Sub-Saharan Africa: Four Very Diverse Regions

In contrast with Northern Africa, the vast Sahara Desert buffered sub-Saharan Africa from outside influences for centuries. In sub-Saharan Africa, most people are descendants of Nilotic (originating in the southwestern Ethiopian Highlands), Cushitic (originating in the Ethiopian Highlands), and Bantu (originating in eastern Nigeria) ancestors—considered Black Africans. These main groups are divided into hundreds of other ethnic groups, many of which have their own language and religion.

Nearly 75 percent of the people who live in Africa south of the Sahara live in rural villages; however, country people have been steadily moving to cities over the years. In 1960 only a few cities in Africa had populations over 500,000. The countries of sub-Saharan Africa with little industry have economies based mainly on subsistence farming and the exporting of raw materials.

Africa's Economy

Farming in Africa can be risky. In the tropical, wet climate of the rain forests, the soil is poor due to leaching—the dissolving and washing away of nutrients. In dry areas, frequent droughts cause crop failures.

After winning their independence, many African governments borrowed large sums of money to pay for modernization. Loan repayments are now a major part of many African national budgets.

Many African nations depend on one or two exports. If the world price drops, entire economies crumble. Thus governments are trying to diversify, or increase the variety of, their exports.

The People of Sub-Sahara Africa

As previously mentioned, the majority of the people living in sub-Saharan Africa are Black Africans, yet there are hundreds of different ethnic groups within this classification, many with their own language and religion. Some of these ethnic groups along with the region of sub-Saharan Africa in which they reside include:

- **East Africa—Oromo, Amhara, Somalis, Ganda, Maasai, Hutu, and Tutsi**

- **West Africa—Fulani, Hausa, Asante, Ewe, Mende, Bambara, Malinke, and Dogon**

- **Central Africa—Baya, Azande, Ovimbundu, Kongo, Tonga, Luba, Mbuti, and Fang**

- **Southern Africa—Sotho, Zulu, Swazi, Herero, Shona, Ndebele, Xhosa, and Ovambo**

Minorities in sub-Saharan Africa include:

- **In East Africa—Asians mainly from India; Europeans; and groups of mixed Black African, Arab, and Persian (Iranian) descent such as the Swahili**

- **In West Africa—Moors of mixed Arab, Berber, and Black African descent who make up a majority of the population in Mauritania**

- **In Southern Africa—Africaners of mixed Dutch, French, German, and Black African descent considered the "white" minority in South Africa; Cape Coloreds and Cape Malays of mixed European, Asian, and Black African descent; Madagascans of mixed Black African and southeast Asian descent; and Indians whose ancestors came to work on British plantations in the 1800s**

In addition to the hundreds of African languages related to particular ethnic groups, languages of former colonial powers are spoken in sub-Saharan Africa and are often recognized as the official languages of countries. A common language, usually a language used formerly for trading, may also be spoken throughout an entire region—for example, Swahili in East Africa, Arabic and Hausa in West Africa, and Shona in Southern Africa. For these reasons, many people in sub-Saharan Africa speak more than one language.

In addition to the many African religions related to particular ethnic groups, both Islam and Christianity are practiced in sub-Saharan Africa. Islam spread, of course, through contact with the Arabs and is followed mostly in the northern countries of East and West Africa, in the area often referred to as the transition zone between Arab North Africa and sub-Saharan Africa. Moving south away from North Africa are smaller percentages of people practicing Islam, with very few in Central or Southern Africa.

Africa's Inhabitants

North of the Sahara, populations are less diverse than in the rest of Africa. Nearly 3,000 ethnic groups live south of the Sahara. They speak a total of more than 800 languages.

Africa is the world's second most populous region, after Asia, and is the fastest-growing continent in the world. Today almost 720 million people live in the region.

Keeping people healthy is a challenge in Africa. Life expectancy is only 55 years, lower than any other continent. Many diseases that afflict Africans are carried by tropical insects and parasites. Africans' health is also weakened by poor diet due to constant problems of drought and famine.

Throughout Africa, women's work is important to the economic and social well-being of the community. Women produce food, most of which is consumed within the country and not exported.

Christianity was brought to the continent by European missionaries and is widely practiced in Southern and Central Africa and in the southern countries of East and West Africa, with smaller percentages of practicing Christians in the countries approaching North Africa. In some cases, a mix of an African religion with Christianity or Islam is practiced.

West Africa

Figure 2.6.6 shows a physical map of West and Central Africa. For centuries, the West African coast was an important trade route, supplying ivory, gold, and slaves for American plantations. In addition to trade, colonialism brought export crops and urbanization to the coast, while much of the interior remained untouched. It also led to political and ethnic strife once colonial powers withdrew. In Nigeria and Chad, as in Sudan, there have been conflicts between the Muslim northerners and southerners who are mainly Christians or followers of an African religion. Civil wars as recent as the 1990s have occurred in Sierra Leone and Liberia.

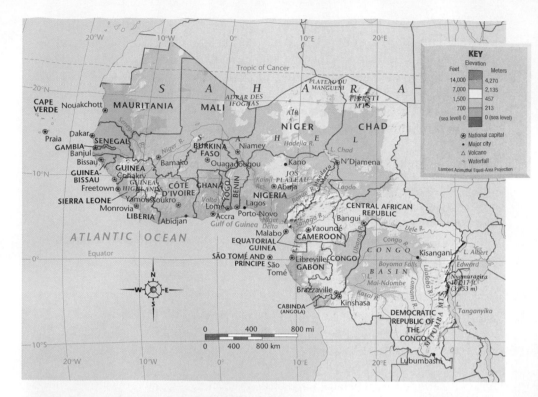

Like North Africa, much of West Africa is plateau. The eastern boundary of West Africa is the Adamawa Highlands, partly created by molten rocks from volcanoes in the area. This volcanic soil provides fertile farmland in Cameroon. In contrast, the southern reaches of the Sahara, as well as the Sahel, lie in West Africa's northernmost land.

In the Sahel, desertification in certain regions has resulted from droughts and overuse of the fragile land (see Figure 2.6.7). Nomadic peoples have been encouraged to remain in one place resulting in populations too large to be supported by the land. Droughts in the latter part of the twentieth century have severely affected crops and brought great hardship to populations in Niger, Mali, Mauritania, and Chad. Understandably, most people live in the southern half of the region along coastlines and rivers. In fact, about one-third of Africa's total population lives in West Africa, with most in Nigeria.

Figure 2.6.7:
Desertification in
Mauritiania.

Courtesy of Photo
Researchers.

Although many West Africans are employed in subsistence agriculture, crops grown for export include cocoa, coffee, peanuts, and timber. Irrigation of land comes from rivers like the Niger, the largest in the region, Gambia, and Senegal, and from lakes like Chad and Volta. Volta is an artificial lake formed by the Akosombo Dam. These rivers also provide transportation for goods and people, and the rivers, lakes, and coastlines support fishing.

Unlike East Africa, West Africa possesses many mineral resources, including gold, diamonds, oil, natural gas, phosphates, and bauxite. Although Nigeria is oil-rich, it is deeply in debt, and its people have a very low per capita income. The region is slightly more industrialized than East Africa.

Central Africa

The Zaire River basin covers much of Central Africa (see Figure 2.6.6). To the basin's north in the Central African Republic and its south in Angola and Zambia are highland areas, with a thin strip of coastal lowlands in the west and the Great Rift Valley as a border in the east. With the Equator running through it, this region gets heavy rain and is very hot. Some of the low-lying areas are swampy, breeding mosquitoes and flies that spread dangerous diseases. This region is also the most heavily forested in Africa, supporting a productive timber industry that has also led to deforestation in some areas.

Central Africa is rich in mineral resources such as diamonds, copper, iron, oil, and manganese (see Figure 2.6.8). Countries such as Gabon, Zaire, and Congo are more industrialized than their neighbors, yet still over half the population exists on subsistence farming. In Zaire, which has territory deep in the African interior, the economy is hindered because of poor transportation systems through the difficult vegetation and along the Zaire River, which has many rapids. Zambia, a landlocked country, is hurt by transportation costs associated with the long distance to a coastline. Central Africa's economy has also been hindered by a lengthy civil war in Angola and other conflicts in the region.

Figure 2.6.8: Copper mine in the democratic Republic of Congo.

Courtesy of Aurora Photos.

In addition, while Africa in general has one of the world's largest refugee populations, Central Africa, in particular, has huge refugee populations—both from people fleeing from one country to another within the region, as well as from people in surrounding regions seeking haven there. In the 1990s, Zaire accepted over one million refugees from Rwanda alone because of fighting in that country. Problems associated with refugee populations include lost labor and income for the country losing the refugees and unemployment for the country gaining them. Political conflicts often erupt between the countries. Furthermore, the large concentrations of people in a particular area can lead to environmental problems.

East Africa

East Africa is Africa's most mountainous region, including its highest peak, Mount Kilimanjaro, and the Ethiopian Highlands (see Figure 2.6.9). The region also includes the Somali Peninsula, or Horn of Africa, and many lakes and rivers that help feed the Nile. The Horn of Africa is mostly semi-desert, while grassy plains, most above 600 feet in elevation, cover much of Tanzania, Uganda, and Kenya. These plains support Africa's famous herds of wildlife, and Tanzanian and Kenyan national parks and game reserves are major tourist destinations. Unfortunately, while the parks and reserves protect wildlife, many also exclude local people who once used the land to graze livestock.

Figure 2.6.9: East and Southern Africa.

Courtesy of maps.com.

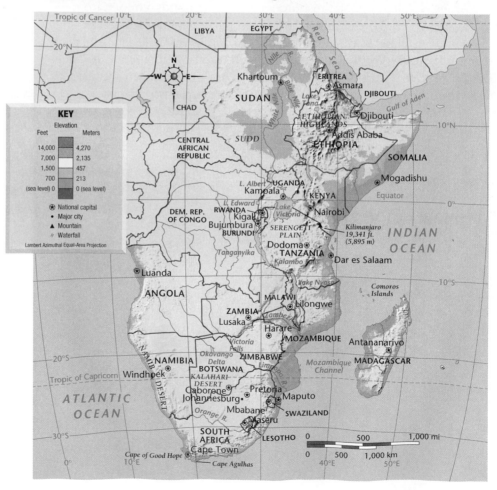

East Africa is the poorest region in Africa. Except for diamonds in Tanzania and copper in Uganda, it has few mineral resources, and there is little industry for processing raw materials. In addition, ethnic and political conflicts have hurt the region's economy. Some of the most recent conflicts (as of the 1990s) include the civil war in which Eritrea separated from Ethiopia; the ethnic fighting between Hutus and Tutsis in Rwanda and Burundi; and fighting between clans in Somalia.

Most people in East Africa make a living by farming, many at a subsistence level. Because they are growing just enough to survive, it is devastating when crops are ruined due to insufficient rainfall. In the past, widespread famines have resulted. Export crops grown in the region, historically on the best land, include coffee, tea, tobacco, and cotton. Intensive farming and **deforestation** have further weakened the already fragile soil in much of the region.

Key Note Term

deforestation – the act of clearing forests, often to earn income from timber, create farmland, or expand urban areas; may result in the permanent loss of forest areas and soil erosion

Global Issues: Water Use in Africa

Much of Africa suffers from a severe shortage of water. This problem is a cause for concern on both local and international levels.

More than half of all of Africa's people lack safe drinking water and live with inadequate sanitation. As the region's population grows, the situation gets worse. Aquifers, or underground reservoirs, and rivers that have been used as water sources for thousands of years are being drained. In some places renewable fresh water has dropped by more than 65 percent over the past 40 years. Many people are forced to use unclean water for both drinking and cooking.

Most farmers in Africa depend on rainfall to water their crops, but rainfall is unpredictable. Since the late 1960s, a series of droughts have destroyed crops and brought repeated famine to many African countries. In addition, droughts have sped up desertification.

The scarcity of clean water in Africa is often a threat to health. Cholera and other diseases carried by dirty water kill over 5 million people a year. Many of the victims are children. Famine brought on by drought has also taken the lives of millions of Africans. Over the years, developed nations have sent billions of dollars in aid to suffering nations in Africa.

Governments, international aid agencies, and individuals in different African nations have made some progress developing new water resources.

Governments in Africa and international donors have invested billions of dollars in building dams and desalination plants that provide fresh water for irrigation and drinking. In addition, giant pipelines are being built that will carry fresh water from aquifers in Libya and Lesotho to places that need water.

Villages and towns across Africa are trying to improve their water supply by using low-cost technologies that they can manage and maintain themselves. In Zambia, for example, a group of women got together and financed the drilling of wells to supply their town with fresh water. In other places, farmers operate their own simple irrigation systems.

Many experts say that a long-term solution to the water crisis depends less on securing water than on changing the way it is used. In the poorest countries 90 percent of the available water is used for irrigation. Much of it is wasted in the process. Alternative methods of irrigation, such as drip irrigation, can reduce the amount of water wasted. Some experts suggest it might be wiser for Africa's food to be grown in places that are rich in water. They support a movement that encourages Africa's people to develop other commodities that can be traded for water.

Southern Africa

Much of Southern Africa's interior is a plateau surrounded by mountainous highlands, including the Drakensburg (see Figure 2.6.10). These highlands drop off steeply to narrow coastal lowlands in the west and south and to a wider coastal plain in the east, especially in southern Mozambique. Rivers in the region cannot be used by ships because of their many waterfalls. The highlands are sparsely populated, as are Botswana and Namibia, covered by the Kalahari and Namib Deserts. As with the Sahara, desertification has occurred along the fringes of these two deserts.

Figure 2.6.10: Drakensberg Mountains.

Courtesy of eStock Photo.

The country of South Africa dominates this region. Considered the most developed and wealthiest country on the continent, it boasts the richest gold mine in the world. Here also are diamond and coal mines, fertile farmland, large cities, transportation networks, factories, and ports. Most of the wealth, however, is held by a small, white minority and was earned over years of racial segregation and inequality.

South Africa's policy of apartheid, forced ethnic groups to live in ethnic-specific "homelands" consisting of the least desirable land, and denied them the right to vote, to an adequate education, and to work as a skilled professional—which forced them to work on white-owned farms and mines. In addition, South Africa interfered in the government of neighboring countries by supporting rebel forces and white-minority rule and even occupying Namibia in an attempt to preserve its own policies.

Many countries throughout the world cut political and economic ties with South Africa because of apartheid, which was finally abolished in 1991 after years of internal and external opposition. Still, the effects of apartheid, such as inequalities in wealth, ownership, education, and so on, will not be easily overcome.

Many people in this region are employed by agriculture (see Figure 2.6.11), and there is a wide variety of export crops including wheat, apples, cotton, and citrus. In Madagascar and Mozambique, however, subsistence farming is prevalent, and these countries are some of the poorest in the world. Madagascar's growing population and deforestation threatens the island's unique plant and animal life, while Mozambique's economy has been hindered by civil war and drought.

Figure 2.6.11: Agriculture in Zimbabwe.

Courtesy of Getty Images, Inc.

Many of the remaining countries are rich in mineral wealth, and as a result many people are employed in mining. The economies of Botswana, Swaziland, and Lesotho are tied to South Africa, with many people employed as laborers on farms and in mines in that country. Botswana, which has the richest diamond mine in the world, and Zimbabwe are two of the most stable countries in the region.

Conclusion

Africa is an enormous continent with breath-taking terrain, history and people. The first trace of modern humans emerged over 100,000 years ago in what is now called the Great Rift Valley of Africa. One of the world's first great civilizations arose in Egypt about 5,000 years ago. European colonialism strongly impacted Africa, though there are still thousands of different languages and religions on the continent. Africa is becoming a less mysterious place as more and more people choose it as a tourist destination. However, the African people still deal with issues of poverty, famine and disease.

The following lesson profiles Australia and Oceania, which consists of about 25,000 islands divided into three broad geographic-cultural areas—Micronesia, Melanesia, and Polynesia. Each of these areas is made up of several island countries, most of which are groups of many small islands.

Lesson Review

1. What physical feature divided the continent of Africa into two major regions?

2. What makes North Africa so different from Sub-Saharan Africa?

3. Why was Africa so desirable to European colonial powers?

4. List some of the major economic activities in Sub-Saharan Africa.

Lesson 7
Australia and the Rest of Oceania

Key Terms

coral reef
Micronesia
Melanesia
Polynesia
Outback
maritime

WHAT YOU WILL LEARN TO DO

- Explore the unique geographic characteristics of Australia and Oceania

LINKED CORE ABILITIES

- Communicate using verbal, non-verbal, visual, and written techniques
- Apply critical thinking techniques

SKILLS AND KNOWLEDGE YOU WILL GAIN ALONG THE WAY

- Describe principal physical features of Australia and Oceania
- Summarize the physical and human characteristics of countries and regions of Australia and Oceania
- Explain how the interactions between groups of people in Australia/Oceania can affect the areas cultural, economic and political characteristics
- Compare places in Australia and Oceania to other areas of the earth's surface
- Define key words contained in this lesson

Introduction

Collectively, the islands located in the Pacific Ocean away from the Asian continent are known as Oceania. Unlike the islands previously discussed in this text, these islands (with the exception of Australia which is itself a continent) are not considered part of any continent.

In this lesson, you learn about the people and cultures of Australia and Oceania. You learn how the geographic location and terrain of these areas are unique when compared to the rest of the world.

Australia: The Island Continent

Australia (Figure 2.7.1) is the smallest continent and the only continent that is also a single country. Situated south of the Equator, it is nicknamed "the land down under." Australia is completely separated by water from any other continent, which led to another nickname "the island continent." Because it is an island, Australia has plant and animal life that is indigenous to this area, including the kangaroo, wallaby, wombat, and koala.

Figure 2.7.1: Australia and New Zealand.

Courtesy of maps.com.

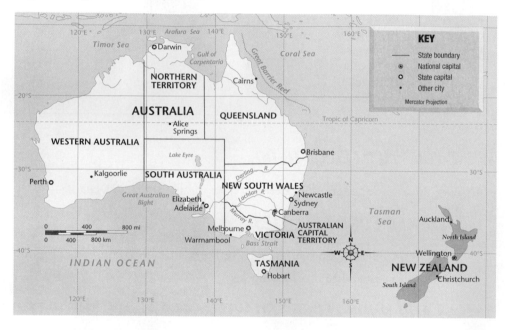

In general, Australia is flat, consisting mainly of plains and plateaus. It has the lowest average elevation of any of the continents. It is also dry—note the continent's location in relation to the Tropic of Capricorn—and much of the plateau land is desert including the Great Sandy, Gibson, Great Victoria, and Simpson Deserts. In fact, desert and semi-desert areas in western and central Australia cover about 66 percent of the entire continent and are known as the **Outback**. Although about 25 percent of the continent's land is unusable for agricultural purposes, the semi-desert areas support huge sheep and cattle ranches.

Between the desert plateau in central Australia and the Great Dividing Range (a highland area that parallels the east coast from Cape York in the north to the island of Tasmania in the south) is a lowland area covered by grassy plains that support livestock grazing. Between the Great Dividing Range and the sea as well as in the Murray River basin in the southeast are fertile lowlands that receive reliable rainfall and support huge commercial wheat farms, as well as livestock. A small piece of the southwest coast around the city of Perth also receives adequate rainfall that supports agriculture.

Off the east coast in the Coral Sea is the Great Barrier Reef (see Figure 2.7.2). This area of coral is over 1,240 miles long and is the largest known accumulation of **coral reef** in the world, making it a major tourist attraction for snorkeling and scuba diving.

Key Note Term

coral reef – found in the warm clear shallow waters of tropical oceans, coral reefs are among the most diverse and productive communities on Earth; reefs have functions ranging from providing food and shelter to fish and invertebrates to protecting shore from erosion

Figure 2.7.2: Scuba diving in the Great Barrier Reef.

Courtesy of Woodfin Camp and Associates.

Important Historical/Political Considerations of Australia

Australia's original inhabitants were Aborigines arriving from Southeast Asia about 40,000 years ago. European explorers landed on the continent in the 1600s. Great Britain claimed it in 1770, establishing New South Wales as a prison colony and sending shiploads of convicts there. Free settlers came to the continent looking for economic opportunities, especially after the discovery of gold. The last convict ship arrived in 1849. Meanwhile, the Aborigine population began to decrease significantly, mostly because of European diseases.

Similar to Canada, Australia is a self-governing dominion within the British Commonwealth of Nations. It consists of six states (New South Wales, Victoria, Queensland, Western Australia, South Australia, and Tasmania) and two territories (Northern Territory and the Australian Capital Territory, where the nation's capital, Canberra, is located).

The People of Australia

Australia's immigration policy from the early 1900s to the 1960s excluded non-Europeans from migrating to the country and was specifically aimed at keeping out Asians, people from other islands in Oceania, and Africans. International pressure stopped this unofficial "white-only" policy. Yet, for labor reasons, Australian immigration policy remains selective, ensuring immigrants are skilled workers with job opportunities waiting for them. Because of this former policy and Australia's colonial history, most Australians are of European descent—particularly British. Asians make up four percent of the population, and Aborigines make up one percent. Most people speak English and follow a Christian religion.

Similar to Canada, Australia has a small population for its great size—it is the sixth largest country in the world. About 85 percent of Australians live in towns and cities (see Figure 2.7.3) along the east coast from Brisbane to Adelaide and in the southwest around Perth.

Figure 2.7.3: The Sydney Opera House in Sydney Harbor.

Courtesy of Getty Images, Inc.

"My Brilliant Career" by Miles Franklin

Under the pen name of Miles Franklin, Stella Franklin (1879–1954) wrote the novel "My Brilliant Career" when she was just 16 and living in the Australian outback of New South Wales. In this excerpt, Sybylla Melvyn and her family have just moved from the mountains to a farm near Golburn, south of Sydney.

"My first impression of Possum Gully was bitter disappointment—an impression which time has failed to soften or wipe away.

How flat, common, and monotonous the scenery appeared after the rugged peaks of the Timlinbilly Ranges!

Our new house was a ten-roomed wooden structure, built on a barren hillside. Crooked stunted gums [Australian evergreen trees] and stringybacks, with a thick underscrub of wild cherry, hop [leafy vine], and hybrid wattle [woody plants with flower clusters], clothed the spurs which ran up the back of the detached kitchen. Away from the front of the house were flats, bearing evidence of cultivation, but a drop of water was nowhere to be seen. Later, we discovered a few round, deep, weedy waterholes down on the flat, which in rainy weather swelled to a stream which swept all before it. Possum Gully is one of the best watered spots in the district, and in that respect has stood to its guns in the bitterest drought. Use and knowledge have taught us the full value of its fairly clear and beautifully soft water. Just then, however, coming from the mountains where every gully had its limpid creek, we turned in disgust from the idea of having to drink this water.

I felt cramped on our new run [sheep-grazing property]. It was only three miles wide at its broadest point. Was I always, always, always to live here, and never, never, never to go back to Bruggabrong? That was the burden of the grief with which I sobbed myself to sleep on the first night after our arrival.

Mother felt dubious of her husband's ability to make a living off a thousand acres, half of which were fit to run nothing but wallabies [small kangaroos], but father was full of plans, and very sanguine concerning his future. He was not going to squat henlike on his place as the cockies [small farmers] around him did. He meant to deal in stock, making of Possum Gully merely a depot on which to run some of his bargains until reselling.

Dear, oh dear! It was terrible to think he had wasted the greater part of his life among the hills where the mail came but once a week, and where the nearest town, of 650 inhabitants, was forty-six miles distant. And the road had been impassable for vehicles. Here, only seventeen miles from a city like Goulburn, with splendid roads, mail thrice weekly, and a railway platform only eight miles away, why, man, my fortune is made! Such were the sentiments to which he gave birth out of the fullness of his hopeful heart."

Excerpt from "My Brilliant Career" by Miles Franklin. Published by St. Martin Press.

The Economy of Australia

Australia is a modernized, rich country, and its people enjoy a high living standard. It is the world's largest wool producer, a major exporter of beef, and a large exporter of wheat, sugar, fruit, and dairy products. It has an abundance of minerals including coal, bauxite, iron, nickel, lead, zinc, and uranium, as well as petroleum and natural gas reserves.

Australia's diverse manufacturing produces machinery, equipment, textiles, and food products. Manufacturing is limited, however, owing to the continent's small domestic market and the long distances to foreign markets.

New Zealand

Because of its original inhabitants, New Zealand (Figure 2.7.1) is considered part of **Polynesia**. Nevertheless, because of its location and cultural ties to Great Britain, today it is more closely associated with Australia. New Zealand was originally settled by Maoris, a Polynesian people probably from the Marquesas Islands. Like Australia, it was claimed by Great Britain and today is a self-governing dominion within the British Commonwealth. Most New Zealanders are of British descent, speak English, and are Christian. Nine percent of the population is Maori, many of whom speak the Maori language.

Unlike Australia, New Zealand is mostly mountainous (see Figure 2.7.4). North Island has hot springs and volcanoes, while South Island has glaciers and fjords. New Zealand is sparsely populated with more people living on North Island and roughly 35 percent of the total population living in or around Auckland.

Key Note Term

Polynesia – the islands of Central and South Pacific including Hawaii, The Line, Phoenix, Tonga, Cook and Samoa Islands, Tuvalu, Easter Island, French Polynesia, and often New Zealand

Figure 2.7.4: Sheep grazing on the hills below Mt. Cook, New Zealand.

Courtesy of Getty Images, Inc.

Like Australians, most New Zealanders have high standards of living. The economy is based mainly on agriculture, and New Zealand is a major dairy and wool exporter (see Figure 2.7.5). It has coal and natural gas reserves, and its natural beauty supports a growing tourism market. It has a diverse manufacturing sector, yet is limited for the same reasons as Australia.

Figure 2.7.5: Wellington, New Zealand, is a major harbor for exports.

Courtesy of Woodfin Camp and Associates.

The Rest of Oceania

In addition to Australia, Oceania consists of about 25,000 islands divided into three broad geographic-cultural areas—**Micronesia**, **Melanesia**, and Polynesia each made up of several island countries, most of which are groups of many small islands (see Figure 2.7.6).

Key Note Terms

Micronesia – the islands of the West Pacific east of the Philippines and north of Melanesia including Caroline, Kiribati, Mariana, and Marshall groups

Melanesia – the islands in the Pacific northeast of Australia and south of Micronesia including Bismarck Archepelago, the Solomons, Vanuatu, New Caledonia, and the Fijis

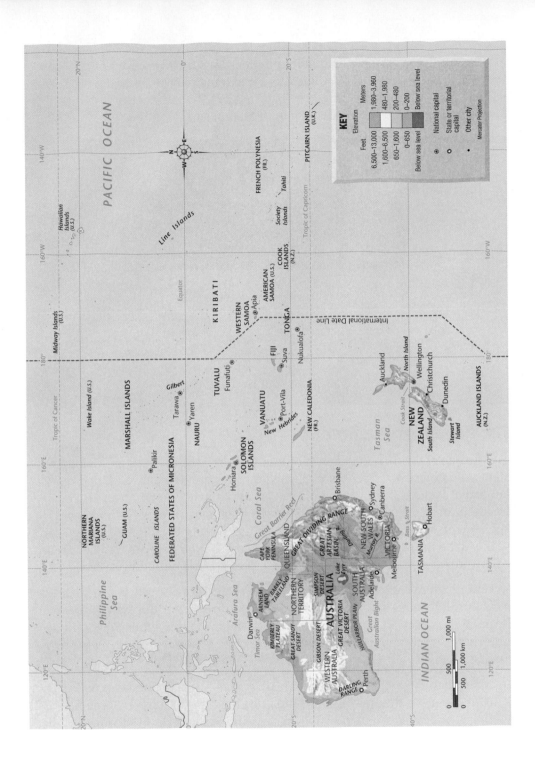

Figure 2.7.6: Oceania.

Courtesy of GeoSystems Global Corporation.

In general, Polynesia forms a triangle in the eastern Pacific extending from the Hawaiian Islands in the north to New Zealand and Easter Island in the south. In the western Pacific, excluding those islands considered part of Asia, Micronesia includes the islands north of the Equator, and Melanesia includes the islands south of the Equator.

Note that the island of New Guinea, which is often included geographically in its entirety as part of Oceania, is split for political reasons. The western half, Irian Jaya, is part of Indonesia and, therefore, considered part of Southeast Asia. The eastern half, Papua New Guinea (see Figure 2.7.7), is a member of the British Commonwealth and is considered part of Melanesia.

Figure 2.7.7: Traditional housing in Papua, New Guinea.

Courtesy of Wolfgang Kaehler Photography.

The People of Oceania

The people of the three regions, known ethnically as Micronesians, Melanesians, and Polynesians, are distinguished by physical appearance, blood type, language, social organization, and even art and housing. Yet, because of the fragmentation of land throughout Oceania, there are hundreds of languages spoken and a diversity of cultural traits. Of the three groups, Polynesian culture seems to be the most consistent from island to island. There are also European, Asian, and groups of mixed minorities scattered throughout these islands.

In Hawaii, there is a large minority of Japanese descent, as well as many Americans from the mainland U.S., however, U.S. culture predominates. Like New Zealand's association with Australia, the Hawaiian Islands, while Polynesian, are now more closely associated with the U.S. having become the 50th state on August 21, 1959.

In addition to the many ethnic-specific languages spoken, English is widely spoken and used as a mutually understandable language throughout Oceania. French is also spoken in French Polynesia, Vanuatu, and New Caledonia. Christian religions are widely practiced throughout the three regions, in addition to island-specific and ethnic-specific religions.

Important Historical/Political Considerations of Oceania

In the past century, most of the islands have been under the protection of or administered by another country for some period of time. In fact, most of the island countries of Micronesia were administered by the U.S. as United Nations Trust Territories until they made the transition to self-rule.

The Economy of Oceania

The main economic activities on most of these islands are agriculture and fishing, depending in part on the physical characteristics of the island itself. Those islands that are mountainous and volcanic have fertile soil that supports agriculture. Smaller, low-lying, coral islands tend to have poor soil, requiring people to look to the sea for their livelihood. In general, Melanesia has larger, volcanic islands, while a majority of Micronesian and Polynesian islands are smaller, coral islands. Trading for food between the people of the two types of islands is common. The Polynesians, in particular, are renowned as great **maritime** peoples who have traveled hundreds of miles across the ocean to fish and trade.

Although many people practice subsistence agriculture, one of the most important export crops is copra, the kernel of the coconut from which coconut oil is extracted. Other exports include tropical fruit, cotton, sugarcane, fish, and handicrafts of the native people. In Melanesia, timber is an important resource. Other resources are sparse on most of the islands—a few exceptions include phosphate in Nauru; copper, gold, and petroleum in Papua New Guinea; gold in Fiji; and nickel in New Caledonia. Island countries also earn income by selling other countries fishing rights to their waters. Tourism is an important economic activity, particularly in Polynesia.

> **Key Note Term**
>
> **maritime** – of, relating to, or bordering on the sea

Conclusion

Australia is a vast land with diverse physical characteristics and a relatively small population. Australia's physical geography limits its population to the coastal areas. Mountainous New Zealand is known for its beauty and sheep population. The 25,000 Pacific Islands, while beautiful, struggle with ethnic conflict, economic development and natural hazards like typhoons, volcanic activity, and earthquakes.

This chapter provided you with an overview of world geography within the familiar framework of continents and countries. It discussed aspects of both the physical and human landscapes that make up our world and demonstrated how places can be grouped into regions based on common characteristics. This basic insight and background into world geography is an important skill to possess in today's age of information, global economics, and accessible worldwide travel. As a citizen of a leading world power, it will help you understand events around the globe—economic crises, political and ethnic conflicts, natural disasters, and so on—and how they can impact your country and, in some cases, your own life. In the following chapter, you will learn about local and global environmental issues, and what you can do to help make our world more environmentally sound.

Lesson Review

1. What are the key economic activities of Australia?

2. What culture groups make up the population of New Zealand?

3. What kinds of natural resources can be found on the Pacific Islands?

4. How is tourism both a blessing and a curse for the Pacific Islanders?

Environmental Awareness

Chapter 3

LESSONS

Lesson 1
Local Environmental Issues

Key Terms

air emissions
ash
combustion
composting
incineration
landfill
leachate
liners
methane
pelletize
pollutants
pollution
recycling
searing
solid waste
source reduction
synthetic
toxicity

WHAT YOU WILL LEARN TO DO

- Investigate the causes and effects of a local environmental issue

LINKED CORE ABILITIES

- Take responsibility for your actions and choices
- Do your share as a good citizen in your school, community, country, and the world

SKILLS AND KNOWLEDGE YOU WILL GAIN ALONG THE WAY

- Identify examples of air and water pollution
- Describe types of waste material
- Identify the components that enable modern-day, properly engineered sanitary landfills to meet environmental standards

Chapter 3

- Explain how communities address environmental issues
- Describe recycling processes
- Define key words contained in this lesson

Introduction

How many of you take for granted your existence on this earth — the air you breathe, the water you drink, and the land upon which you live, work, and play. You might want to stop and think about why the air and water are relatively clean and the land is relatively free from **pollution**.

Most Americans are not aware of decisions that governmental agencies and/or state and federal legislatures make to ensure the purity of our environment or to protect our health — that is, until it affects them directly. Even though environmental issues are often very diverse and technical in nature, many non-technical community leaders and citizens are making the decisions on these issues. Consequently, society is forcing these decision makers to gain a significant understanding of the technology, terminology, and laws governing environmental issues.

This lesson helps you to become more sensitive to local environmental issues, thoughtful in your actions, and aware of the contributions that you can make to help protect your environment. After completing this lesson, you should have a better appreciation for the environment around you; know how to safeguard its upkeep; and be prepared to prevent its breakdown.

Background: Examples of Environmental Impacts

More than a century of advanced technology has taken its toll on the natural environment of North America. For decades, the federal government ignored the growing problems of water and air pollution. In 1970, the White House and Congress worked together to establish the EPA in response to the growing public demand for cleaner water, air and land. The EPA was assigned the task of repairing the damage already done to the natural environment and to establish new criteria to guide Americans in making a cleaner environment a reality. The EPA is responsible for leading the nation's environmental science, research, education and assessment efforts.

The environment is a very dynamic and complex subject. Listed below are three examples of environmental impacts on today's society.

Various medical geographers and scientists have linked many forms of cancer, especially lung cancer, to environmental conditions. As a result of an intensified effort to study this finding, these experts have discovered that the distribution of respiratory-system cancers in the United States coincides with a number of major manufacturing and refining centers.

Acid rain is a serious pollution problem. Acid rain comes from sulfur dioxide (SO2) and nitrogen oxides (NOx) reacting in the atmosphere with water and returning to earth as rain, fog, or snow. Acid rain has a variety of effects, including damage to forests and soils, fish and other living things, materials, and human health. The region surrounding the United States Manufacturing Belt (particularly Ohio, Illinois, Indiana, and Michigan—which produce about 75 percent of North America's sulfur and nitrogen emissions), is one of the areas worst affected by acid rain.

Smog is an example of a severe air pollution problem that faces the large metropolitan areas in the United States. Air pollution is the presence of "unwanted material" (substances that are in sufficient concentrations to interfere with a person's health, comfort, welfare, or their enjoyment of property) in the air in excess of certain standards. Dozens of major cities experience this hazard, with Los Angeles and Denver among the most frequently exposed. Smog (a contraction of the words "smoke" and "fog") occurs when the warmer atmospheric air prevents cooler surface air from rising, thereby causing the surface air to become stagnant. The stagnant air then traps automobile and industrial emissions, thus intensifying the air pollution.

The list of local environmental issues goes on. Every community struggles with the balance of progress and protection. It is inevitable that human activity will affect the land we inhabit. Even in our own homes—each and every day—we contribute to a local environmental issue: waste management.

Types of Waste Material

The management of solid waste is a fundamental local environmental concern. Before discussing the key issues of **solid waste** and its disposal, an introduction is in order on the types of wastes and disposal facilities, as well as the different disposal procedures. The following lists the major categories of wastes that communities must pick-up, transport, process, landfill, and/or take appropriate measures for disposal.

- **Domestic or Household Waste.** Solid waste, composed of garbage and rubbish, that normally originates in the household.

- **Garbage.** Solid waste that consists of putrescible (defined on this page) animal and vegetable waste materials, resulting from the handling, preparation, cooking, and consumption of food. It also includes waste materials from markets, and storage facilities, as well as the handling and sale of produce and other food products.

- **Hazardous Waste.** Waste that because of its quantity; concentration; or physical, chemical, and/or infectious characteristics may pose a substantial hazard to human health or to the environment when improperly treated, stored, transported, disposed of, or otherwise managed.

Key Note Term

solid waste – garbage, refuse, sludges and other discarded solid materials including those from industrial, commercial, and agricultural operations, and from community activities

- **Inorganic Waste.** Non-combustible waste material made from substances composed of matter other than plant, animal, or certain chemical compounds of carbon (for example, metals and glass).

- **Municipal Solid Waste.** Waste that includes non-hazardous material generated in households, commercial and business establishments, and institutions. It excludes industrial-process, demolition, agricultural, and mining wastes; abandoned automobiles; ashes; street sweepings; and sewage sludge.

- **Organic Waste.** Waste material that consists of substances composed of carbon and hydrogen compounds that are generally manufactured in the life processes of plants and animals. It includes paper, wood, food wastes, plastics, and yard wastes.

- **Putrescible Waste.** Decaying solid wastes that can decompose rapidly causing foul odors and possibly attracting animals and/or disease carrying insects.

- **Residential Waste.** Waste material generated in houses and apartments. It includes paper, cardboard, beverage and food cans, plastics, food wastes, glass containers, old clothes, garden wastes, etc.

- **Solid Waste.** Garbage, refuse, sludges, and other discarded solid materials including those from industrial, commercial, and agricultural operations, and from community activities. It does not include solids or dissolved materials in domestic sewage or other significant **pollutants** in water resources, such as silt.

Types of Disposal Facilities and Procedures

Collection is the service of picking up and moving solid waste from its location of generation to a disposal area or facility, such as a transfer station, resource recovery facility, or **landfill**. Most disposal facilities have the necessary equipment and required land area to receive and dispose of wastes. These facilities may operate one or more disposal methods.

A sanitary landfill is just one method of disposing refuse on land without creating nuisances or hazards to public health or safety. Communities must ensure careful preparation of the fill area and control of water drainage to assure proper landfilling. To confine the refuse to the smallest practical area and reduce it to the smallest practical volume, facilities use heavy tractor-like equipment. This equipment spreads, compacts, and usually covers the waste daily with at least six inches of compacted soil.

The modern, properly engineered sanitary landfills have compacted clay or artificial (plastic) **liners, leachate** collection systems (which remove the leachate for treatment and disposal), and/or systems to collect and remove **methane** gas generated in the landfill.

These modern facilities also use volume reduction to decrease the amount of space the waste materials occupy. Such facilities use three major processes to accomplish volume reduction.

- **Mechanical Process**—Uses compacting techniques (baling, sanitary landfills, etc.) and shredding.
- **Thermal Process**—Uses heating techniques (**incineration**) and can reduce volume by 80 to 90 percent.
- **Biological Process**—Uses bacterial action (**composting**, etc.) to degrade the organic waste.

Contents of a Landfill

Figure 3.1.1 shows how the contents of a typical landfill in the United States have changed over several decades. Some types of solid waste have increased, others have decreased, and still others have stayed about the same.

Key Note Terms

incineration – an engineered process involving combustion to thermally break down organic waste materials

composting – controlled biological decomposition of organic solid waste into soil amendments such as mulch under aerobic (in the presence of oxygen) conditions

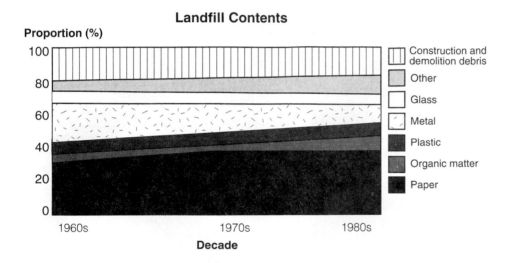

Figure 3.1.1: The changing contents of a typical landfill.

Courtesy of Rathje, W., and Murphy, C. *Rubbish!* (New York: HarperCollins, 1992), p. 104

Some of the contents of the landfill are biodegradable. This means they are capable of being broken down by natural biological processes, such as decay, and then absorbed into the environment as reusable raw material. Others are not.

By studying the information presented in Figure 3.1.1, you can answer the following questions:

- **Which waste products decreased in volume during the period covered by the information in Figure 3.1.1? Why? Which waste products increased in volume?**
- **Which waste product do you think people should work hardest to reduce? How might people go about reducing the volume of this waste product?**
- **Picture this experiment: One sheet of newspaper is buried. Another is left exposed to the elements. After several months, which sheet do you expect will have decomposed more? Why?**
- **Many communities have made a major effort to encourage recycling during the 1990s. How would you expect the graph in Figure 3.1.1 to look in the 1990s based on that fact?**

Solid Waste Issues

Every community faces numerous issues when dealing with the collection, transport and disposal of solid waste. Unfortunately, there is no ideal solution. However, improved research, new technology and increased governmental regulation have worked to mitigate these concerns in recent years.

Effect on Water Supply

In the past, communities used unlined landfills that allowed for the contamination of groundwater—a source of drinking water in some areas. This exposure of small quantities of chemical waste leaching into an unfiltered groundwater supply can result in human health risks.

Today, communities operate state-of-the-art structures (sanitary landfills) to limit water pollution through the use of **synthetic** liners that guide the wastewater to a separate treatment system. To assist communities in these efforts and reduce the number of contaminated sites, the U.S. Congress passed the Comprehensive Environmental Response, Compensation and Liability Act. This law imposes strict liability measures for hazardous waste pollution and creates a "superfund" of money to clean up the worst hazardous waste sites across the country.

SUPERFUND

The Comprehensive Environmental Response, Compensation, and Liability Act (CERCLA), commonly known as Superfund, was enacted by Congress in 1980. This law created a tax on the chemical and petroleum industries and enabled the Federal government to respond directly to releases or threatened releases of hazardous substances that may endanger public health or the environment.

The Superfund Program helps clean up the environment. Many areas of the environment are contaminated with hazardous waste. Years ago, people did not know that throwing hazardous waste on the ground might hurt humans, animals, and the environment. Many wastes were dumped on the ground, thrown into rivers, or left out in the open. The waste was polluting the environment and making a mess. When Superfund started in 1980, the EPA started to clean up the some of these areas, called Superfund sites. There are over 1,300 Superfund sites across the country.

Some superfund sites are old factories where chemicals were dumped on the ground. Others are landfills where garbage was dumped along with other poisonous waste. Some Superfund sites are remote places where people secretly dumped hazardous waste because they did not know what to do with it. Still other Superfund sites are old mines where people used to dig in the ground for things like coal, iron ore, or silver.

Almost 90 percent of all of the Superfund sites across the country have been cleaned up or are in the process of being cleaned up. There is still a lot of work to be done, since new Superfund sites are being discovered every year. Superfund has helped to make our environment a cleaner and safer place to live.

Other landfill problems facing communities are cost, intolerance, and odor. First, it is very costly and difficult for communities to site a new landfill or to close a landfill that is at its capacity. There are also costs associated with transporting the solid waste to another facility.

Intolerance can become a major problem when siting new landfills because of the "Not In My Back Yard," or NIMBY, concept. Few people want a landfill in or near their neighborhood. Most of us want trash picked up on time, but once collectors pick it up, it is "out of sight and out of mind."

Effect of Landfill Gases on Air Quality and Health

Odors are always a concern of landfills. In an attempt to reduce odors, modern structures install piping and collection systems for the recovery of gases produced by the breakdown of the wastes.

Additionally, landfills risk the possibility of explosion from excessive concentrations of methane (an odorless, explosive gas) as well as the long-term risk of pollution caused by gases escaping into the atmosphere. Because methane comes from the deterioration of organic matter within the landfill, the natural decomposition process over time will result in buried waste giving off methane and water.

Furthermore, the production of methane pockets can continue at a landfill for 10 to 20 years after collectors bury the solid waste products. Because methane is heavier than water, it accumulates and seeks the lowest point. Its accumulation and subsequent migration can result in explosions in low built structures such as sewers and basements of buildings.

Control of Waste Volume

Communities can control waste volume through **recycling, source reduction**, and incineration. However, to make such controls work, consumers must be willing to separate recycled goods and reusable containers, and they must be willing to purchase recyclable products and products made from recycled goods. Otherwise, recycled and/or recyclable products will not survive in a competitive enterprise economy.

Although, incinerators can reduce waste volume and kill bacteria in wastes, their **ash** and **air emissions** can be problematic. Communities must educate their citizens on the technological advances of incineration if they desire community acceptance and cooperation. Furthermore, through the use of established emission standards, community leaders must strictly enforce or regulate the amount of pollutants that landfills or industries discharge into the atmosphere.

Recycling

Recycling is one of the best environmental success stories of the late 20th century. Recycling, including composting, diverted 68 million tons of material away from landfills and incinerators in 2001, up from 34 million tons in 1990. By 1999, more than 9,000 curbside collection programs served roughly half of the American population. Curbside programs, along with drop-off and buy-back centers, resulted in a diversion of about 30 percent of the nation's solid waste in 2001. (from epa.gov)

There are several definitions of recycling waste which include:

- **The commonly accepted meaning is to use discarded materials in their original or changed form rather than wasting them.**

- **The precise meaning refers to sending material back into the process by which industry first formed it.**

- **The general meaning refers to the separation of recyclable materials such as newspapers, cardboard/corrugated papers, plastics, glass products, or metals (aluminum, steel, tin, etc.) from the waste system at the point of generation (households, industries, etc.). This also includes the separation and recycling of materials from municipal waste by individuals or specially designed recovery facilities, industrial in-plant recycling, and/or recycling by commercial establishments. Source separation makes recycling simpler and easier.**

A successful recycling program must consider the needs of the entire community. Although different communities have different sets of priorities, the following three-step process can apply to any recycling effort.

1. **Collect waste materials that have potential value. Collection methods include voluntary measures such as drop-off or curbside service, mandatory curbside service, or private collection (when citizens or firms pay private operating agencies to collect the solid waste—also known as private disposal).**

2. **Sort or process the above waste materials to a condition useful for industry.**

3. **Market those materials to industry for manufacture of a useful end product. This step is key to the recycling process. If there is no market to buy the product, recycling cannot be successful and the community would have to dispose of the recycled goods in another manner after collection.**

Many citizens share a common concern for wanting to protect the environment; however, they are uncomfortable with mandatory recycling for two reasons. First, it takes some effort to separate the materials. Secondly, once recycling becomes mandatory within a community, lawmakers may have to impose fines or penalties for those people who do not comply.

Source Reduction

Source reduction is the process of keeping waste out of the waste system through buying practices, conservation, etc. Buying products with less packaging is an example of source reduction. Some supermarkets even offer discounts if you use your own bags. Source reduction also means purchasing products as free of toxins as possible. However, source reduction does not by itself solve a community's waste disposal problems.

Communities frequently resort to a combination of options, especially since they must landfill the residue of recycling and take incinerator ash to a landfill for disposal. Therefore, an alternative such as landfill disposal is important even when communities use source reduction and other options.

> **Note**
>
> According to the EPA, from 1980 to 1990 the average yearly increase of garbage discarded by each American was 69 pounds.

Environmental Risks of an Incineration System

The main point of incineration is to reduce consumption of landfill volume. Incineration is an option that communities should consider only after they have explored recycling and source reduction. The remaining trash must go somewhere, and landfill space is becoming increasingly limited in certain communities.

Often, because of the NIMBY factor, communities do not readily welcome large waste burning facilities. Residents associate landfills with chronic **toxicity** problems (conditions which structures can easily correct with liners), as well as the previously mentioned air pollution and odor concerns.

Even though disposal facilities eliminate 70 to 90 percent of the solid waste volume, communities must landfill the remaining ash. Ash is the residue that remains after a landfill has burned a fuel or solid waste, which consisted primarily of non-combustible materials. The incineration process produces two types of ash: filter (or "fly") ash and bottom ash.

Fly ash is all solids (including ash, charred papers, cinders, dusty soot, or other matter) that rise with the hot gases from **combustion** rather than falling with the bottom ash. Fly ash is only a minor portion (or about 10 percent) of the total ash produced from combustion of solid waste, but environmentalists consider it to be more toxic than the cinders and metal bits of bottom ash.

Bottom ash is the non-airborne combustion residue from burning fuel in a boiler. The ash falls to the bottom of the boiler and landfills remove it mechanically. Bottom ash constitutes the major portion (or about 90 percent) of the total ash created by the combustion of solid waste.

The most common types of incinerators are mass-burn plants, refuse-derived fuel facilities, and modular small units (or other types of combustors).

- **Mass-burn Plant:** Takes virtually all non-hazardous waste and burns it collectively.

- **Refuse-derived Fuel Facility:** Separates, crushes, and **pelletizes** waste for burning alone or with fossil fuel.

- **Modular Small Unit:** Includes a variety of different combustion technologies.

Communities currently dispose of ash by mixing truckloads of fly and bottom ash with truckloads of unburned wastes at municipal solid waste landfills. Although these landfills usually do not attempt alternative processing methods to contain the toxic materials found in the ash (leading to potential health problems), governmental agencies are classifying such airborne emissions of gases and toxic chemicals as hazardous under the Clean Air Act, which the Federal Government passed in 1990 to set limits on the amount of pollutants that can be in the air anywhere in the United States.

Cost is another factor in using incineration. Incineration is a very expensive option. As of 1990, incineration costs range from $40 to $90 per ton, translating into an additional $30 to $40 per household each year.

Key Note Term

toxicity – the level of poison or harm of a particular substance

Key Note Term

combustion – a burning, a chemical exchange, especially oxidation, accompanied by the production of heat and light

Key Note Term

pelletize – to form or compact debris into pellets

What You Can Do

As an individual or a family, there are numerous steps you can take to prevent further damage to the environment. Many of these you may be doing already!

Recycle

There are two distinct ways that you can do recycling. You can recycle at home. Find out if there is a recycling program in your community. If so, participate in the program by separating and putting out your recyclables for curbside pickup or taking them to your local drop-off or buy-back center.

Another way to recycle is to shop smarter. Use products in containers that can be recycled in your community and items that can be repaired or reused. Also, support recycling markets by buying and using products made from recycled materials.

Compost

Backyard composting, in a fenced-off area or bin, provides a convenient way to reduce the volume of trash a household produces. It also provides a valuable product that can enhance the soil and increase the growth and health of the yard. Yard trimmings can be composted as well.

Celebrate

April 22, 2005 will mark the 35th Anniversary of Earth Day. On April 22, 1970, 20 million Americans took to the streets, parks, and auditoriums to demonstrate for a healthy, sustainable environment. Since then, Earth Day has become an annual event in many communities around the world. Some communities schedule events for "Earth Week"—the week before and after April 22. It is a time to celebrate the environment and get the community motivated to think about and act towards protecting our planet. (*note: from www.earthday.net*)

Join an Environmental Group

Environmental groups from across the country celebrated their accomplishments and pointed to the challenges ahead. These groups range from very large—the Nature Conservancy and Sierra Club—that take on a wide range of environmental efforts, to the smaller, local groups that usually fight more defined battles.

While deciding if you want to join any of the dozens of environmental groups, ask yourself, "What does the group really do?" "What level of commitment do I plan to give—time, money, or both?" and, "What will the group expect from me?" Some groups may want you to simply make telephone calls or write letters, whereas others may want you to become involved in environmental restoration projects where you roll up your sleeves and grub around in the soil, muck, and briers.

The following is a sampling of national environmental groups:

Blue Earth Alliance - www.blueearth.org

Environmental Defense Fund - www.environmentaldefense.org

Greenpeace - www.greenpeace.org

League of Conservation Voters - www.lcv.org

Legal Environmental Assistance Foundation - www.leaflaw.org

Nature Conservancy - www.nature.org

Sierra Club (includes the Sierra Club Legal Defense Fund) - www.sierraclub.org

World Wildlife Fund - www.worldwildlife.org

Whether you join a group or not, remember that environmentalism should start in each person's backyard, grow to consume a neighborhood, and finally, expand until it encompasses the entire community.

Grenada: A Local Environmental Dilemma

The city of Grenada has a population of two million people. It has reached a solid waste crisis.

Trashmore, located on the south side of Grenada, is the larger of two solid waste landfills. It accepts over three-fourths of the city's solid waste and has disposal capacity for ten more years. This landfill has existed for 25 years, long before there were any environmental laws governing landfill disposal. Therefore, in addition to household garbage, it also has handled many substances that the government now considers to be hazardous. Trashless, the city's smaller landfill, has reached its capacity. Grenada does not have a recycling program.

Less than three miles from Trashmore is the Grenada River, which is the city's primary source of drinking water. However, a serious drinking water problem exists for the city. Governmental inspectors have discovered that the Trashmore facility does not have a protective liner, causing hazardous substances from the landfill to contaminate the groundwater.

Additionally, residents have reported isolated cases of uncommon illnesses in the area of the landfill, but it is uncertain if the illnesses are the result of the emission of methane gas.

State and federal environmental agencies have contacted the Grenada city council regarding these environmental problems. The council must decide what course of action to take to solve the city's problems. It must exercise one of the following options:

- Keep Trashmore open since it has the additional capacity

- Build a new state-of-the-art landfill

- Contract with a commercial disposal facility elsewhere in the city, either temporarily or permanently

- Build an incinerator to burn the solid waste

- Develop a recycling program (Consider this option in conjunction with any one of the above options)

Next, the city has to control and clean up the contamination to the drinking water supply by treating the water with chemicals. This means they must also select a location for and build a new water treatment facility. In the meantime, the city must provide enough drinking water to its citizens, which is a very costly undertaking.

Finally, the city council must deal with its air pollution problem by controlling the methane gas emissions. The council may also want to consider decreasing the use of cars within the city limits. Regarding the air pollution, the city should consider using alternative fuels. For the vehicle problem, one option the council should consider is to create High Occupancy Vehicle (HOV) lanes. These lanes encourage carpooling, thereby reducing the number of vehicles on the road.

The city council is holding a town meeting to consider the options for solving their environmental problems. There are citizens in attendance who have varying opinions on these issues. Many citizens oppose the community locating any facility in their neighborhood. The residents of Southside are particularly strong in their opposition.

Imagine that you are a city-council member. Using the information provided in this lesson and the background information given with the case study, what would you select as the best option for Grenada's landfill problem? Remember that you must also consider the city's water and air pollution problems when determining the best possible course of action. Use the problem-solving/decision-making models to assist you throughout this case study. Be prepared to present the option you select with your reasons to your JROTC instructor.

The Future: Two Examples of What to Expect

As human populations increase and concerns over the disposal of solid waste continue, scientists will place a high priority on devising solutions to these problems. In some cases, the technology already exists and just needs to be made commercially viable.

Methane as Fuel for Power Plants

Methane is a basic ingredient of natural gas and the fuel for stoves, water heaters, and industrial machines like power plants. Since rotting garbage in landfills naturally creates methane, about 360 landfills nationwide (as of 2003) sell methane. Pipes are inserted into hills of rotting garbage at landfills to collect methane, which is then cleaned of water and grit, and pumped to power plants.

For example, in Orlando, Florida, the Orlando Utilities Commission power plant uses methane from the county-owned landfill to supplement its coal-burning plant. Each day this provides enough electricity for 10,000 homes, while reducing methane emissions from the landfill. In this way, the county benefits because it receives payment for the landfill methane from the power plant. The power plant, in turn, benefits by reducing its fuel costs, and the environment benefits because landfill methane is not released into the atmosphere. Additional sites for landfill methane gas projects are currently being identified all over the country.

Man-Made Lightning

Man-made lightning, **searing** at up to 18,000 degrees, will soon turn hazardous (toxic) and municipal wastes into harmless blocks of glass at a fraction of the cost of current disposal techniques. The process would transform much of the

Key Note Term

searing – to burn or scorch with a sudden application of intense heat

nation's garbage and poisonous waste into paving material. Plus, gases from this process would be about a tenth of that from conventional incinerators.

Continuous bolts of artificial lightning would arc across a nitrogen-filled furnace chamber to create a superheated plasma that would melt most waste products and neutralize molecules of highly toxic chemicals. The electrical charge and high temperatures of the furnace would blow apart toxic chemicals such as solvents, causing the atoms to recombine into simpler, less toxic, and more manageable molecules.

Conclusion

Governmental agencies from the local level up to the U.S. executive and legislative branches must constantly be alert to the growing environmental problems that face our nation. Then, they must create and enforce pro-environmental legislation to fight those problems. However, saving the environment is not just the government's responsibility.

All Americans must become more sensitive to environmental issues and determine what they can do to help. After all, environmentalism begins in everyone's backyard—it is everyone's responsibility to preserve and protect the environment in which we live.

The next lesson helps you examine environmental issues on a global level. You will learn what you can do to become a better global citizen by understanding worldwide environmental issues.

Lesson Review

1. **Describe ways in which pollutants enter our air and water.**

2. **What is Superfund and what is its purpose?**

3. **How do modern-day, properly engineered sanitary landfills meet environmental standards?**

4. **How does recycling work?**

Lesson 2
Global Environmental Issues

Key Terms

acid rain
carbon dioxide
deforestation
global warming
nuclear waste
treaty

WHAT YOU WILL LEARN TO DO

- Examine an environmental issue that has global impact

LINKED CORE ABILITIES

- Take responsibility for your actions and choices

- Do your share as a good citizen in your school, community, country, and the world

SKILLS AND KNOWLEDGE YOU WILL GAIN ALONG THE WAY

- Explain how countries work together to address global environmental problems

- Describe the challenges that the international community faces in addressing global environmental problems

- Describe the possible consequences of not addressing global environmental problems

- Compare the differing opinions of scientists regarding the causes and solutions of environmental problems

- Define key words contained in this lesson

Introduction

The Earth's human population is approximately 6 billion and rising. As the population continues to increase, there is the fear of more and more strain on the Earth's environment. This lesson explores the role of human activities in shaping and changing the global environment.

The Earth is constantly changing. Much of the change taking place on Earth is part of natural cycles. Human activity, however, can also cause environmental changes. Many changes are not evident because they occur over intervals longer than a human lifetime or because the changes are not easily seen. And environmental problems that originate in one location can impact many other locations around the world—its climate, human population, resources, and ecosystems.

During the past several decades, humans have become much more aware of their impact on the environment. This lesson explains several of the most significant global environmental issues, such as global warming, biodiversity, genetic engineering, and nuclear waste disposal.

Global Warming

Global warming refers to an average increase in the Earth's temperature, which in turn causes changes in climate (see Figure 3.2.1). A warmer Earth may lead to changes in rainfall patterns, a rise in sea level, and a wide range of impacts on plants, wildlife, and humans.

Key Note Term

global warming – the gradual increase in the overall temperature of the Earth's atmosphere due to the greenhouse effect caused by increased levels of carbon dioxide, CFCs, and other pollutants

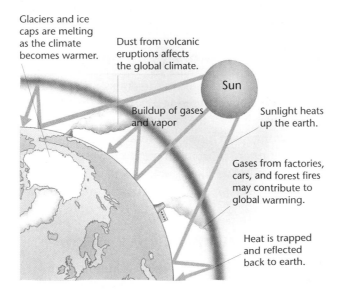

Figure 3.2.1: Global warming.

Courtesy of Peter Bull/Dorling Kindersley.

Some believe that natural events and human activities are contributing to an increase in average global temperatures. The most popular theory is that this is caused primarily by increases in "greenhouse" gases such as **carbon dioxide** (CO_2). The greenhouse effect works as follows.

Energy from the sun drives the earth's weather and climate, and heats the earth's surface. In turn, the earth radiates energy back into space. Some atmospheric gases (water vapor, carbon dioxide, and other gases) trap some of the outgoing energy, retaining heat somewhat similar to the glass panels of a greenhouse. These gases are therefore known as greenhouse gases. The greenhouse effect is the rise in temperature on Earth as certain gases in the atmosphere trap energy.

The greenhouse effect is actually life-enabling because without it, heat would escape back into space and the Earth's average temperature would be considerably colder. If the greenhouse effect becomes stronger, however, more heat gets trapped than needed, and the Earth might become less habitable for humans, plants and animals.

It is the rapid pace at which the temperature will rise that will result in many negative impacts to humans and the environment and this is why there is such a world-wide concern. According to the World Meteorological Organization (WMO), 1998, 2002 and 2003 have been the three warmest years on record; the 1990s was the warmest decade; and the 1900s was the warmest century during the last 1,000 years.

Many scientists believe that the warming of the climate will lead to more extreme weather patterns such as:

- **More hurricanes and drought**

- **Longer spells of dry heat or intense rain (depending on where you are in the world)**

- **Colder weather in Northern Europe as the Arctic Ice Cap begins to melt and send fresher waters further south**

- **In South Asia, the Himalayan glaciers could retreat causing water scarcity in the long run**

The Causes of Global Warming

Global warming comes from the emission of greenhouse gases into the earth's atmosphere. In the United States, approximately 6.6 tons of greenhouse gases are emitted per person every year. Most of these emissions, about 82 percent are from burning fossil fuels to generate electricity and power our cars. The remaining emissions are from methane from wastes in our landfills, raising livestock, natural gas pipelines, and coal, as well as from industrial chemicals and other sources. The U.S. presently emits more greenhouse gases per person than any other country.

Preventing Further Global Warming

As an individual, you can affect the emissions of greenhouse gases by the choices you make in three areas of your life. These areas are: the electricity you use in your homes, the waste you produce, and personal transportation. The other 68 percent of emissions are affected more by the types of industries in the U.S., the types of offices we use, how our food is grown, and other factors.

Cars and the Environment

Cars and light trucks, which include sport utility vehicles, pickups, and most mini-vans, emit more than 300 million tons of carbon into the atmosphere each year in the United States. The transportation sector alone is responsible for about one-third of our nation's total production of carbon dioxide, the greenhouse gas that contributes to global warming. In response to burgeoning consumer demand over the past decade, automakers have shifted their fleets to sport utility vehicles (SUVs) and other light trucks—popular vehicles whose fuel economy standards are generally lower than those of passenger cars.

Because more gas-guzzling SUVs are on the road today and because there is a lack of effective fuel efficiency standards for all classes of vehicles, cars collectively get worse gas mileage today than they did in the mid-1980's. This means they also pollute more. Given the increased threats to world oil supplies, the nation's dependence on foreign sources of oil to fuel our cars' increasing thirst is neither a sound nor secure energy policy.

Biodiversity

Another serious global environmental issue involves biodiversity. The variety of life on Earth—its biological diversity—is commonly referred to as biodiversity. The number of species of plants, animals, and micro-organisms, as well as the different ecosystems on the planet, such as deserts, rainforests and coral reefs are all part of a biologically diverse Earth. Almost all cultures in some way have recognized the importance that nature and its biological diversity has had upon them and the need to maintain it. Yet, human activity has adversely affected the precarious balance.

Unfortunately, human activity is causing massive extinctions, including various animal species, forests, and marine life. One-third of the species in the United States are at risk, while more than 500 U.S. species are already extinct or missing. Of these, at least 100 plants and animals have disappeared forever and are presumed extinct, while another 439 are missing and feared lost. Nearly 60 percent of the United States outside of Alaska has lost most of its natural vegetation, and habitat destruction is the leading threat to U.S. species.

Global Issues: Tropical Rain Forests

Rain forests throughout the world are being destroyed at a rapid rate. Here are a few of the reasons why this is causing international concern.

Improving Their Standard of Living. Governments, hoping to improve the economic well-being of their countries, encouraged people to develop the resources of the rain forests. Beginning in the 1960s, for example, the Brazilian government began carving roads into the forests to give people better access to valuable hardwoods and farmland.

Putting Economic Needs First. People in need of land to farm or wood to sell burn and cut down thousands of acres of rain forests. They sometimes clear whole sections of forest to get a few prized trees. Unfortunately, the soils of the forests have few nutrients so crops grow well for only a few years. Settlers must then move on, cutting and burning still more rain forest.

Global Impact. About one half to two thirds of all of the plant and animal species on earth are found in tropical rain forests. Rain forest plants provide ingredients for at least one quarter of the world's medicines. Scientists fear that the destruction of the rain forests will lead to the extinction of more plants and animals. Valuable medical resources will be lost forever. In addition, dense forest vegetation absorbs a large share of carbon dioxide in the earth's atmosphere. If more forests are cleared, global warming may accelerate.

Governments and nonprofit environmental groups have made some progress in slowing down the rate of rain forest destruction. Here are some of the solutions they are working on.

Balancing Economic and Environmental Concerns. Economic development can take place without further excessive destruction of forests. Researchers are trying to determine which parts of the rain forest regenerate quickly and naturally after they have been cleared. If settlers are directed into these areas and taught soil-conserving techniques, long-term damage may be minimized.

Debt-For-Nature Swaps. Governments have experimented with debt-for-nature swaps. Swaps involve payment of parts of a nation's debt in exchange for its agreement to protect rain forests.

Create New Markets. Companies are trying to change the economic forces that lead to the destruction of rain forests. They are working to increase demand for the nuts, fruits, and oils that can be harvested from rain forests without destroying them.

One type of ecosystem-the coral reefs-are neglected more than any other system and are perhaps also the richest in biodiversity. Reefs are useful to the environment and to people in a number of ways:

- **They protect shores from the impact of waves and from storms**
- **They provide a lot of benefits to humans in the form of food and medicine**
- **They provide economic benefits to local communities from tourism**

However, all around the world, much of the world's marine biodiversity face threats from activities and events, including:

- **Coastal development**
- **Overfishing**
- **Inland pollution**
- **Global climate change (global warming)**

It is feared that very soon, many reefs could die off. This is merely one example of an endless list of species and ecosystems which are threatened by human activity. It is critical to remember that all the organisms of an ecosystem work together, and that the elimination of one species is likely to adversely impact a number of other species, including humans. Conservation needs to be a national as well as global priority, while taking into consideration the needs and aspirations of humans.

Genetic Engineering

Another important global environmental issue is genetic engineering (GE) or genetic modification (GM) of food. Some of food that we eat today contains genetically modified ingredients, usually without our knowledge. Genetic engineering of foods essentially means that scientists are shuffling genes between species to create new and improved species: pest-resistant, disease-resistant or higher yielding crops, for example.

The potential benefits of genetically engineered food are exciting. Supporters of this technology maintain that it ensures and sustains food security around the world as the population increases. At the same time though, there are valid concerns about biodiversity, the ecosystem, and health safety if such food has not been tested properly and guaranteed to be safe.

The reason that genetically engineered food could be dangerous is because there has been no adequate testing to ensure that extracting genes that perform an apparently useful function as part of that plant or animal is going to have the same effects if inserted into a totally unrelated species. It may be that in the long term, genetically modified food could provide us with benefits and be a safe alternative, but we cannot know that at this time due to the lack of safety testing.

The Grocery Manufacturers of America estimates that 70 to 75 percent of processed foods sold in the United States may contain genetically engineered ingredients. Actually, very few commercial crop types are bioengineered. Only four major foods are genetically engineered, those being corn, soybeans, canola and cotton. They are broadly used in countless products, however, especially processed foods. They show up on ingredient labels as high-fructose corn syrup, soy lecithin, corn oil, soybean oil, or generically, "vegetable oil." There's also canola oil and cottonseed oil.

Most of the world's industrialized nations require labeling of genetically modified foods. The U.S. government , however, maintains that the act of gene splicing doesn't significantly change a food. As long as an engineered food is nutritionally the same as its conventionally grown version, the government says labels aren't necessary.

Many people think that genetically engineered foods should not be on our grocers' shelves without sufficient testing and mandatory labeling. And no one is sure what kind of impact genetic engineering will have on the environment, particularly ecosystems that are near where genetically engineered crops are grown.

International Cooperation

The issues discussed in this lesson do not pertain to the United States alone. The nations of the world must work together to manage natural resources and deal with environmental concerns. International environmental agreements are a key mechanism by which this is done. These agreements enable nations to search for equitable and efficient solutions to problems that arise from the intersection of natural and human systems that affect the entire globe. Environmental laws and institutions have been strongly developed over the past few years in almost all countries. But we must work together. There are also global-level agreements, including those on global warming and biodiversity that resulted from the United Nations Earth Summit, held in Rio de Janeiro, Brazil, in 1992 and attended by 172 Governments.

An example of an international agreement is the Kyoto Protocol. In 1997, the Kyoto Conference on Climate Change took place in Kyoto, Japan. There, developed countries agreed to specific targets for cutting their emissions of greenhouse gases. A general framework was defined for this, with specifics to be detailed over the next few years. This became known as the Kyoto Protocol.

The world mostly agrees that something needs to be done about global warming and climate change. However, the United States has been vocally against effective action on climate change due to its reliance upon fossil fuels for its economy. Being a producer of oil and coal, they feel more threatened by action on climate change. Europe, on the other hand, is calling for stronger action. In both regions, people have a high awareness of environmental issues. However, in the US, the business lobbies (mainly fossil fuel based industries) are very strong and powerful and have been able to affect decisions and outcomes.

At the Kyoto Conference, the U.S. proposed to just stabilize emissions and not cut them at all, while the European Union called for a 15 percent cut. In the end, there was a trade off, and industrialized countries were committed to an overall reduction of emissions of greenhouse gases to 5.2 percent below 1990 levels for the period 2008 through 2012. (The Intergovernmental Panel on Climate Change said in its 1990 report that a 60 percent reduction in emissions was needed.)

The United States refuesd to sign the Kyoto Protocol despite the fact that over 36 countries, including all members of the European Union, signed it. Those who have argued against the Kyoto conference and global warming in general, claim that it will hurt the global (or US) economy and affect people's jobs. As a result, the world's top producer of greenhouse gases has chosen not to participate in a worldwide commitment to curbing global warming. (The United States has also failed to ratify the Biodiversity Convention, a similar international agreement).

Nuclear Waste Disposal

The end of the arms race between the United States and the former Soviet Union reduced the possibility of a large-scale nuclear war. Now the global community has a new issue. It must deal with the disposal of the radioactive waste created when nuclear weapons are dismantled.

Over the course of the Cold War, the United States and the former Soviet Union manufactured nearly 50,000 nuclear warheads. In the process, tons of radioactive materials were produced. Little thought was given to the future and how these materials could be disposed of safely.

Now the United States and Russia are left with a massive cleanup. But a number of experts say "cleanup" is the wrong word. Many nuclear wastes will take hundreds of centuries to break down so that they are no longer toxic. The most that can be hoped for is to stabilize, or contain, the wastes safely. And this, according to the U.S. Department of Energy, will cost between $230 and $500 billion and take 75 years to accomplish in the United States alone.

Some experts have great concerns about the long-term impact of **nuclear wastes** on the environment. Much of the stored wastes are in old containers that could leak toxins into the environment at any time. According to the U.S. Department of Energy, more than 161 million people in the U.S. reside within 75 miles of temporary stored nuclear waste. Nuclear wastes in some locations have already seeped into the soil and ground water (see Figure 3.2.2)

Key Note Term

nuclear waste – radioactive waste material, especially for the use or reprocessing of nuclear fuel

Figure 3.2.2: Pathways of contamination.

Courtesy of Prentice Hall.

Radioactive wastes are highly toxic to humans and the environment. Studies link higher rates of illness and cancer to exposure to radioactivity. When these wastes leak into the air or water supply, they can be spread over huge distances and affect large populations.

Finding Solutions to Nuclear Waste

Scientists and other experts have made some progress in finding ways to safely contain the waste from nuclear weapons production.

The United States plans to store the most highly radioactive materials deep underground in special metal containers. But until an appropriate site is established, the materials must be stored above ground. New and stronger tanks are being built. Others are being repaired to stop leakage.

Experts are also working on ways to change liquid nuclear wastes into solid forms, which are more stable and easier to store. Radioactive wastes can also be reprocessed into powder and glass, and then placed in storage containers.

Scientists are discussing what should be done with the supply of plutonium, one of the main components of nuclear warheads. As the warheads are dismantled, the supply of plutonium is increasing. Because it costs billions of dollars to produce, some argue that it should be used to fuel nuclear power plants. Others say that plutonium should be disposed of as permanently and quickly as possible. One suggestion is to dispose of it beneath the ocean floor. However, many environmentalists are opposed to this plan.

Conclusion

Global warming, biodiversity, and genetic engineering are controversial but important topics. These are not the only environmental issues facing the inhabitants of planet Earth. We must also be aware of the impact of human activity on our natural world. None of these issues is clear-cut. Controversy and debate constantly follow these and other environmental topics. But the important thing to remember is that we as humans do have a responsibility to preserve the earth for future generations as well as for the living things who share this planet with us right now.

Lesson Review

1. What are the primary causes of global warming?

2. What types of human activity can have a negative impact on biodiversity?

3. What is the primary concern over genetic engineering of foods?

4. How can international cooperation help the global environment?

Unit 5: Geography, Map Skills, and Environmental Awareness Correlated to:
McRel Standards for Geography, Life Work, Thinking and Reasoning, and Working with Others

McRel Standards	Unit 5: Geography, Map Skills, and Environmental Awareness
GEOGRAPHY STANDARDS (G) **The World in Spatial Terms**	
Geo 1. Understands the characteristics and uses of maps, globes, and other geographic tools and technologies	The Globe: An Overview, 3–13; Introduction to Maps, 14–22; Introduction to Topographic Maps, 23–30; Grid Reference System, 31–40; Contours and Landforms, 41–52; Determining Distance, 53–59; Determining Direction, 60–68; Converting the Grid-Magnetic Angle, 69–75; Determining Location, 76–87; Orienteering, 88–99; Air Navigation, 100–111; additional Maps & Map Activities, 116, 119, 122, 123, 126, 128, 130, 133, 136, 139, 142, 143, 161, 163, 165, 168, 169, 171, 173, 176, 179, 182, 187, 188, 191, 196, 200, 201, 204, 207, 213, 215, 218, 222, 224, 230, 235
Geo 2. Knows the location of places, geographic features, and patterns of the environment	Contours and Landforms, 46–52; Maps & Map Activities, 116, 126, 128, 130, 133, 136, 139, 142, 143, 161, 163, 165, 168, 169, 171, 173, 176, 179, 182, 187, 188, 191, 196, 200, 201, 204, 207, 213, 215, 218, 222, 224, 230, 235; Before You Get Started, 118–123; Local Environmental Issues, 241–253; Global Environmental Issues, 254–262
Geo 3. Understands the characteristics and uses of spatial organization of Earth's surface	The Globe: An Overview, 3–13; Introduction to Topographic Maps, 23–30; Contours and Landforms, 41–52; Determining Distance, 53–59; Determining Direction, 60–68; Determining Location, 76–87; Orienteering, 88–99; Air Navigation, 100–111; Spatial Perspective, 114

Copyright © 2004 McREL
Mid-continent Research for Education and Learning
2550 S. Parker Road, Suite 500
Aurora, CO 80014
Telephone: 303/337-0990
www.mcrel.org/standards-benchmarks

McRel Standards	Unit 5: Geography, Map Skills, and Environmental Awareness
Places and Regions	
Geo 4. Understands the physical and human characteristics of place	Contours and Landforms, 46–52; Before You Get Started, 113–123; North America-From Tundra to Tropics, 124–148; South America-Through the Tropics Toward Antarctica, 149–159; Europe-The Peninsular Continent, 160–185; Asia-The Largest, Most Populous Continent , 186 –211; Africa-The Plateau Continent, 212–228; Australia and the Rest of Oceania, 229–239; Local Environmental Issues, 241–253; Global Environmental Issues, 254–262
Geo 5. Understands the concept of regions	Polar Region, 10; Physical Geography, 114; Cultural Geography, 115; Economic Geography, 116; What is a Region?, 117–118; Climate, 120–121; North America's Climate Regions, 137; Regions of South America, 154–159; Europe-The Peninsular Continent, 160–185; Asia-The Largest, Most Populous Continent, 186 –211; Africa-The Plateau Continent, 212–228; Australia and the Rest of Oceania, 229–239
Geo 6. Understands that culture and experience influence people's perceptions of places and regions	Cultural Geography, 115; Economic Geography, 116; Political Geography, 117; History: Settlement of the Americas, 127–128; Canada: A Plural State, 129–130; The Canadian People, 131–132; People of the United States, 135; Mexico: Merging Cultures, 138–140; Important Historical/Political Considerations of Central America, 142; People of Central America, 143; Important Historical/Political Considerations of the West Indies, 144–146; Important Historical/Political Considerations of South America, 152; People of South America, 153–154; Important United Kingdom Historical/Political Considerations, 166–167; People of Western Europe, 169; People of Scandinavia, 172; People of the Mediterranean, 174; People of European Russia, 178; People of the Northern Countries, 179; Important Historical/Political Considerations of the Southern Countries, 182–183; People of the Southern Countries, 184; Important Historical/Political Considerations of Asia, 190; People of Asian Russia, 193–194; People of the Middle East, 198–199; People of South Asia, 202–203; People of Southeast Asia, 205; Important Historical/Political Considerations of East Asia, 208; People of East Asia, 208–209; Urbanization in China, 210; Important Historical/Political Considerations of Africa, 215–216; People of North Africa, 217–218; People of Sub-Saharan Africa, 220–221; Important Historical/Political Considerations of Australia, 231; People of Australia, 231–232; People of Oceania, 236

McRel Standards	Unit 5: Geography, Map Skills, and Environmental Awareness
Physical Systems	
Geo 7. Knows the physical processes that shape patterns on Earth's surface	Physical Geography, 114–115; Climate, 120–122; United States of America: From Sea to Shining Sea, 132–133; North America's Weather Patterns, 147; Western Europe: The Continental Core, 167–169; Eastern Europe, 176–177; The Middle East (climate), 196; South Asia, 201; Monsoon Climate, 203; Southeast Asia, 204; Tsunami, 206; Africa's Climate Regions, 214; West Africa, 222; Water Use in Africa, 225; Global Environmental Issues, 254–262
Geo 8. Understands the characteristics of ecosystems on Earth's surface	Physical Geography, 114–115; North America's Climate Regions, 137; The West Indies: Island Paradise, 144; South America, 150, 152; Regions of South America, 154–156; South America's Vegetation, 157; Europe, 161–162; Asia, 188–190, 191–192; South Asia, 201; East and Southeast Asia's Terrain, 208; Africa, 214–215; West Africa, Central Africa, 223; East Africa, 224; Water Use in Africa, 225; Southern Africa, 226; Australia, 230–231; Local Environmental Issues, 241–243
Human Systems	
Geo 9. Understands the nature, distribution and migration of human populations on Earth's surface	Cultural Geography, 115; Political Geography, 117; History: Settlement of the Americas, 127–128; Canada: A Plural State, 129–130; The Canadian People, 131–132; People of the United States, 135; Mexico: Merging Cultures, 138–140; People of Central America, 143; Christopher Columbus and the Foods We Eat Today, 145; People of South America, 153–154; People of Western Europe, 169; People of Scandinavia, 172; People of the Mediterranean, 174; People of European Russia, 178; People of the Northern Countries, 179; People of the Southern Countries, 184; People of Asian Russia, 193–194; People of the Middle East, 198–199; People of South Asia, 202–203; People of Southeast Asia, 205; People of East Asia, 208–209; Urbanization in China, 210; People of North Africa, 217–218; People of Sub-Saharan Africa, 220–221; People of Australia, 231–232; People of Oceania, 236

McRel Standards	Unit 5: Geography, Map Skills, and Environmental Awareness
Human Systems *(continued)*	
Geo 10. Understands the nature and complexity of Earth's cultural mosaics	Cultural Geography, 115; Political Geography, 117; History: Settlement of the Americas, 127–128; Canada: A Plural State, 129–130; The Canadian People, 131–132; People of the United States, 135; Mexico: Merging Cultures, 138–140; Important Historical/Political Considerations of Central America, 142; People of Central America, 143; Important Historical/Political Considerations of the West Indies, 144–146; Important Historical/Political Considerations of South America, 152; People of South America, 153–154; Important United Kingdom Historical/Political Considerations, 166–167; People of Western Europe, 169; People of Scandinavia, 172; People of the Mediterranean, 174; People of European Russia, 178; People of the Northern Countries, 179; Important Historical/Political Considerations of the Southern Countries, 182–183; People of the Southern Countries, 184; Important Historical/Political Considerations of Asia, 190; People of Asian Russia, 193–194; People of the Middle East, 198–199; People of South Asia, 202–203; People of Southeast Asia, 205; Important Historical/Political Considerations of East Asia, 208; People of East Asia, 208–209; Urbanization in China, 210; Important Historical/Political Considerations of Africa, 215–216; People of North Africa, 217–218; People of Sub-Saharan Africa, 220–221; Important Historical/Political Considerations of Australia, 231; People of Australia, 231–232; People of Oceania, 236
Geo 11. Understands the patterns and networks of economic interdependence on Earth's surface	Economic Geography, 116–117; Canada's Economy, 132; Mexico's Economy, 141; Central America's Economy, 144; Economy of the West Indies, 146; Regions of South America, 154–158; The European Union, 164; The European Economy, 166–167; The Economy of Western Europe, 170–171; The Economy of Scandinavia, 172; The Economy of Mediterranean Europe, 175; The Economy of European Russia, 178; The Economy of the Northern Countries, 180; Economy of the Southern Countries, 184; The Economy of Asian Russia, 195; The Economy of the Middle East, 199–200; The Economy of South Asia, 203; The Economy of Southeast Asia, 205; The Economy of East Asia, 209–210; North Africa: The Most Prosperous Regions, 217; The Economy of North Africa, 219; Central Africa, 223; East Africa, 224–225; The Economy of Australia, 233; The Economy of Oceania, 237

McRel Standards	Unit 5: Geography, Map Skills, and Environmental Awareness
Human Systems *(continued)*	
Geo 12. Understands the patterns of human settlement and their causes	Cultural Geography, 115; Political Geography, 117; History: Settlement of the Americas, 127–128; Canada: A Plural State, 129–130; The Canadian People, 131–132; People of the United States, 135; Mexico: Merging Cultures, 138–140; People of Central America, 143; Christopher Columbus and the Foods We Eat Today, 145; People of South America, 153–154; People of Western Europe, 169; People of Scandinavia, 172; People of the Mediterranean, 174; People of European Russia, 178; People of the Northern Countries, 179; People of the Southern Countries, 184; People of Asian Russia, 193–194; People of the Middle East, 198–199; People of South Asia, 202–203; People of Southeast Asia, 205; People of East Asia, 208–209; Urbanization in China, 210; People of North Africa, 217–218; People of Sub-Saharan Africa, 220–221; People of Australia, 231–232; People of Oceania, 236
Geo 13. Understands the forces of cooperation and conflict that shape the divisions of Earth's surface	Political Geography, 117; History: Settlement of the Americas, 127–128; Canada: A Plural State, 129–130; Mexico: Merging Cultures, 138–140; Important Historical/Political Considerations of Central America, 142; Important Historical/Political Considerations of the West Indies, 144–146; Important Historical/Political Considerations of South America, 152; Important United Kingdom Historical/Political Considerations, 166–167; Important Historical/Political Considerations of the Southern Countries, 182–183; Important Historical/Political Considerations of Asia, 190; Important Historical/Political Considerations of East Asia, 208; Important Historical/Political Considerations of Africa, 215–216; Important Historical/Political Considerations of Australia, 231

McRel Standards	Unit 5: Geography, Map Skills, and Environmental Awareness
Environment and Society	
Geo 14. Understands how human actions modify the physical environment	Local Environmental Issues, 241–253; Global Environmental Issues, 254–262
Geo 15. Understands how physical systems affect human systems	Physical Geography, 114–115; Climate, 120–122; United States of America: From Sea to Shining Sea, 132–133; North America's Weather Patterns, 147; Western Europe: The Continental Core, 167–169; Eastern Europe, 176–177; The Middle East (climate), 196; South Asia, 201; Monsoon Climate, 203; Southeast Asia, 204; Tsunami, 206; Africa's Climate Regions, 214; West Africa, 222; Water Use in Africa, 225; Global Environmental Issues, 254–262
Geo 16. Understands the changes that occur in the meaning, use, distribution and importance of resources	Economic Geography, 116–117; Canada's Economy, 132; Mexico's Economy, 141; Central America's Economy, 144; Economy of the West Indies, 146; Regions of South America, 154–158; The European Union, 164; The European Economy, 166–167; The Economy of Western Europe, 170–171; The Economy of Scandinavia, 172; The Economy of Mediterranean Europe, 175; The Economy of European Russia, 178; The Economy of the Northern Countries, 180; Economy of the Southern Countries, 184; The Economy of Asian Russia, 195; The Economy of the Middle East, 199–200; The Economy of South Asia, 203; The Economy of Southeast Asia, 205; The Economy of East Asia, 209–210; North Africa: The Most Prosperous Regions, 217; The Economy of North Africa, 219; Central Africa, 223; East Africa, 224–225; The Economy of Australia, 233; The Economy of Oceania, 237

McRel Standards	Unit 5: Geography, Map Skills, and Environmental Awareness
Uses of Geography	
Geo 17. Understands how geography is used to interpret the past	Political Geography, 117; History: Settlement of the Americas, 127–128; Canada: A Plural State, 129–130; Mexico: Merging Cultures, 138–140; Important Historical/Political Considerations of Central America, 142; Important Historical/Political Considerations of the West Indies, 144–146; Important Historical/Political Considerations of South America, 152; Important United Kingdom Historical/Political Considerations, 166–167; Important Historical/Political Considerations of the Southern Countries, 182–183; Important Historical/Political Considerations of Asia, 190; Important Historical/Political Considerations of East Asia, 208; Important Historical/Political Considerations of Africa, 215–216; Important Historical/Political Considerations of Australia, 231
Geo 18. Understands global development and environmental issues	Local Environmental Issues, 241–253; Global Environmental Issues, 254–262
LIFE WORK STANDARDS (LW)	
LW 1. Makes effective use of basic tools	Determining Distance, 53–59; Determining Direction, 60–68; Converting the Grid-Magnetic Angle, 69–75; Determining Location, 76–87; Orienteering, 88–99; Air Navigation, 100–111
LW 2. Uses various information sources, including those of a technical nature, to accomplish specific tasks	Introduction to Topographic Maps, 23–30; Grid Reference System, 31–40; Contours and Landforms, 41–52; Determining Distance, 53–59; Determining Direction, 60–68; Converting the Grid-Magnetic Angle, 69–75; Determining Location, 76–87; Orienteering, 88–99; Air Navigation, 100–111
LW 5. Makes general preparation for entering the work force	Orientation to Service Learning, 265–270; Plan and Train for Your Exploratory Project, 271–276; Project Reflection and Integration, 277–284
LW 6. Makes effective use of basic life skills	Orientation to Service Learning, 265–270; Plan and Train for Your Exploratory Project, 271–276; Project Reflection and Integration, 277–284
LW 7. Displays reliability and a basic work ethic	Orientation to Service Learning, 265–270; Plan and Train for Your Exploratory Project, 271–276; Project Reflection and Integration, 277–284

McRel Standards	Unit 5: Geography, Map Skills, and Environmental Awareness
LIFE WORK STANDARDS (LW) *(continued)*	
LW 8. Operates effectively within organizations	Orientation to Service Learning, 265–270; Plan and Train for Your Exploratory Project, 271–276; Project Reflection and Integration, 277–284
THINKING AND REASONING STANDARDS (TR)	
TR 3. Effectively uses mental processes that are based on identifying similarities and differences	Contours and Landforms, 41–52; Determining Distance, 53–59; Determining Direction, 60–68; Converting the Grid-Magnetic Angle, 69–75; Determining Location, 76–87; Orienteering, 88–99; Air Navigation, 100–111
TR 4. Understands and applies basic principles of hypothesis testing and scientific inquiry	Plan and Train for Your Exploratory Project, 271–276
TR 5. Applies basic trouble-shooting and problem-solving techniques	Plan and Train for Your Exploratory Project, 271–276; Project Reflection and Integration, 277–284
TR 6. Applies decision-making techniques	Plan and Train for Your Exploratory Project, 271–276
WORKING WITH OTHERS STANDARDS (WO)	
WO 1. Contributes to the overall effort of a group	Orientation to Service Learning, 265–270; Plan and Train for Your Exploratory Project, 271–276; Project Reflection and Integration, 277–284
WO 4. Displays effective interpersonal communication skills	Plan and Train for Your Exploratory Project, 271–276; Project Reflection and Integration, 277–284
WO 5. Demonstrates leadership skills	Plan and Train for Your Exploratory Project, 271–276; Project Reflection and Integration, 277–284

solid waste. garbage, refuse, sludges and other discarded solid materials including those from industrial, commercial, and agricultural operations, and from community activities

source reduction. the process of keeping waste out of the waste system through buying practices, conservation, and so on

spatial. in terms of geography, relating to space (area) on the surface of the earth

spur. a sloping line of high ground projecting out from the side of a ridge

standard of living. a measurement of a person's or group's education, housing, health care, and nutrition

statute mile. a unit of measurement that is approximately 5,280 feet (it is commonly referred to as a "mile")

steering mark. an easily identifiable feature in the landscape not shown on the map, and is used by the orienteer to follow a bearing

sultanate. a country governed by a sultan, the title given to the supreme authority usually of a Muslim state

superimpose. to place over or on top of something else

synthetic. man-made or artificial; not of natural origin

tectonic plates. slowly moving plates of the Earth's crust that carry the continents; where two plates meet, one slides under the other, crumpling the crust and producing mountains, volcanoes, and earthquakes

terrain. a region or tract of land; the character (or topography) of a tract of land

timekeeper. one who keeps track of time and plans the schedule.

topographic map. a map that shows relief and the position of natural and man-made features**toxicity.** the level of poison or harm of a particularsubstance

training. to form by or undergo instruction, discipline, or drill; to teach so as to make fit, qualified, or proficient.

true north. a line from any position on the earth's surface to the geographic north pole; symbolized by a line with a star at the apex

tundra. a treeless area between the icecaps and the tree line of Arctic regions, having a permanently frozen subsoil and supporting low-growing vegetation such as lichens, mosses, and stunted shrubs

Universal Transverse Mercator Grid System. a grid system that has been designed to cover the part of the world between latitude 84 degrees north and latitude 80 degrees south, and, as its name implies, is imposed on the transverse Mercator projection

Index